The Hebrides
A GUIDE TO THE ISLANDS
OF WESTERN SCOTLAND

Celtic Birds of Friendship (Croft Studio, Dunvegan, Skye).

The Hebrides

A GUIDE TO THE ISLANDS
OF WESTERN SCOTLAND

Martin Coventry

GOBLINSHEAD
Musselburgh

The Hebrides

First Published 1999
© Martin Coventry 1999

Published by **GOBLINSHEAD**
130B Inveresk Road, Musselburgh EH21 7AY, Scotland
Tel: 0131 665 2894 Fax: 0131 653 6566 Email: goblinshead@sol.co.uk

British Library Cataloguing in Publication Data
A catalogue record for this book is available from the British Library.

ISBN 1 899874 21 6

Typeset by **GOBLINSHEAD** using Desktop Publishing

Goblinshead offices, Musselburgh.

Contents

List of Maps and Illustrations   vi
Acknowledgements   vii
How to Use the Book   viii
Preface   ix

Serious, Sensible and Useful
   Information   1
Some Useful Addresses   3
Tourist and Visitor Information   5

Introduction   11

OUTER HEBRIDES   **19**
Lewis and Harris   22
Lewis   24
Great Bernera   25
Harris   28
St Kilda   40
North Uist   43
Berneray   45
Grimsay   45
Benbecula   53
South Uist   58
Eriskay   60
Barra   64
Vatersay   65

INNER HEBRIDES   **69**
Skye and Raasay   72
Raasay   77
Small Isles (Rum, Eigg,
   Canna and Muck)   92
Coll   97
Tiree   100
Mull   106
Staffa   108
Ulva   109
Iona   119
Lismore   122
Kerrera   125
Slate Islands (Seil, Luing,
   Lunga and Scarba)   127
Colonsay and Oronsay   134
Jura   138
Islay   142
Gigha   152
Bute   157
Cumbrae   163
Arran   165
Other Inshore Islands   175

Index of Islands   177
Index of Places of Interest   179

Illustrations

Map 1: The Hebrides – main ferry routes
and TICs   9
Map 2: The Hebrides   10
Map 3: Lewis and Harris   20-21
Map 4: North Uist and Benbecula   42
Map 5: South Uist and Barra   57
Map 6: Skye and Raasay   70-71
Map 7: Small Isles   92
Map 8: Coll and Tiree   97
Map 9: Mull, Iona and Slate Islands   104-105
Map 10: Islay, Jura, Colonsay, Gigha   132-133
Map 11: Arran, Bute and Cumbrae   156

Birds of Friendship (Croft Studio)   frontispiece
Iona (MC)   11
Callanish, Lewis (MC)   13
Teampull na Trionaid, North Uist (MC)   14
Abandoned settlement, Mull (MC)   18
Tolsta Chaolais, Lewis (MC)   22
Stornoway, Lewis (MC)   25
Butt of Lewis (MC)   27
St Clement's Church, Rodel, Harris (MC)   28
Callanish Standing Stones, Lewis (MC)   30
Dun Borranish, Uig, Lewis (MC)   32
Dun Carloway, Lewis (MC)   33
Arnol blackhouse, Lewis (MC)   34
St Moluag's Church, Eoropie, Lewis (MC)   36
St Kilda – Boreray (NTS)   40
St Kilda – the Street (NTS)   41
Beach, Baleshare, North Uist (MC)   43
Thatched house, North Uist (MacGillivrays)   44
Barpa Langass, North Uist (MC)   46
Dun an Sticar, North Uist (MC)   49
Pobull Fhinn Stone Circle, North Uist (MC)   50
Island Crafts, Lochmaddy, North Uist (IC)   51
Taigh Chearsabhagh, North Uist (TC)   52
Beach, nr Sollas, North Uist (MC)   52
Nunton, Benbecula (MC)   54
Museum nan Eilean, Benbecula (MnE)   55
Loch Hermidale, South Uist (William Neill)   56
Howmore, South Uist (MC)   59
Luatharan Glas, South Uist (William Neill)   60
Book ends, Uist Craft Workshop (UCW)   63
Airstrip, Barra (JM)   64
Kiessimul Castle, Barra (DR)   66
Trotternish, Skye (Trotternish Art Gallery)   73
Cuillin mountains, Skye (MC)   74

Cuillin mountains from Elgol, Skye (MC)   76
Raasay and Skye from Applecross (MC)   78
Dun Beag, Skye (MC)   80
Colbost Croft Museum, Skye (MC)   83
Dunvegan Castle, Skye (MC)   84
Duntulm Castle, Skye (MC)   84
Glendale Water mill, Skye (MC)   85
Raasay House, Raasay (RHAC)   86
Skye Museum of Island Life (MC)   87
Trumpan Church, Skye (Dandelion Designs)   88
Dragon, Dandelion Designs, Skye (DD)   88
Goblet, Edinbane Pottery (EP)   89
Uig Pottery, Uig, Skye (UP)   91
Rum (DR)   93
Eigg (DR)   94
Canna (NTS)   94
Canna (NTS)   96
Coll (AILLSTTB)   98
Tiree (AILLSTTB)   101
Glen Mor, Mull (MC)   107
Staffa (MC)   108
Calgary Sands, Mull (MC)   110
MacCulloch's Tree, Burg, Mull (NTS)   111
Lochbuie, Mull (MC)   113
Duart Castle, Mull (Mary MacLean)   114
Moy Castle, Mull (MC)   115
Pennygown Chapel, Mull (MC)   116
Iona Abbey (MC)   118
Cross, Iona Abbey (MC)   120
Mhian Arts, Iona (Mhian Arts)   121
Lismore (MC)   122
Kerrera (AILLSTTB)   125
Seil (AILLSTTB)   127
Colonsay (AILLSTTB)   134
Oronsay Priory (AILLSTTB)   135
Paps of Jura (MC)   139
Standing Stone, Tarbert, Jura (MC)   140
Bowmore, Islay (MC)   143
Kilchoman Cross, Islay (MC)   144
Dunyvaig Castle, Islay (MC)   146
Kildalton Cross, Islay (MC)   148
Lagavulin Distillery, Islay (MC)   150
Gigha (Gigha Hotel)   152
Gigha Hotel (Gigha Hotel)   155
Rothesay Castle, Bute (MC)   157
Blackpark Stone Circle, Bute (MC)   159
St Blane's Church, Kingarth, Bute (MC)   161
Cathedral of the Isles, Cumbrae (CoI)   164
Holy Island, Arran (MC)   166
Machrie Moor Standing Stones, Arran (MC)   170
Brodick Castle, Arran (MC)   171
Lamlash Parish Church, Arran (LPC)   173
Lochranza Castle, Arran (MC)   173

Acknowledgements

Thanks to everyone who provided information and illustrations. Especial thanks to Joyce Miller; The National Trust for Scotland; Argyll, the Isles, Loch Lomond, Stirling and Trossachs Tourist Board; Caroline Boyd; Diane Stratton; Hilary Brown; David Reed; Murdo Macdonald; Gigha Hotel; Colonsay Hotel; Coll Hotel.

Thanks also to the staff of the TICs of Stornoway, Tarbert, Lochmaddy, Lochboisdale, Castlebay, Portree, Broadford, Dunvegan, Uig, Mallaig, Oban, Craignure, Tobermory, Bowmore, Tarbert, Campbeltown, Rothesay, Largs and Brodick.

More thanks also the following for supplying information and/or providing illustrations:
Ardbeg Distillery, Islay • An Cala Garden, Seil • An Lanntair, Stornoway •An Tuireann, Portree • Ardencraig Gardens, Bute • Arran Aromatics • Arran Heritage Museum• Ascog Hall Fernery, Bute • Balmichael Visitor Centre, Arran • The Barn, Colonsay • Barra Heritage Centre • Bernera Centre • Borgh Pottery, Lewis • Borvemore Studios, Lewis • Bowmore Distillery, Islay • Bunnahabain Distillery, Islay • Bute Museum • Caol Ila Distillery, Islay • Cathedral of the Isles, Millport • Castle Keep, Portree • Clan Donald Centre, Armadale • Colbost Croft Museum, Skye • Co Leis Thu?, Harris • Colonsay House Garden • Columba Centre, Mull • Crafts of Arran • Croft Crafts, Harris • Croft Studio, Dunvegan • Dandelion Designs, Stein • Duart Castle, Mull • Easdale Folk Museum • Finlaggan Trust •Gaelic Whiskies, Eilean Iarmain • Gearrannan, Lewis • Giant Angus MacAskill Museum, Dunvegan • Glendale Toy Museum, Skye • Gisla Woodcraft, Lewis • Harbour View, Port of Ness • Kildonan Museum, Cafe and Crafts, South Uist • Hebridean Jewellery, South Uist • Iona Heritage Centre • Island Crafts, North Uist • Islay Woollen Mill, Bridgend • Isle of Arran Distillery, Lochranza • Isle of Jura Distillery, Craighouse • Isle of Mull Angora Rabbit Farm • Isle of Mull Museum, Tobermory • Isle of Skye Brewing Company, Uig • Joan MacLennan Tweeds, Harris • Jura House Garden • Kenneth MacLeod Harris Tweed Mill, Lewis • Kilmory Workshop, Arran • Kiessimul Castle • Kylerhea Otter Haven • Lagavulin Distillery, Islay • Lamlash Parish Church • Laphroaig Distillery, Islay • Lewis Loom Centre, Stornoway • Little Gallery, Skye • Luib Croft Museum, Skye • Luskentyre Harris Tweed Company, Harris • MacGillivrays, Benbecula • Margaret Curtis, Callanish, Lewis • Mhian Arts, Iona • Morven Gallery, Lewis • Mount Stuart, Bute • Mull & West Highland Narrow Gauge Railway, Craignure • Mull Theatre, Dervaig • Museum nan Eilean, Benbecula • Museum nan Eilean, Stornoway • Museum of Islay Life, Port Charlotte • Ness Heritage Centre, Lewis • Oiseval Gallery, Lewis • Port Ellen Pottery, Islay • Raasay Outdoor Centre • Ravenspoint, Lewis • Skye Batiks, Armadale • Skye Jewellery, Broadford • Skye Museum of Island Life, Kilmuir • Skye Serpentarium • Skyeskyns • Skye Woollen Mill, Portree • Soay Studios • South Bank Farm Park, Arran • Staffin Museum, Skye • Talisker Distillery, Skye • Tobermory Distillery, Mull • Taigh Chearsabhagh Museum and Art Centre, Lochmaddy • Tormisdale Croft Crafts, Islay • Trotternish Art Gallery • Uig Heritage Centre, Lewis • Uig Pottery, Skye • Uist Animals Visitor Centre, Bayhead • Uist Croft Workshop, South Uist • Uist Outdoor Centre, North Uist • West Highland Heavy Horse Tours, Skye • World of Wood, Skye • Anyone else I have forgotten

How to Use the Book

The first section (pp 1-10) consists of useful information, such as driving on single track roads, the country and forest code and advice for climbers. This is followed by a list of addresses and contact information for various bodies (pp 3-4), then a list of which tourist information centres cover which islands (pp 5-9), again with contact information. There is a map of the main ferry routes to the Hebrides and TICs (p 9), as well as a map (p 10) showing the island sections into which the maps in the main text are divided. These maps are: Lewis and Harris (pp 20-21); North Uist and Benbecula (p 42); South Uist and Barra (p 57); Skye and Raasay (pp 70-71); Small Isles (p 92); Coll and Tiree (p 97); Mull, Iona, Lismore, Kerrera and Slate Islands (pp 104-105); Islay, Jura, Colonsay and Gigha (pp 132-133); Arran, Bute and Cumbrae (p 156).

A concise introduction to the islands covers the history of the Hebrides from earliest times to the present day (pp 11-18).

The main section (pp 19-176) is a listing by island of all the Hebrides. The tour starts with the Outer Hebrides (pp 19-68), beginning in Lewis and concluding with Barra; then goes on to the Inner Hebrides (pp 69-176), starting with Skye and finishing with Arran. Fuller listings of the islands can be found in the contents (p v) and the island index (p 177).

The entry for each island and group of islands consists of the following: map of area; the name and its derivation and pronunciation; location; how to get there; tourist information centre(s); notes; basic info; wildlife; history; and today.

Following the main island entries are listings of any nearby islands.

At the end of each island or island group is a gazetteer of places of interest, which can be visited. This part is divided into prehistoric; historic and heritage; arts, crafts and industry; gardens, animals and miscellaneous. These entries are made up of location, description, opening times and facilities, and contact information. £ sign indicates admission price range: £ = £3.50 and less; ££ = £3.50-£5.00; £££ = more than £5.00.

There is an index of islands towards the end of the book (pp 177-178), as well as comprehensive index of all the places of interest (pp 179-182).

Preface

The Hebrides are a beautiful and fascinating group of islands, diverse in landscape and wildlife, and rich in history and archaeology. My first Hebride, Islay, was visited in 1991, when we stayed at Bunnahabain on the picturesque Sound of Islay. This was a revelation for me, helped – it must be said – by a week of stunning sunny weather. We went to the magnificent Kildalton Cross, took a tour of Bowmore Distillery, and visited Finlaggan, once base to the Lords of the Isles, and the Museum of Islay Life at Port Charlotte. The scenery was spectacular: from peat moors to grand hills to dramatic cliffs to sandy beaches to soft, rolling countryside.

Over the next eight years we visited as many of the islands of western Scotland as time and opportunity would allow, and each one revealed itself as fascinating and yet very different from the last. Our tour concluded two years ago in Bute with the great castle at Rothesay and the remains of the ancient monastery of St Blane at Kingarth.

Vivid memories come back of these trips. Calgary Bay on Mull on a beautiful sunny day with a wind so bitter and persistent that it cut you in half. Staffa, grim and spectacular, with a rising sea. The Callanish stones on Lewis just after a dusting of snow. Dawn at Sollas on North Uist and a sky of liquid fire. Uig sands in a blinding sun and the ruins of Dun Borranish. The chambered cairn of Barpa Langass and finding the chamber and passage still roofed. A sea of mud at Teampull na Trionaid. Spray at the Butt of Lewis. Moy Castle at Lochbuie. Iona. Dunyvaig Castle on a still evening. Machrie Moor stone circles. The causeways at Dun an Sticar. A lone sheep following us for miles round Tolsta Chaolais. So many wonderful memories.

This book is an introduction to the western isles of Scotland, providing background on all of the Hebrides, from Lewis to Barra, Arran to Skye, both large and small. The text covers ferry and traveller information, history and location, and a wealth of useful facts and advice. Also included are over 400 places of interest, which can be visited, to help the traveller or tourist get as much as possible from their trip. These sites span important and impressive prehistoric monuments, Christian sites, burial grounds, carved stones and castles, museums, crofts and distilleries, gardens, animals and wildlife, and a wide selection of arts and crafts from around the islands.

I hope this book encourages visits to the Hebrides of Scotland so that others can appreciate the beauty, history and peace of these wonderful islands.

MC, Musselburgh, May 1999

To Anna Banana
1933-1997

Serious, Sensible and Useful Information

Many of the islands of the Hebrides are much larger than some think, and travel by ferries and roads – particularly single-track roads – is usually slower than on most of the mainland. Allow enough time to explore the islands – a couple of days will not do justice to any of the larger islands.

Although the weather in the islands is not always as bad as some people think, many activities involve long periods out of doors. It is wise to have sensible footwear, even walking boots, and waterproof and warm clothing. The Ordnance Survey provide excellent ranges of maps, which are also indispensable for getting the most from visits. Tourist Information Centres (TICs) provide a wide range of maps, guides and leaflets.

There are several travel options getting to, and travelling between, the different islands. Some involve considerable discounts, combining rail and ferry, so check with TICs – Caledonian MacBrayne (CalMac), a ferry company which travels to most of the islands, offers a range of packages. Always remember to ask about any special fare deals which may be on offer from the ferry, air, rail and bus operators. It is advisable to book all ferry journeys well in advance for vehicles and make sure arrival at ferry ports is well before the ferry loading time. Inter-island travel timetables can depend on tides and weather, so check with travel operators before setting out.

Accommodation can be booked through TICs or increasingly through the Internet.

Driving
- Remember to drive on the left (if you do not usually do so!)

Single Track Roads

These roads are only wide enough for one vehicle, but have passing places which are identified by posts, either with the legend 'Passing Place' attached or alternatively by poles, which are usually striped.

- Stop at a Passing Place on your **left** to allow approaching traffic to pass
- If the Passing Place is on your right, you must wait opposite to allow traffic to pass. You must **stay on the left** and do not cross to a Passing Place on your right

- Do not hold up following traffic: stop in a passing place on your left to allow them to overtake
- If you are overtaking a vehicle that has stopped in a Passing Place, look out for approaching traffic
- Be prepared to give way to traffic coming uphill
- Do not park in Passing Places
- Look out for pedestrians and cyclists
- Watch out for animals on all unfenced roads, particularly deer and sheep

Country and Forest Code

- Use local shops and garages (although check opening times for food and fuel – many outlets are open shorter hours than in cities and are closed on Sundays and sometimes a half-day during the week)
- Look out for local crafts and produce to buy, and support local events
- Park your car responsibly – farm gateways are 'work place' entrances
- Shut gates behind you if found shut – it can take many hours to round up stray animals. If you find a gate open, leave it that way: the farmer has probably chosen to do that
- Keep dogs on leads and under control at all times and always away from livestock. Take especial care during lambing
- All birds and nests are protected by law, and so are many mammals including otters and all bats
- Guard against all risk of fire: protect trees, plants and wildlife
- Leave things as you find them: take nothing away
- Leave no litter

Climbing and Serious Hill Walking

- Do not attempt climbs unless you are experienced and well equipped
- Wear good boots and have waterproofs and warm clothing
- Take water and something to eat
- Take a good map and compass
- Tell someone where you are going and when you intend to return

All the information in this book has been checked with the visitor attractions and other sites, including access, facilities and opening, wherever possible. Although every care has been taken, please check with TICs, ferries and visitor sites before setting out on any journey. Inclusion in the text should not be taken as an indication the site is open to the public and should be visited. Permission to visit sites on private property should be sought in advance. Many places, particularly ruinous brochs, duns, castles and other similar sites, are located in difficult and inaccessible locations as well as being in potentially dangerous conditions: great care should be taken during any visit. The sites listed in the following pages are a personal selection and should not be considered as either a recommendation or comment on the various places.

Useful Addresses and Phone Numbers

For visitor information and Tourist Information Centres see next section..

British Airways Reservations
Tel: 0345 222111

Caledonian MacBrayne (CalMac)
The Ferry Terminal
Gourock PA19 1QP
General enquiries
Tel: 01475 650100
Fax: 01475 637607
Web: www.calmac.co.uk
Car ferry reservations
Tel: 0990 650000
Fax: 01475 635235
Email: reservations@calmac.co.uk
Also Oban
General Enquiries
Tel: 01631 566688
Fax: 01631 566588

Forest Enterprise
231 Corstorphine Road
Edinburgh EH12 7AT
Public enquiry line
Tel: 0131 314 6322
fax: 0131 316 4891
Email: enquiries@forestry.gov.uk
Web: www.forestry.gov.uk

Historic Scotland
Longmore House
Salisbury Place
Edinburgh EH9 1SH
Tel: 0131 668 8800
Fax: 0131 668 8888
Web: www.historic-scotland.gov.uk

Macdonald Coaches
(operates between Inverness and Ullapool)
Tel: 01851 706267

National Rail Enquiry Service
Tel: 0345 484950

The National Trust for Scotland
5 Charlotte Square
Edinburgh EH2 4DU
Tel: 0131 226 5922
Fax: 0131 243 9501
Email: information@nts.org.uk
Web: www.nts.org.uk
(from early 2000 the postal address will be:
The National Trust for Scotland
26-31 Charlotte Square
Edinburgh EH2 4ET)

Royal Society for the Protection of Birds

Dunedin House
25 Ravelston Terrace
Edinburgh EH4 3TP
Tel: 0131 311 6500
Fax: 0131 311 6569
Web: www.rspb.org.uk

Scotland's Gardens Scheme

31 Castle Terrace
Edinburgh EH1 2EL
Tel: 0131 229 1870
Fax: 0131 229 1443
Email: sgsoffice@aol.com

Scotrail

Tel: 0345 550033
Web: www.scotrail.co.uk

Scottish Citylink Coaches

Tel: 0990 505050

Scottish National Heritage

12 Hope Terrace
Edinburgh EH9 2AS
Tel: 0131 447 4784
fax: 0131 446 2277
Web: www.snh.org.uk

Scottish Wildlife Trust

Cramond House
Kirk Cramond
Cramond Glebe Road
Edinburgh EH4 6NF
Tel: 0131 312 7765
Fax: 0131 312 8705
Email: scottishwl@cix.co.uk
Web: www.wildlifetrust.org.uk

Scottish Youth Hostels Association

Head Office
7 Glebe Crescent
Stirling FK8 2JA
Tel: 01786 891400
Fax 01786 891333
Email: syha@syha.org.uk
Web: www.syha.org.uk
Central booking telephone number: **Tel: 0541 553255**

Strathclyde Transport

Tel: 0345 484950

Sustrans (Cycle Network)

Information Service
PO Box 21
Bristol BS99 2HA
Tel: 0117 929 0884
Fax 0117 915 0124

Tourist and Visitor Information

Tourist Information Centres (TICs)

Lewis, Harris, North Uist, Benbecula, South Uist and Barra

General Enquiries
Western Isles Tourist Board
26 Cromwell Street
Stornoway HS1 2DD
Lewis
Tel: 01851 703088
Fax: 01851 705244
Email: witb@sol.co.uk
Web: www.witb.co.uk

Lewis
Stornoway TIC
26 Cromwell Street
Stornoway HS1 2DD
Tel: 01851 703088
Fax: 01851 705244
Open Jan-Dec

Harris
Tarbert TIC
Pier Road
Tarbert HS3 3DG
Tel: 01859 502011
Fax: 01859 502011
Open Jan-Dec

North Uist
Lochmaddy TIC
Pier Road
Lochmaddy HS6 5AA
Tel: 01876 500321
Fax: 01876 500321
Open end-Mar to Oct – contact Stornoway TIC during winter

South Uist
Lochboisdale TIC
Pier Road
Lochboisdale HS8 5TH
Tel: 01878 700286
Fax: 01878 700286
Open Apr to Oct – contact Stornoway TIC during winter

Barra
Castlebay TIC
Main Street
Castlebay HS9 5XD
Tel: 01871 810336
Fax: 01871 810336
Open mid-Mar to mid-Oct – contact Stornoway TIC during winter

Skye, Raasay and Small Isles

General Enquiries
Highlands of Scotland Tourist Board
Peffery House
Strathpeffer IV14 9HA
Tel: 01997 421160
Fax: 01997 421168
Email: admin@host.co.uk
Web: www.host.co.uk

Skye and Raasay
Portree TIC
Bayfield House
Bayfield Road
Portree IV51 9EL
Tel: 01478 612137
Fax: 01478 612141
Email: portree@host.co.uk
Open Jan-Dec

Broadford TIC
Broadford IV49 9AB
Tel: 01471 822361
Fax: 01471 822141
Open Easter to Oct – contact Portree TIC during winter

Dunvegan TIC
2 Lochside
Dunvegan IV55 8WB
Tel: 01470 521581
Fax: 01470 521582
Open all year: Oct-Mar part-time – contact Portree TIC if unavailable

Uig TIC
Caledonian MacBrayne Ferry Office
Uig Pier
Uig IV51 9XX
Tel: 01470 542404
Fax: 01470 542404
Open Apr-Oct – contact Portree TIC during winter

Small Isles (Eigg, Muck, Canna and Rum)
Mallaig TIC (mainland)
Mallaig PH41 4QS
Tel: 01687 462170
Fax: 01687 462064
Email: mallaig@host.co.uk
Open all year: Oct-Mar open part-time – contact Fort William TIC (tel: 01397 703781; fax: 01397 705184) if unavailable

Mull, Islay, Jura, Colonsay, Gigha, Coll, Tiree, Slate Islands (Seil, Luing, Lunga and Scarba), Lismore, Kerrera, and Bute

General Enquiries
Argyll, the Isles, Loch Lomond, Stirling and Trossachs Tourist Board
Old Town Jail
St John Street
Stirling FK8 1EA
Head office tel: 01786 470945
Fax: 01786 471301
Email: info@scottish.heartlands.org
Web: www.scottish.heartlands.org

Mull
Craignure TIC
The Pier
Craignure PA65 6AY
Tel: 01680 812377
Fax 01680 812497
Open Jan-Dec

Tobermory TIC
Tobermory PA75 6NT
Tel: 01688 302182
Fax: 01688 302145
Open Apr-Oct – contact Craignure TIC in winter

Islay and Jura
Bowmore TIC (Islay)
Bowmore PA43 7JP
Tel: 01496 810254
Fax: 01496 810363
Open Jan-Dec

Colonsay, Coll, Tiree, Slate Islands (Seil, Luing, Lunga and Scarba), Lismore and Kerrera
Oban TIC (Argyll mainland)
Argyll Square
Oban PA34 4AN
Tel: 01631 563122
Fax: 01631 564273
Email: info@oban.org.uk
Open Jan-Dec

Gigha
Campbeltown TIC (Kintyre mainland)
Mackinnon House
The Pier
Campbeltown PA28 6EF
Tel: 01586 552056
Fax: 01586 553291
Open Jan-Dec.

Bute
Rothesay TIC (AILLSTTB)
15 Victoria Street
Rothesay PA20 0AJ
Tel: 01700 502151
Fax: 01700 505156
Open Jan-Dec

Arran and Cumbrae

General Enquiries
Ayrshire and Arran Tourist Board
Burns House
Burns Statue Square
Ayr KA7 1UP
Tel: 01292 288688
Fax: 01292 288686
Email: ayr@ayrshire-arran.com;
Web: www.ayrshire-arran.com

Arran
Brodick TIC
The Pier
Brodick KA27 8AU
Tel: 01770 302140/401
Fax: 01770 302395
Email: aatbayr@aol.com
Open Jan-Dec

Cumbrae
Millport TIC
28 Stuart Street
Millport KA28 0AJ
Tel: 01475 530753
Fax: 01475 530753
Open Easter-Jun wknds only; Jun-Sep open seven days; closed Oct-Easter – contact Largs TIC (mainland) if unavailable

Largs TIC (Ayrshire mainland)
Promenade
Largs KA30 8BQ
Tel: 01475 673765
Fax: 01475 676297
Email: ayr@ayrshire-arran.com
Open Jan-Dec

Scotland – General

Scottish Tourist Board
23 Ravelston Terrace
Edinburgh EH4 3TP
Tel: 0131 332 2433
Fax 0131 315 4545
Web: www.holiday.scotland.net
(phone and correspondence only)

Scottish Tourist Board
19 Cockspur Street
London SW1Y 5BL
Tel: 0171 930 8661
Fax: 0171 930 1817
Web: www.holiday.scotland.net
(Also Britain Visitor Centre Scotland Desk,
1 Regent Street, London SW1Y 4XT –
personal callers only; open seven days)

Map 1: The Hebrides – main ferry routes and TICs

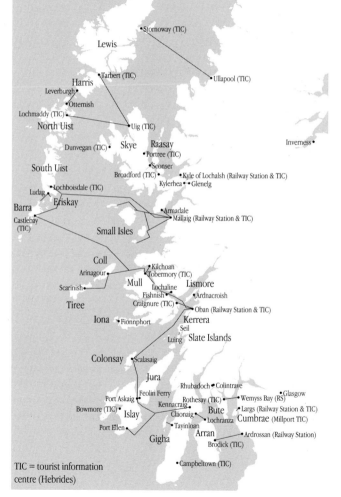

Stornoway (TIC)

Lewis

Tarbert (TIC)

Harris

Leverburgh

Otternish

Lochmaddy (TIC)

North Uist

Uig (TIC)

Ullapool (TIC)

Dunvegan (TIC) Skye Raasay

Portree (TIC)

Inverness

South Uist

Sconser

Broadford (TIC) Kyle of Lochalsh (Railway Station & TIC)

Kylerhea Glenelg

Ludag Lochboisdale (TIC)

Barra Eriskay

Castlebay
(TIC)

Small Isles

Armadale

Mallaig (Railway Station & TIC)

Coll

Kilchoan

Arinagour Tobermory (TIC)

Mull Lismore

Lochaline

Scarinish Fishnish Ardnacroish

Craignure (TIC) Oban (Railway Station & TIC)

Tiree

Iona Fionnphort Kerrera

Seil

Luing Slate Islands

Colonsay Scalasaig

Jura Rhubadoch Colintrave

Port Askaig Feolin Ferry Rothesay (TIC) Wemyss Bay (RS) Glasgow

Kennacraig Bute Largs (Railway Station & TIC)

Bowmore (TIC) Islay Claonaig Lochranza Cumbrae (Millport TIC)

Port Ellen Tayinloan Arran Ardrossan (Railway Station)

Gigha Brodick (TIC)

Campbeltown (TIC)

TIC = tourist information
centre (Hebrides)

Map 2: The Hebrides

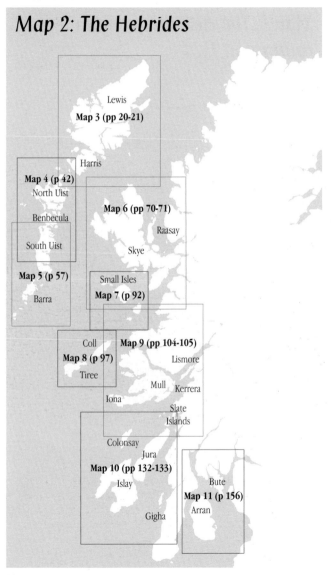

Lewis
Map 3 (pp 20-21)

Harris

Map 4 (p 42)
North Uist

Benbecula

South Uist

Map 5 (p 57)

Barra

Map 6 (pp 70-71)

Raasay

Skye

Small Isles
Map 7 (p 92)

Coll
Map 8 (p 97)
Tiree

Map 9 (pp 104-105)

Lismore

Mull   Kerrera

Iona

Slate
Islands

Colonsay

Jura
Map 10 (pp 132-133)

Islay

Gigha

Bute
Map 11 (p 156)
Arran

Introduction

The western islands of Scotland were called the *Hebudes* by Pliny the Elder in 77 AD – at which time the Romans were conquering their way up the length of Britain – and *Ebudae* in Greek by Ptolemy. Apparently following a misprint, this became 'Hebrides', by which name they are known to this day.

Iona.

This book covers the Hebrides, both the Outer and Inner islands. The Outer Hebrides run from the Butt of Lewis in the north to the small islands of Mingulay and Berneray in the south. The larger of the islands are Lewis and Harris, St Kilda, North Uist, Benbecula, South Uist and Barra. The Inner Hebrides consist of Skye, Raasay, the Small Isles (Rum, Eigg, Canna and Muck), Coll, Tiree, Lismore, Kerrera, Mull, Iona, Slate Islands, Colonsay, Jura, Islay, Gigha, and (at least anciently) Bute, Cumbrae and Arran.

The Hebrides of Scotland are a picturesque and magnificent collection of islands. The climate is softened by the Gulf Stream – warmer water which flows up from the south – and the range of diversity of landscapes is breathtaking. Although the weather can be wet and windy, Tiree gets more sunshine than any other place in Britain and the climate is often fine, sunny and warm. Parts of many of the islands are fertile and lush, while others area are rough, heather-clad and mountainous. The Cuillin mountains of Skye, the hills of Harris, and St Kilda and Rum all present an impressive aspect. There are fantastic beaches throughout, from Coll and Tiree, the Uists, Uig sands on Lewis, Barra, Mull, Islay and Bute. Spring flowers are also particularly impressive on the machair (sandy fertile land) on many islands, and the peat moors of Lewis, North Uist and Islay have their own grandeur. There are also the towering cliffs on many islands, and the interesting geological features of the Quirang and Storr on Skye and the Carsaig Arches on Mull.

Because of the diversity of habitats, the islands are home to a huge range of plant life and wildlife. There are hundreds of species of birds and wildfowl, including eagles, swans, ducks, geese, owls, and of seabirds: puffins, fulmars, terns, kittiwakes and cormorants to name but a few. There are also otters, deer, wild goats, pine marten, hares and seals, and dolphins, porpoises and whales. One slightly less welcome inhabitant is the dreaded midge, which stalk the summer months. Bad times for getting bitten are on still summer evenings or in sheltered places near water. There are also lots of sheep, many of which wander over roads without taking any notice of traffic – because they were there first.

The Hebrides have been inhabited from at least 5000 or 6000 BC. These earliest people were probably nomads, but by 4000 BC farmers had settled, bringing with them domestic animals. To some the Hebrides may now seem remote, but in prehistoric times and indeed through medieval times, transport by boat was quicker and easier. This made the Hebrides an ideal area both to settle in and travel, trade and raid from.

There are a huge number of fine prehistoric sites on the islands, including the splendid standing stones at Callanish on Lewis which is the centre of a large complex of prehistoric monuments, believed to have been a lunar observatory. Machrie Moor on Arran has the remains of at least six circles. There are many interesting burial cairns, including Barpa Langass on North Uist, standing stones and circles and the remains of ancient settlements, including the site at Bosta on Great Bernera. Many of these sites have yet to be excavated.

The climate deteriorated from around 1000 BC, and peat began to form, and there may have also been an influx of people from the continent as the centuries passed. Whatever the reason, the inhabitants chose to live in forts, duns and brochs, built to defend the population against invaders or rival tribes. Duns were fortified sites, usually on a rocky crag or cliff top, further defended by a strong wall; while brochs were round dry-stone towers with a gallery running up inside the wall. There are hundreds of these sites throughout the western isles. Dun Carloway on Lewis is the best preserved broch in the Hebrides.

Callanish, Lewis.

The Picts appear to have controlled many of the islands. Evidence of their occupation survives in some Pictish carved stones: Clach Ard at Tote on Skye and a sculpted stone in the garden of Raasay House. Pictish stones have also been found on some of the outer isles, including Benbecula and Pabbay, south of Barra. From 300 AD Scots from Ireland began to arrive in the southern Inner Hebrides and Argyll, and in 500 AD Fergus MacErc was made king of Dalriada, and whose kingdom covered this area.

Christianity probably came to Scotland with the Romans along Hadrian's Wall by the 4th century AD, and St Ninian was active in Galloway from 430 and possibly also on Bute. Other early missionaries founded monasteries in the Hebrides in the 6th century, including St Blane at Kingarth on Bute, St Brendan at Eileach nan Naoimh in the Garvellachs, St Colmac on Eilean Mor off the coast of Jura, St Moluag on Lismore, and of course St Columba on the peaceful island of Iona. Many kings were buried on the island by the Reilig Odhrain – 'Street of the Dead': kings of Scots (including Duncan and Macbeth), Irish, Norwegian and even French rulers, as well as the Lords of the Isles. From Iona Columba converted the northern Picts and increased the power of the Dalriadic kings. Later ecclesiastical sites include the Priory on Oronsay, several sites on Islay, Howmore on South Uist, Teampull na Trionaid on

North Uist, Teampull Eoropie at Ness on Lewis, and Inch Kenneth off the coast of Mull. There is also a well-preserved early Christian monastic site on Rona, forty or so miles north of the Butt of Lewis.

Teampull na Trionaid, North Uist.

From the 8th century Vikings from Scandinavia savagely raided along the coasts of the islands in their longships, devastating Iona and slaughtering the monks. They then came as settlers, forming an often unruly Viking province. The Picts lost influence in the islands, and the Scots were sorely beset in the southern isles and in Argyll, eventually being driven eastwards.

In the Outer Hebrides Norse place names predominate. The Vikings had a profound effect on all the islands from Islay (and the Isle of Man) all the way north to Lewis. The Norsemen even fought among each other until the northern islands were controlled by Ketil Flatnose around the turn of the 10th century. They remained lawless, however, and men from the Hebrides began to raid the coasts of Norway. The islands were seized by the Danes of Dublin, who were then driven out by Sigurd the Stout, Earl of Orkney, in 990, who added the islands to his own earldom of Orkney and Shetland. When he was killed at the battle of Clontarf in Ireland in 1014, they passed to his son Thorfinn the Mighty, who held them until he died. In the 1070s Godred Craven became king of Man and extended his influence to the north, but the islands remained disputed and rebellious. Godred died on Islay.

To enforce his overlordship and pacify the area, Magnus Barelegs, king of Norway, sailed south in his longships and harried the islands. He reached an agreement with the king of Scots that any island on the western seaboard around which he could sail a helmed ship was a possession of the Norwegians. This included all the Inner and Outer Hebrides, as well as the islands in the Firth of Clyde: Arran, Cumbrae and Bute, the Isle of Man and the peninsula of Kintyre. Magnus wanted the isthmus of Kintyre and had his longship dragged over the short strip of land between East and West Tarbert. The southern islands, at least, were subject to the kingdom of Man, itself subject to Norway, and were to remain under the control of the Norwegians for the next 150 years.

In 1158 Somerled, of mixed Scots and Norse blood, raised a force and drove out the king of Man and made himself virtually the independent ruler of the Hebrides. So powerful was Somerled that he threatened the then king of Scots, Malcolm the Maiden, and he landed at Renfrew with an army. Somerled was assassinated in his tent, however, and his forces disbanded. The southern islands were held by his sons, through which both the MacDonalds and the MacDougalls were descended.

The kings of Scots were increasingly determined to control the Hebrides, and in the reign of Alexander II – when relations with England were relatively peaceful – the king of Scots mounted an expedition to wrest control from the Norwegians. Alexander II died on Kerrera in 1249, but his son, Alexander III, pursued the policy. He wreaked havoc in the north, and king Haco of Norway assembled a large force of longships and sailed south in 1263. His armada was wrecked by storms, and his men were beaten at a battle at Largs, and he retired to Orkney, where he died. Three years later the islands were ceded to the Scots. From this time Gaelic increasingly predominated in the islands and Viking influence waned.

Angus Og MacDonald of Islay was a supporter and friend of Robert the Bruce in the 14th century. After the victory at Bannockburn (where Angus had fought along side Bruce), Angus controlled most of the southern Hebrides. The MacDonalds' position was further strengthened when John of Islay married Amy MacRuari, heiress of the MacIans. With this marriage, John assumed control of all the Hebrides and used the title Lord of the Isles. John divorced Amy – although it is from her that the Clan Ranald branch of the MacDonalds were descended – and married Margaret, daughter of the future Robert II.

Gaelic culture and learning flourished throughout the Hebrides, and the Lords of the Isles rivalled even the kings of Scots in splendour, sophistication and power. They were great patrons of medicine and the church, and stone carving flourished at Iona and Oronsay, as well as on Argyll, with the sculpting of fabulous stone crosses and gravestones. There had been a tradition of carving for centuries, and the (earlier) crosses at Kildalton on Islay and at Iona are the finest in the islands or even Scotland. The Lords had an important base at Finlaggan on Islay, where they were inaugurated, although they were buried at Iona by the Street of the Dead.

In 1425 the Lords also gained the earldom of Ross, after a dispute which had led to the bloody battle of Harlaw, near Aberdeen, in 1411. The strength and independence of the Lords brought them into conflict with the kings of Scots, whose high-handedness in dealing with the lords further worsened the situation. This culminated with an expedition to the Hebrides by James IV, king of Scots, in 1493. The last Lord was forfeited that year, and died in Paisley Abbey. The MacDonalds tried to regain their former power but never succeeded – losing influence to other clans, particularly the Campbells of Argyll. James V made another expedition to restore order in 1540, but unrest of one kind or another followed until the middle of the 18th century.

The islands of the Hebrides belonged to various clans and families: the major ones are listed below. In the Outer Hebrides, Lewis was held by the MacLeods of Lewis, who had a castle at Stornoway; Harris by the MacLeods of Dunvegan and Harris, who also held much of Skye – Dunvegan Castle has been continuously occupied from the 13th century and they also had the fine church of St Clement's at Rodel on Harris. North Uist, Benbecula and South Uist were held by the MacDonalds of Clan Ranald – who had a stronghold at Borve on Benbecula – as were the Small Isles. Barra was held by the MacNeils who had a castle at Kiessimul in Castlebay. Tiree, Coll and Mull were held by the MacLeans of Duart, while Ulva was held by the MacQuarries from Dun Ban. Colonsay was held by the MacDuffies; Islay and south Jura to Tarbert by the MacDonalds from their stronghold of Dunyvaig; and the north of Jura and Slate Islands by the MacLeans in Glengarrisdale. Lismore by the Stewarts of Appin and Kerrera by the MacDougalls. Arran was held by the Hamiltons from Brodick, Cumbrae by the Montgomerys from Ballikillet, and Bute by the Stewarts from Rothesay. Ownership changed over time as the Campbells became increasingly powerful, while the fortunes of other clans waxed and waned. Long-running feuds between the MacLeods and MacDonalds led to the atrocities at Trumpan, on Skye, and on Rum.

The islands were seen as a source of good fighting men from the 17th century. Many of the clans were loyal to the Stewart kings and fought with the Marquis of Montrose in the 1640s in support of Charles I during the Civil War (they also took part in an attempt to reduce the power of the Campbells). This led to a punitive and brutal expedition through the islands by the Covenanter forces of David Leslie. There was also resistance to Cromwell after Charles's execution, and Cromwell took Stornoway Castle in Lewis by force, although his garrison were slaughtered.

Many of the clans were Jacobites during all, or part, of the Jacobite Risings, supporting Bonnie Dundee at the early battle of Killiecrankie in 1689, although enthusiasm wavered for later risings. By 1745, after he had landed at Eriskay, Bonnie Prince Charlie was disappointed by his lack of support. Clans – or at least their chiefs – such as the MacDonalds of Sleat, MacLeods of Dunvegan and MacNeils of Barra were lukewarm at best.

After defeat at Culloden in 1746, Bonnie Prince Charlie was sheltered in the Outer Hebrides and on Skye, where he was helped by Flora MacDonald. He eventually managed to get back to the mainland, from where he fled Scotland never to return. The measures following the 1745 Rising were proscriptive: the wearing of tartan and plaid was banned, as was the playing of bagpipes and the carrying of weapons. This was done to destroy the clans and their Gaelic culture. Supporters of the prince were harshly treated.

A long-term outcome of these measures was the disintegration of the clan system. Landlords were no longer content to calculate their wealth by manpower and increasingly looked for monetary rewards from their lands and estates. This led to land being cleared of people and replaced by sheep – the Clearances – in the late 18th and through the 19th centuries. Many islanders emigrated to the lowlands of Scotland, and abroad to North America, Australia and New Zealand. Others were forced on to marginal coastal land, from where crofting developed: fishing was supposed to augment the limited agricultural potential as was the kelp industry. Many men also joined the British army, creating outstanding regiments who were to be crucial in creating the British empire.

The rate of clearances varied down the years, and at times landlords even tried to prevent their people leaving when they needed manpower for the flourishing kelp industry and burgeoning fishing of the early 19th century. When the kelp industry collapsed in the 1820s, the Clearances began afresh, also spurred on by rent rises, poverty and famine, particularly the potato famine of 1846. The people had been replaced by sheep, and later sporting estates, and their lot was dire. The Clearances were particularly harsh on the Uists, Skye, Raasay, Rum and Tiree. The speaking of Gaelic was at best ignored and, at worst, discouraged by the authorities.

Eventually some islanders rose, refused to pay their rents, and there were disturbances in many places, including the Battle of the Braes of

Abandoned settlement, Mull.

1882 on Skye and at Sollas on North Uist. Some improvements were put in place following the Napier Commission and the Crofter's Act of 1886, giving crofters greater rights of land tenure. The position, however, could still be further improved, and there are still many absentee landlords with feudal power over the tenants. Community co-operative purchasing of estates seems to be a way forward, both in the Hebrides and the rest of the Highlands.

Tourism is now a major industry throughout the islands, along with crofting, fishing and fish farming, whisky and arts and crafts. Gaelic still flourishes in many places, particularly the Outer Hebrides and on Skye where there is now a Gaelic college at Sabhal Mor Ostaig. Many Gaelic-speaking areas follow the Free Church of Scotland, a Presbyterian church which broke from the Church of Scotland in the 19th century, although Barra and South Uist are predominantly Roman Catholic.

The Outer Hebrides

Lewis, Harris, St Kilda, North Uist, Benbecula, South Uist, Barra and nearby islands

Map 3: Lewis and Harris

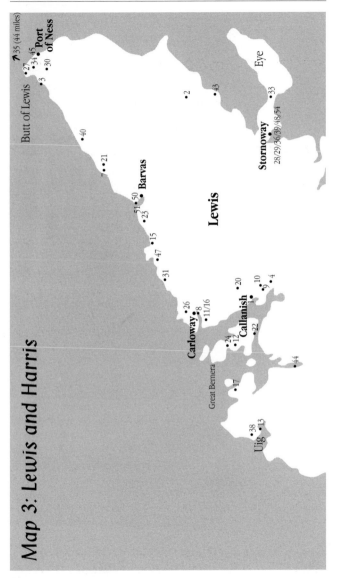

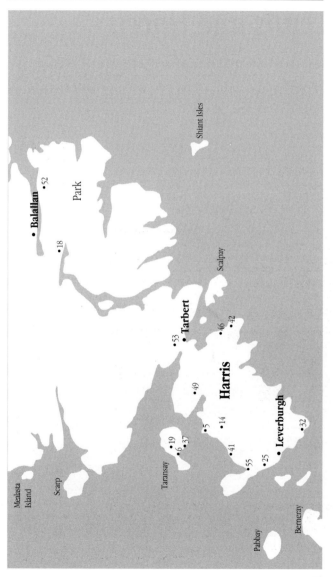

Lewis and Harris

(Lewis 'marshy place' or 'place/house of song')
(Harris 'high island' from Norse; Na Hearadh in Gaelic)

All the islands offer a wide range of outdoor activities, including hill walking, climbing, cycling, diving, boat trips, bird watching, fishing and visiting a wide and splendid range of archaeological and historic sites, museums, arts and crafts, beaches and viewpoints.

The deeply held religious beliefs on all the islands of the Outer Hebrides mean that most shops and petrol stations are closed on a Sunday, and there is no scheduled public transport.

In Lewis and Harris most hotel bars, public houses and restaurants are also closed on Sundays, although some hotels are open to non-residents for meals.

Many shops also close on Wednesday afternoons, and there is a restricted bus service on Wednesdays.

The Western Isles Tourist Map has both English and Gaelic place names. The Western Islands Tourist Board has its own website on the Internet: www.witb.co.uk

There are a large number of music, arts and activities throughout the islands, including this small selection: Lewis Half Marathon, Harris Mod, Lochmaddy Boat Festival, Hebridean Celtic Music Festival, South Uist Highland Games and Twin Peaks Hill Race – contact TIC for full schedule. The Royal National Mod is to be held in the islands in 2001.

Tolsta Chaolais, Lewis.

In Brief

Callanish Standing Stones. Dun Carloway Broch. Uig Sands. Sheep. St Clement's Church, Rodel. Arnol blackhouse. Waves, beaches, moors and hills. Sunsets. Gaelic.

Location (see map 3, pp 20-21)

OS Landranger maps 8, 13, 14, 18
Off NW coast of Scotland, 20 miles N of Skye

Tourist Information Centres

Stornoway, Lewis (tel: 01851 703088; fax: 01851 705244; email witb@sol.co.uk)
Open Jan-Dec
Tarbert, Harris (tel: 01859 502011; fax: 01859 502011)
Open Jan-Dec

How to Get There

By vehicle ferry from Ullapool on mainland to Stornoway on Lewis (2hrs 40 mins; CalMac tel: 01854 612358 or 01851 702361)
By vehicle ferry from Uig on Skye to Tarbert on Harris (1hr 45 mins; CalMac tel: 01470 542219 or 01859 502444)
By passenger ferry from Otternish on North Uist to Leverburgh on Harris (50 mins; Cal Mac 01876 500337 or 01859 502444)
By air from Glasgow, Inverness, Barra or Benbecula (British Airways tel: 0345 222111)
By bridge from Scalpay

Although Lewis and Harris are thought of as being separate, and were in fact in different administrative areas, they are in fact one island. This is the largest of the Hebrides (and the largest island in the British Isles except for Ireland).

Wildlife

Seabirds and wildfowl, including gannets, terns, cormorants, skuas, fulmars, kittiwakes, oystercatchers, ringed plovers, corncrakes, waders and greylag geese, as well as wintering birds such as Greenland and white-fronted geese, whooper swans and redwing. Basking sharks, dolphins and whales. Seals and otters.

Notes

In most places sheep are timid creatures who are likely to run from humans and cars – and normally are kept within fields. In Lewis, however, the sheep roam everywhere and are friendly and bold. They will happily stand chewing in the middle of the road, blocking the traffic, seemingly for hours, or will single-mindedly follow the walker for miles. Be warned: being stalked by a whole flock of sheep can be surprisingly disconcerting.

When emptying ranges or peat fires, do not put the embers into a plastic bin unless you mean to generate smoke.

Most signposts are in Gaelic as well as English.

LEWIS

Notes

There is a sign-posted walk from Garenin to Dalbeg and from Tolsta to Ness. Many events throughout the year. Fishing, sea angling and sea cruises. Guided and study tours. There is an eighteen-hole golf course. Hostels.

Basic Info

Lewis is about 45 miles long and 30 miles at its widest. It covers some 600 square miles, and has a population of 20,200. The island is relatively flat, and much of it is covered by peat moor, which only started forming some 5000 years ago. The south of the island is a mass of lochans and sea inlets, and is hillier than the north: Benmore and Mealsabhal are both about 1750 feet high.

There are superb sandy beaches at Traigh Mhor and Port Geiraha, Port of Ness, Bosta on Great Bernera, Traigh na Berie and Uig Sands, where the famous Lewis chessmen were found. Other particularly scenic places are the viewpoints from the cliffs and lighthouse at Butt of Lewis, built in 1862, where the waves can be spectacular. Tiumpan Head Lighthouse on Point; Valtos; and North Lochs are also picturesque. There are impressive cliffs, rising straight out of the sea, with flocks of seabirds at Swordale.

The largest town in Lewis (and the Hebrides) is Stornoway, which is also the centre of the Islands Council 'Comhairle nan Eilean'. The town has an excellent harbour and a fish market, and there are more than 8000 inhabitants. There are also many settlements along the west and east coasts.

There is a thriving Gaelic-speaking culture in Lewis, with a Gaelic local radio station, Gaelic television programmes, and the Gaelic publisher Acair. Most of the population are presbyterian. There are many Gaelic events held on the islands, contact the TIC at Stornoway for details – 01851 703088.

History

Lewis has some of the foremost prehistoric sites in Scotland, most notably the stones at Callanish, the standing stone at Ballantrushal, and the well-preserved broch at Dun Carloway.

The Outer Hebrides were first raided by the Vikings in the 9th century, and then held by them until 1266. There are several interesting churches on Lewis, including the 12th-century chapel at Eorrapaidh and the ruins on the isthmus of the Eye Peninsula near Stornoway.

The lands were long a property of the MacLeods of Lewis, who had a castle at Stornoway – although nothing remains of it – but Lewis was granted to the Mackenzies, later Earls of Seaforth, in 1610 by James VI. In 1599 Fife adventurers, with 600 mercenaries, had tried to 'colonise' the island, but their base at Holm, near Stornoway, was stormed by a force of islanders led by Tormod MacLeod, and many were slain. Stornoway was occupied by Cromwellian forces in 1653 and the 5th Earl of Seaforth was forfeited for his part in the Jacobite Risings of 1715 and 1719. The 6th Earl recovered his estates in 1741, and did not take part in the Jacobite Rising of 1745-6. The island was sold by the Mackenzies to Sir James Matheson in 1844 and he held it until his death in 1878. He built Lews Castle on the site of an old house of the Mackenzies.

The blackhouse at Arnol is an interesting example of a Lewis house from the 19th century.

Stornoway, Lewis.

The blackhouses at Gearrannan, a traditional crofting village, are being restored and used as hostels. The men of Ness were famous for 'guga' hunting – killing and preserving young gannets – each year on Sula Sgeir, a rock in the open sea some 40 miles north of the Butt of Lewis – which is now a nature reserve. Near to it is the island of Rona with its oratory.

Matheson's factor was responsible for trying to evict many crofters, and this resulted in much discontent in Lewis and Great Bernera. South Lochs, also known as Park, was the location of the Park Deer Raid in 1887, when crofters drew attention to the hardships they faced by occupying part of the area and killing some of Matheson's deer. A cairn has recently been erected to commemorate the event, and there are others to mark the Highland Land Raids at Aignish, Greiss and Balallan.

The ship *Iolaire*, carrying 260 seaman back to Lewis after the First World War sank off Stornoway harbour with the loss of over 200 men. This was added to the high loss of life (over 1000 men) the relatively small population had to suffer during that war.

From 1918 Lewis and Harris were a property of Lord Leverhulme. Leverhulme spent a fortune trying to make Lewis and Harris more prosperous by exploiting herring, but was ultimately unsuccessful, although he did give much land to the islanders. One of his projects was to build a road up the east coast of the island to Ness. The project was abandoned, leaving the 'bridge to nowhere' north of New Tolsta.

Great Bernera

Located in Loch Roag on the south-west coast of Lewis, Great Bernera is about 5.5 miles long and up to three miles wide. The island is reached over the 'bridge over the Atlantic', and is relatively flat, only reaching just over 200 feet, with many lochans and rocky outcrops. There is a superb beach at Bosta, with stunning white sand. Wildlife includes multitudes of birds, including eagles and gannets, otters, seals and dolphins.

There is a restored Norse mill and community centre and museum, standings stones, and Dun Baravat, an Iron Age dun. There was a 'riot' here in 1872, when local crofters – angered at eviction notices and the arrogance of Sir James Matheson's factor – were engaged in scuffles with the local law enforcement officers. The mainstay of the local population is fishing for lobsters. Loch fishing is available.

Little Bernera

Small island to the north of Great Bernera, which is about one mile long. Little remains of two old chapels, dedicated to St Michael and St Donan, and the associated burial ground is being eroded by the sea.

Pabay Mor

Small island, about one mile long, off coast at Valtos and west of Great Bernera. There are traces of an old church, dedicated to St Peter.

Other islets in Loch Roag include **Vacsay**, **Vuia Mor** and **Vuia Beag**, **Floday**, **Eilean Kearstay**, **Orasay Island** and **Keava**.

Eilean Chaluim Chille

Small island, with a church dedicated to St Columba, in the mouth of Loch Erisort, where there are several other islets.

Eilean Iubhard

Small island, one mile long, at the mouth of Loch Shell.

Seaforth Island

Island in Loch Seaforth, 1.5 miles long, and rising to over 700 feet high. The Mackenzies were made Earls of Seaforth in 1623, but forfeited for their part in the Jacobite Rising of 1715.

Shiant Isles

Group of picturesque islands ('sacred or charmed isles') some four miles south-east of Lewis mainland across Sound of Shiant. The main island – Garbh Eilean and Eilean an Tighe – is two miles long, with a smaller island to the east, Eilean Mhuire. The islands have high cliffs and columns similar to those found on Staffa and Ulva, and they support a large colony of puffins, guillemots and fulmars.

The isles were once thought to be the 'resort of fairies, elves and other supernatural beings' – hence the name. There are the ruins of a chapel, dedicated to St Mary, on Eilean Mhuire; and there has been a small Christian monastery or hermitage on Eilean Garbh. The island had a small population (of eight) in 1900, but is now abandoned. Sir Compton Mackenzie spent some time living and writing here in the 1930s.

Rona

Small island ('rough island' or 'St Ronan's Isle'), also known as North Rona, 45 miles north of the Butt of Lewis, one mile long, and rises to 355 feet. There was a cell or hermitage here [HW 809323], dedicated to St Ronan, which consists of a small oratory, dating from the 7th or 8th century, and cashel. A stone cross from the island is now at St Moluag's Church at Eoropie. The last inhabitant of the island left in 1844. The island is accessible from Ness (in calm weather). It is a National Nature Reserve, in the care of Scottish National Heritage, from who permission should be sought in advance (tel: 0131 447 4784).

Flannan Isles

Group of islands, 21 miles north-west of Lewis at Gallan Head. Standing on Eilean Mor, the largest of the group, are the remains of a small chapel or oratory, which has a corbelled roof and dates from the 7th or 8th century. It was dedicated to St Flannan, a 7th-century Irish saint, and islanders from the west of Lewis are said to have made pilgrimages to the isles, even after the Reformation. The islands are also known as the Seven Hunters, and are home to flocks of seabirds, which at one time were exploited by islanders from Lewis at great peril to their own lives. There is a lighthouse on Eilean Mor, the scene of a mystery when the three lighthouse keepers disappeared in 1900.

Butt of Lewis.

Harris

Basic Info

Harris is divided from Lewis by the long sea lochs of Loch Seaforth and Loch Resort, and is 21 miles long, at most, by 18 miles wide. Harris is nearly cut in two by East and West Loch Tarbert, and has an area of 90 square miles. The area is much more mountainous than Lewis, and Clisham is the highest hill at 2622 feet. There are superb beaches on the west coast, including Traigh Scarista, Luskentyre, Taobh Tuath, and Huisinis Bay, with views to Scarp. The east of the island is rougher: rocky with many lochans and sea inlets, although many people live here now: again the island was cleared, and folk were moved to the east from the more fertile west side of the island.

The population is about 2200, and many of the population speak Gaelic and are presbyterian. The largest settlement is Leverburgh, followed by Tarbert, which is the administrative capital and has a local history exhibition in the Old School Hostel. The island has a nine-hole golf course at Scarista, and there are fine views from Manish.

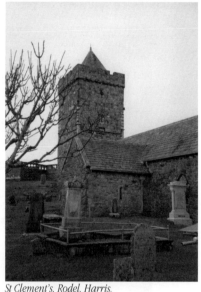

St Clement's, Rodel, Harris.

History

Harris was occupied from earliest times, but there are relatively few prehistoric remains. There is the fine standing stone known as Clach Mhic Leod, a ruinous dun at Borve, and the remains of the chapel at Rubh an' Teampull which is built on the site of a broch. Harris was held by the Norsemen, part of the Lordship of the Isles, and then long a property of the MacLeods of Dunvegan and Harris, confirmed in 1498. Alasdair Crotach MacLeod built himself the spectacular tomb in the church at Rodel.

The lands passed to the Murray Earl of Dunmore, who built Amhuinnsuidhe Castle [NB 045085], then the soap magnate Lord Leverhulme, who bought the islands in 1918-9 and tried to make Harris more prosperous by buying fishing boats and improving communications: Leverburgh is named after him. With his death in 1925, his schemes failed.

The island was the centre of the Harris Tweed industry, and although more of the fabric is now produced on Lewis, there are fine examples to be had on Harris. The whaling industry was once important, employing many local people until 1930, and there are the remains of a

Norwegian whaling station at Bunavoneadar [NB 130045]. Lord Leverhulme purchased the station and boats in 1922, and over the next few years it processed 6000 tons of whale meat, but closed in 1929.

Today
Crofting and fishing. Tourism. Harris Tweed.

Scalpay

Island ('ship river island') in East Loch Tarbert, 3.5 miles south-east of Tarbert. The island is three miles long by two miles wide, and there are several islets off the west coast. Scalpay has a substantial and relatively dense population of 450, and there is a bridge connecting it to Harris. Fishing is the main industry.

 The lighthouse on the south-eastern tip is built on the site of one of the first four lighthouses erected by the Commissioners of Northern Lights in 1787, although the lighthouse was rebuilt in 1826. The lighthouse is no longer manned, and the original light mechanism is in the Museum of Scotland.

 Scotasay lies one mile to the north-west.

Stockinish Island

Small island at mouth of Loch Stockinish, six miles south of Tarbert.

Scarp

Island ('scarped or cliff isle') 0.5 miles off the west coast of North Harris, three miles long and two wide. The island is extremely hilly and rocky, and rises to over 1000 feet. The island supported a population of over 200 in the 19th century, but has since been abandoned except for holiday cottages.

 Gasker is an islet five miles south-west of Scarp.

Soay Mor and Soay Beg

Islets ('sow's islands') 0.5 miles west of North Harris, and one mile north-east of Taransay. The bones and dagger of a murderer who fled from Lewis are said to have been found in a cave here [NB 067045], known as Tigh Dugan or 'Duncan's House'.

Taransay

Substantial island ('St Taran's Isle') 1.5 miles west of Harris at the entrance to West Loch Tarbert. The island is 4.5 miles long and about 3 miles at its widest, and Loch na h-Uidhe nearly divides it in two. It is a rough and hilly island, and Ben Raah is 881 feet high, with sandy beaches on its eastern side. There is a cross-incised stone, and the remains of two chapels, one dedicated to St Taran or Torrannan a 6th-century saint.

There are many islands in the Sound of Harris, between Harris and North Uist (see entry on North Uist). Berneray is still inhabited, but the rest of the islands were cleared of people during the 19th century.

Ensay

Small island in the Sound of Harris, two miles west of Leverburgh. It is one mile long, and is fertile and reasonably flat, and there are the remains of a chapel.

Killegray

Small island, just south of Ensay, and two miles east of the northern coast of Berneray. The island is also one mile long.

Pabbay

Round island ('priest's island') five miles west of Leverburgh and two miles north-west of Berneray. The island rises to 1000 feet, but formerly had much good land – fine harvests of corn are said to have been got from here. There are sandy beaches along its south-east coast, and the remains of two churches, the larger of which Teampull Mhoire is believed to have been dedicated to St Mary, while the smaller Teampull Beag was dedicated to St Moluag. There is an islet **Shillay** one mile to the north.

Callanish Standing Stones, Lewis.

Places of Interest

Prehistoric

Callanish Standing Stones

Off A858, 14 miles W of Stornoway, Callanish, Lewis.

HS NB 213330 LR: 8 (Map ref: 1)

Probably constructed between 3000 and 1500 BC, this is one of the most important and unique sites in Britain, and forms only part of a much larger complex of stones and circles, said to cover some twenty sites in all.

The main setting consists of an avenue of nineteen upright stones, leading north from a circle of thirteen stones, with rows of more stones fanning out to the south, east and west. The tallest stone is over fifteen feet tall, and inside the central circle is a small burial cairn. The stones seem to have been aligned to mirror, with outlying settings, the position of the moon at the summer and winter solstices, and at the equinoxes. The stones, incidentally, were far less impressive until a thick layer of peat was removed in 1857.

The visitor centre, which is not visible from the stones, has an exhibition 'The Story of the Stones' and interpretative information about Callanish.

There are further interesting and accessible circles at Cnoc Ceann a' Gharaidh [NB 223326] (Callanish II) down a track off the A858, Cnoc Fillibhir [NB 225327] by foot south of the A858 and Garynahine or Ceann Hulavig [NB 230305], west of the B8011 (all of which also have separate entries).

The stones were evidently quarried from a rocky outcrop at Druim nan Eum [NB 230336], where there are several prostrate slabs.

Sites open all year; visitor centre open Apr-Oct, Mon-Sat 10.00-19.00; Oct-Mar, Mon-Sat 10.00-16.00.

Visitor Centre: Explanatory displays. Gift shop. Tearoom. WC. Disabled access. Car and coach parking.

Tel: 01851 621422 Fax: 01851 621446
Email: calanais.centre@btinternet.com

Carn a' Mharc

Off B895, 6.5 miles NE of Stornoway, Loch a' Chairn, Lewis.

NB 472439 LR: 8 (Map ref: 2)

Located 1.5 miles north-west of Griais is a cham-

bered burial cairn, some 100 feet by 80 feet, and surviving to a height of ten feet. Part of the kerb can be traced, and the chamber lies in the middle of the cairn.

Carnan a' Ghrodhair Souterrain

Off A857, 2 miles W of Port of Ness, 1 mile N of Habost, Lewis.

NB 512640 LR: 8 (Map ref: 3)

A souterrain consists of an underground passageway, which is about ten feet long, and the ruins of a cell. The entrance is blocked, and the structure is near the burial ground.

Ceann Hulavig Stone Circle

Off B8011, 2 miles SE of Callanish, Ceann Hulavig, Lewis.

NB 230304 LR: 13 (Map ref: 4)

A stone circle, just west of the main road, now consists of five upright stones, varying in height from seven to nine feet. There are traces of a burial cairn within the stones. This circle is probably associated with the main site at Callanish [NB 214330], and is also known as Callanish IV.

Clach Mhic Leoid

Off A859, 6 miles N of Leverburgh, Nisabost, Harris.

NG 041973 LR: 18 (Map ref: 5)

A tall and impressive standing stone, over ten feet high.

Clach an Teampull

E side of Loch na h-Uidhe, S coast of Taransay.

NB 013008 LR: 18 (Map ref: 6)

A standing stone, about six feet tall, has a cross cut into one side. There was probably a chapel nearby.

Clach an Trushal

Off A857, 2.5 miles N of Barvas, Ballantrushal, Lewis.

NB 375538 LR: 8 (Map ref: 7)

An impressive standing stone, at a slight angle, some twenty feet or so high. It is said to mark the site of a battle, and to be one of the tallest standing stones in Scotland.

Clach an Tursa

Off A858, 6 miles N of Callanish, Carloway, Lewis.

NB 204430 LR: 8 (Map ref: 8)

A standing stone, 7.5 feet in height, with two fallen stones nearby. Clach an Tursa means 'stone of sorrow'.

Cnoc Ceann a' Gharaidh Stone Circle

Off A858, 1 mile SE of Callanish, Cnoc Ceann a' Gharaidh, Lewis.

NB 222326 LR: 8 (Map ref: 9)

At the end of a track south of the main road is a stone circle – apparently actually an ellipse – of which five stones remain upright, the tallest of which is around ten feet tall. The circle surrounds a burial cairn. Also known as Callanish II.

Cnoc Fillibhir Bheag Stone Circle

Off A858, 1 mile SE of Callanish, Cnoc Fillibhir Bheag, Lewis.

NB 225327 LR: 8 (Map ref: 10)

Two concentric stone circles. The outer ring consists of thirteen stones, eight of which are still upright and vary in height from six to three feet. The inner ring has four upright stones, the tallest of which is over seven feet high. Also known as Callanish III.

Doune Broch Centre

Off A858, 14 miles NW of Stornoway, Carloway, Lewis.

NB 190412 LR: 8 (Map ref: 11)

The centre features an interpretative chamber called 'Scenes from the Broch' and a graphics display, which recreates views of nearby Dun Carloway broch (see separate entry) – when complete – and illustrates the life of the inhabitants.

Open Apr-Oct, Mon-Sat 10.00-18.00.

Explanatory displays. Gift shop. WC. Car and coach parking.

Tel: 01851 643338/01851 621422

Fax: 01851 621446

Email: calanais.centre@btinternet.com

Dun Baravat

Off B8059, 3.5 miles NW of Callanish, Loch Baravat, Great Bernera.

NB 156356 LR: 13 (Map ref: 12)

Standing on a small island on the east side of Loch Baravat are the remains of a dun or broch, the walls of which survive to a height of eleven feet.

Dun Borranish

Off B8011, 8.5 miles W of Callanish, Uig Sands, Lewis.

NB 050332 LR: 13 (Map ref: 13)

A dun is located on a rocky crag at the edge of the splendid Uig sands, connected to the mainland by a causeway. This is said to be the place where a giant, Cuithach, who was terrorising the area, was slain

Dun Borranish, Uig, Lewis.

by the Fians, the guard of an ancient king or prince. The giant was allegedly buried at Cuithach's Grave [NB 035364], where a small setting of stones are said to mark the spot.

Dun Borve

Off A859, 6.5 miles N of Leverburgh, Borve, Harris.

NG 032940 LR: 18 (Map ref: 14)

Standing on a rocky crag is a round dun or broch with an outwork. The entrance can be traced, and the walls survive to a height of about six feet. About 80 feet to the east and south is a rock with 80 cup marks, small carved depressions in the stone.

Dun Bragar

Off A858, 5 miles NE of Carloway, Loch an Duna, Lewis.

NB 285474 LR: 8 (Map ref: 15)

Standing on an island in a small lochan, Dun Bragar is a ruinous broch, the walls of which survive to a height of fourteen feet. The broch may still have been in use as late as the 16th and 17th centuries.

Dun Carloway

Off A858, 15 miles NW of Stornoway, Carloway, Lewis.

HS NB 190412 LR: 8 (Map ref: 16)

Dun Carloway is a well-preserved broch, which

stands to about 30 feet high, although one half of the building has fallen away to the lintel of the entrance passageway. A covered gallery within the wall can be seen, as can an entrance passage and guard cell.

In the 17th century the Morrisons of Ness used the broch as their stronghold against the MacAulays of Uig. However, one of the MacAulays climbed the wall, and the sleeping Morrisons were then suffocated by throwing smouldering heather over them.

The Doune Broch Centre is located nearby.

Open all year.

Car and coach parking.

Tel: 0131 668 8800

Kneep Prehistoric Settlement

Off B8011, 7 miles NW of Callanish, Kneep, Lewis.

NB 098366 LR: 13 (Map ref: 17)

A well-preserved Iron Age wheel-house complex with two roofed cells, covered by a sand dune, which was exposed by winter gales.

Loch Seaforth Stone Circle

Off A859, 2.5 miles S of Balallan, Loch Seaforth, Lewis.

NB 278166 LR: 13 (Map ref: 18)

The reduced remains of a stone circle, consisting of three stones in their original positions, on the north side of Loch Seaforth. The tallest upright stone is over five feet tall.

Loch an Duin Dun, Taransay

Loch an Duin, Taransay.

NB 022013 LR: 18 (Map ref: 19)

A ruinous dun, enclosing a small island in Loch an Duin, with a causeway to the main island. The walls survive to a height of six feet.

Margaret Curtis

On A858, 18 miles W of Stornoway, Olcote, Callanish, Lewis.

NB 217346 LR: 8 (Map ref: 20)

Archaeological exhibition and publications, videos and guides. Comprehensive guided tours of the Callanish standing stone sites for individuals or groups by appointment. Knitwear and spinning.

Open daily all year except Sun.

Parking. Sales area.

Tel: 01851 621277

Dun Carloway, Lewis.

Steinacleit Prehistoric Site

Off A857, 3 miles NE of Barvas, S of Loch an Duin, Shader, Lewis.

HS NB 393541 LR: 8 (Map ref: 21)

The remains of an enigmatic building of early prehistoric date, variously described as a stone circle and denuded cairn or a defensible homestead. The site was in use from around 3000 to 1500 BC.

Access at all times.

Parking nearby.

Tel: 0131 668 8800

Tursachan Standing Stones, Barraglom

On B8059, 3 miles W of Callanish, Barraglom, Great Bernera.

NB 164342 LR: 13 (Map ref: 22)

Three standing stones are located by the roadside, just to the north of the bridge. The tallest stone is over nine feet high, while the others are eight feet and three feet.

Historic and Heritage

Arnol Blackhouse Museum

Off A858, 3 miles W of Barvas, Arnol, Lewis.

HS NB 312495 LR: 8 (Map ref: 23)

A traditional Lewis dwelling, a 'blackhouse', built without mortar and roofed with thatch on a timber framework. The people lived at one end of the house, while the beasts were housed at the other. It has a central peat fire in the kitchen, although no chimney, and retains many of its original furnishings. Blackhouses are said to have been used for hundreds of years, but were still being built as late as 1885 and their use only declined after World War I.

Open Apr-Sep, Mon-Sat 9.30-18.30; Oct-Mar, Mon-Thu & Sat 9.30-4.30; closed Sun all year.

Disabled access. Parking nearby. Group concessions. £.

Tel: 01851 710395

Bernera Centre

Off A8059, Breaclete, Great Bernera.

NB 158367 LR: 13 (Map ref: 24)

The community centre and museum house all the records, photographs and archives of the local history group. Various exhibitions are mounted here, including displays on lobster fishing, a mainstay of the local economy. Historical sites on the island have been way-marked.

There is a restored horizontal grain mill [NB 167370] as well as an Iron Age house restoration next to the archaeological site at Bosta [NB 138401].

Open Apr-Sep, daily 11.00-18.00, except closed Sun.

Refreshments. Sales area. WC. Parking.

Tel: 01851 612331

Arnol blackhouse, Lewis.

Co Leis Thu? Genealogy and Exhibition Centre

On A859, 2.5 miles NW of Leverburgh, Old Schoolhouse, Northton, Harris.

NF 990897 LR: 18 (Map ref: 25)

A genealogical resource and research centre, plus general history exhibitions for Lewis, Harris, Uist and Barra. Geographical and historical publications.

Open all year, Mon-Sat 10.00-18.00; by appt for evenings & Bank Holidays.

Guided tours. Exhibitions. Book shop. WC. Disabled access. Car and coach parking. Group concessions. £.

Tel: 01859 520258 Fax: 01859 520258
Email: 113143.1710@compuserve.com

Gearrannan Blackhouse Village

Off A858, 6 miles N of Callanish, Garenin, Lewis.

NB 192442 LR: 8 (Map ref: 26)

An on-going restoration programme to bring life back to the old blackhouse village of Garenin, which was abandoned in 1973. The thatched buildings, field boundaries and crofting strips are set out on gently sloping ground. Four of the houses have been restored: one as a youth hostel; a second to provide accommodation for up to sixteen people; a third as a public toilet block; while the fourth is a study/resource centre. Work is currently being undertaken to restore the final six buildings in the village, which will provide self-catering blocks, a laundry block, an interpretative blackhouse and a traditional working blackhouse. These further developments should be completed in spring 2000.

Accommodation for sixteen; youth hostel; resource centre.

High-quality accommodation and facilities in traditional and naturally spectacular setting. WC.

Tel: 01851 643477/416 Fax: 01851 643488
Email: seanabheinn@sol.co.uk
Web: www.hebrides.com/gearanan

Luchruban

Off B8013 or B8014, 2 miles NW of Port of Ness, Luchruban, Lewis.

NB 508660 LR: 8 (Map ref: 27)

On a steep rock on the shore are the remains of an early Christian oratory or hermitage with a corbelled cell and adjoining passageway in an enclosure. It is called Luchruban, the name believed to come from the Isle of Pigmies or Little Men.

MacLeod's Castle

Off A866, 2 miles SE of Stornoway, Holm, Lewis.

NB 442305 LR: 8 (Map ref: 28)

Standing on the north side of Stornoway Bay, the site of an old stronghold of the MacLeods, which was demolished by Cromwell's troops in 1653. This may be the 'fort' used by Fife Adventurers in 1599, who landed here with 600 troops. Their camp was stormed by islanders led by Tormod MacLeod, and most were slain.

Museum nan Eilean, Stornoway

Francis Street, Stornoway, Lewis.

LR: 8 (Map ref: 29)

The museum holds collections of objects, photographs and archival material illustrating life in the area from earliest times, including archaeology, fishing and maritime history, domestic life and agriculture. These are featured in a major annual exhibition and changing temporary exhibitions.

Open all year: Apr-Sep, Mon-Sat 10.00-17.30; Oct-Nov, Tue-Fri 10.00-17.00, Sat 10.00-13.00.

Explanatory displays. WC. Limited disabled access. Parking nearby.

Tel: 01851 703773 x266 Fax: 01851 706318
Email: rlanghome@w-isles.gov.uk

Ness Heritage Centre

On A857, 26 miles N of Stornoway, Habost, Ness, Lewis.

NB 520630 LR: 8 (Map ref: 30)

A collection of artefacts relating to crofting life in the district of Ness, with documentary and audio-visual archives. The 10th-century cross is believed to have marked the grave of St Ronan. Current exhibitions include the history of lighthouses in Scotland, with particular reference to the Butt of Lewis lighthouse and the sinking of the *Iolaire* with the loss of many men returning from World War I.

Dell Mill is a restored mill with a full range of equipment and machinery, together with interpretative displays on the mill and local grain production. Access to the mill is available by appointment only.

Open all year: Oct-May, Mon-Fri 9.30-17.30, Sat by prior appt; Jun-Sep, Mon-Sat 9.30-17.30.

WC. Limited disabled access. Car and coach parking.

Tel: 01851 810377 Fax: 01851 810488

Shawbost Crofting Museum

Off A858, 5.5 miles W of Barvas, Shawbost, Lewis.
NB 255465 LR: 8 (Map ref: 31)

The small museum, situated in an old church, illustrates the old way of life in Lewis, with exhibitions of objects relating to crofting, fishing and domestic life in Lewis up to 1950.

Nearby is the restored Norse mill, Mill of the Blacksmiths [NB 244464] and grain kiln (where the grain was dried before milling), both buildings being thatched. This is a horizontal mill and straddles the water channel for the water wheel, and was once very common throughout the Western Isles: mills and kilns like these being used until 1940.

Museum open all year: Mon-Sat 10.00-18.00; if closed, key available from the school caretaker; mill: access all year.

Explanatory displays. WC. Parking nearby.
Donation box.
Tel: 01851 710208 (mill only)

St Clement's Church, Rodel

On A859, 2.5 miles SE of Leverburgh, Rodel, S of Harris.

HS NG 047833 LR: 18 (Map ref: 32)

Fine 16th-century cross-shaped church with a strong square tower. It was dedicated to St Clement, a Bishop of Dunblane. Housed in the church is the splendid carved tomb of Alasdair Crotach MacLeod, built in 1528, although he did not die for another 20 years. MacLeod built the 'Fairy Tower' of Dunvegan Castle, and others of the MacLeods of Dunvegan and Harris are also buried here. The inscription reads: 'this tomb was prepared by Lord Alexander, son of Willielmus MacLeod, Lord of Dunvegan, in the year of Our Lord 1528'. There is another tomb nearby, which also has the effigy of an armoured man and dates from 1539. There are several carved grave slabs preserved in the church, and a disc-headed cross. There is also a Sheila na Gig on the outside of the south wall of the tower, which is quite interesting.

Access at all times.
Parking nearby.
Tel: 0131 668 8800 Fax: 0131 668 8888

St Columba's Church (Ui), Aignish

Off A866, 3.5 miles E of Stornoway, Aignish, Lewis.

NB 484322 LR: 8 (Map ref: 33)

Said to be built on the site of a 6th- or 7th- century cell of St Catan, a contemporary of St Columba, the existing ruinous rectangular church dates from medieval times, perhaps the 14th century. The burial place of the MacLeods of Lewis, there are two carved stones within the church: one is the effigy of a warrior and is believed to be Roderick, 7th chief;

St Moluag's Church, Eoropie, Lewis.

while the other is for Margaret, daughter of Roderick MacLeod of Lewis, who died in 1503.

Access at all reasonable times.

Car parking.

St Moluag's Church, Eoropie

Off B8014 or B8013, 12 miles NE of Barvas, Eoropie, Lewis.

NB 519652 LR: 8 (Map ref: 34)

Although there was probably a Christian settlement here from the 6th century, the present church dates from the 12th century, and is dedicated to St Moluag or St Olaf. An adjoining chapel, possibly used by lepers, only has a squint – or viewing hole – into the main church. The church was restored in 1912. A stone cross outside the church is believed to have been brought here from the island of Rona.

The church was associated with 'hallow-tide sacrifices' to the sea-god Shony as late as the 17th century. There also was a holy well of St Ronan somewhere near the Butt of Lewis. Nearby was Teampull Ronaidh [NB 523654], dedicated to St Ronan, but of which little remains except a mound. The oratory on Rona may have been associated with this church.

Open Easter-Sep during daylight hours.

Parking nearby.

St Ronan's Church, Rona

44 miles NE of Butt of Lewis, Rona.

HW 809323 LR: 8 (Map ref: 35)

On the small island was a cell or hermitage, dedicated to St Ronan, and consisting of a small oratory, dating from the 7th or 8th century, and cashel, and the complex forms one of the most complete groups of buildings from the early Celtic church in Scotland. There are several cross-incised burial markers, dating from the 7th to 12th centuries. A stone cross from the island is now at St Moluag's Church at Eoropie. The last inhabitant of the island left in 1844. The island is accessible from Ness (in calm weather). It is a National Nature Reserve, in the care of Scottish National Heritage, from whom permission should be sought before visiting.

Stornoway Castle

On A857, Stornoway pier, Lewis.

NB 423327 LR: 8 (Map ref: 36)

An early castle here, possibly dating from the 11th century, is said to have been seized from the MacNicol family by a Norsemen called Leod, from whom the MacLeods were descended. It was destroyed by Cromwell's forces in 1653, although the garrison of his nearby small fort, built against the Dutch, is said to have been massacred by the islanders. The site is incorporated into the harbour of 1882.

Teampull Tharain

Paible, Taransay.

NG 031991 LR: 18 (Map ref: 37)

In the old burial ground by the sea are the slight remains of two small chapels, one dedicated to St Torrannan, a 6th-century saint, the other to St Keith.

Uig Heritage Centre

Off B8011, 9 miles W of Callanish, Crowlista, Uig, Lewis.

NB 042340 LR: 13 (Map ref: 38)

The centre contains an exhibition on crofting life in the area, featuring photographs, artefacts and documentary material with detailed histories of the crofting villages and crofting families of the area.

Open Jun-Sep, Mon-Sat 11.00-17.00.

WC. Tea bar. Parking. £.

Tel: 01851 672456

Arts, Crafts and Industry

An Lanntair

Town Hall, South Beach, Stornoway, Lewis.

LR: 8 (Map ref: 39)

Ann Lanntair, the main public arts facility in the Outer Hebrides, is a forum for local, national and international arts, featuring a diverse year-round programme of exhibitions and events.

Open all year, Mon-Sat 10.00-17.30.

Gift shop. Tearoom. WC. Disabled access. Car and coach parking.

Tel: 01851 703307   Fax: 01851 703307

Borgh Pottery

On A857, 4 miles NE of Barvas, Borve, Lewis.

NB 410560 LR: 8 (Map ref: 40)

The pottery features a wide range of pieces, all of which are hand thrown or hand built using traditional techniques with striking or muted glazes. The pottery and showroom can be visited.

Open all year: Mon-Sat 9.30-18.00; open May-Sep until 21.00.

Parking. Shop.

Tel: 01851 850345

Web: www.witb.co.uk/links/borghpottery.htm

Borvemore Studios and Cafe

On A859, 4 miles N of Leverburgh, Scaristavore, Harris.
NG 010931 LR: 18 (Map ref: 41)
An art gallery selling local paintings.
Open daily mid-June-mid-September.
Seasonal cafe. Cottage accommodation available all year (25 max).
Tel: 01859 550222/291 Fax: 01859 550208
Email: borvemore@zetnet.co.uk
Web: www.borvemor.zetnet.co.uk

Croft Crafts

Off A859, Golden Road, 5 miles S of Tarbert, 4 Plocrapool, Harris.
NG 179935 LR: 14 (Map ref: 42)
Harris tweed is woven here, and there are demonstrations of weaving, warping, bobbin winding and wool plying.
Open all year, Mon-Sat 9.00-19.00.
Gift shop. WC. Disabled access. Car and coach parking.
Tel: 01859 511217 Fax: 01859 511249

Fear an Eich

On B895, 6 miles NE of Stornoway, Coll, Lewis.
NB 471402 LR: 8 (Map ref: 43)
Fear an Eich ('the horseman' in Gaelic) is a working pottery, making a wide range of items and with a diverse range of crafts. The working area can be viewed from the shop, and information regarding manufacture is available.
Open Apr-Oct, Mon-Sat 9.00-18.00; Nov-Mar 9.00-17.00.
Gift shop. Tearoom & lunches. WC. Disabled access. Car and coach parking.
Tel: 01851 820219 Fax: 01851 820565
Email: collpot@sol.co.uk
Web: www.hebrides.com/coll

Gisla Woodcraft

On B8011, 7 miles SW of Callanish, Gisla, Lewis.
NB 128257 LR: 13 (Map ref: 44)
Gisla Woodcraft features hand-turned wooden gifts and other quality crafts.
Open daily Mar-Oct.
Tel: 01851 672371 Fax: 01851 672371

Harbour View Gallery

On A857, 27 miles N of Stornoway, Port of Ness, Lewis.
NB 539638 LR: 8 (Map ref: 45)
Harbour View Gallery exhibits contemporary watercolour originals and prints by island-based artist Anthony J. Barber.
Open Mon-Sat, 10.30-17.00.
Gallery.
Tel: 01851 810735 Fax: 01851 810735
Email: AJB@harbourview.FREESERVE.CO.UK
Web: www.HARBOURVIEW.FREESERVE.CO.UK/PAINTINGS/

Joan MacLennan Tweeds

Off A859, 3.5 miles S of Tarbert, 1A Drinishadder, Harris.
LR: 14 (Map ref: 46)
Hand-woven Harris Tweed and knitwear.
Open May-Oct, Mon-Fri 9.00-18.00, Sat 9.00-12.00.
Tel: 01859 511266

Kenneth MacLeod Harris Tweed Mill

Off A858, 4 miles NE of Carloway, 9 North Shawbost, Lewis.
NB 268478 LR: 8 (Map ref: 47)
The mill offers guided tours and there is a range of Harris tweed for sale.

Lewis Loom Centre

3 Bayhead Street, Stornoway, Lewis.
LR: 8 (Map ref: 48)
The centre provides a detailed lecture and guided tour on the history of Harris Tweed, as well as demonstrations of traditional looms, warping, waulking, hand spinning and hand carding. The shop stocks tweeds, quality knitwear, jackets, waistcoats and many other items.
Open Mon-Sat 9.00-18.00.
Guided tours. Explanatory displays. Gift shop. WC. Disabled access. Car and coach parking. £
Tel: 01851 703117 Fax: 01851 704500

Luskentyre Harris Tweed Co

Off A859, 12 miles N of Leverburgh, Luskentyre, Harris.

NG 068991 LR: 14 (Map ref: 49)

The company features hand-woven tweed and tartan for sale and visitors are welcome.

Open all year, Mon-Sat.

Parking. Sales area.

Tel: 01859 550261   Fax: 01859 550308

Web: www.hebrides.com/busi/luskentyre

Morven Gallery

On A857, 12 miles W of Stornoway, Barvas, Lewis.

NB 362499 LR: 8 (Map ref: 50)

The gallery has original paintings, sculpture, photography and textiles, as well as needlepoint, tapestries, knitwear, woodcarving and ceramics.

Open Mar-Sep, Mon-Sat 10.30-17.30.

Explanatory displays. Gift shop. Tearoom. WC. Disabled access. Car and coach parking.

Tel: 01851 840216

Email: morvengal@telinco.co.uk   Web: www.telinco.co.uk/morvengal

Oiseval Gallery

Off A858, 8 miles NE of Carloway, Brue, Lewis.

NB 340496 LR: 8 (Map ref: 51)

An exclusive collection of fine photographs of Hebridean landscapes by local photographer, James Smith, including the island of St Kilda.

Open all year, Mon-Sat 10.00-17.30.

Car and coach parking.

Tel: 01851 840240   Fax: 01851 840240

Email: jamessmith@oiseval.sol.co.uk

Web: www.tullochard.demon.co.uk

Ravenspoint

Off B8060, 22 miles S of Stornoway, Kershader, Lewis.

NB 341200 LR: 14 (Map ref: 52)

Ravenspoint features a range of hand-made Scottish knitwear, island crafts, exhibition on local history, and includes a shop, tearoom and hostel.

Hostel and study centre open by arrangement, Jan-Dec; Cafe and shop open April-Oct, Mon-Sat 11.00-17.00.

Gift shop. Tearoom. WC nearby. Parking. Accommodation available.

Tel: 01851 880236   Fax: 01851 880236

Soay Studio

On A859, 1 mile NW of Tarbert, West Tarbert, Harris.

NB 145008 LR: 14 (Map ref: 53)

The studio features traditional natural dyeing, using plants and lichens. Hand-knitted items, knitting and wools are for sale.

Open May-Sep, Tue-Thu 9.00-16.30; other times by appt.

Parking. Sales area.

Tel: 01859 502361

Gardens, Animals and Miscellaneous

Lews Castle and Lady Lever Park

Off A866, W of Stornoway, Lews Castle, Lewis.

NB 419335 LR: 8 (Map ref: 54)

The pleasant wooded grounds and gardens of Lews Castle, built by the Mathesons in the 19th century, on the west side of Stornoway Harbour. Cnoc na Croich [NB 417323] – 'Gallows Hill' is traditionally the site where criminals were executed, and nearby are the remains of a chambered cairn. The park has shore, woodland, river walks and moorland.

Castle not open; park open all year.

MacGillivray Centre

Off A859, 3 miles NW of Leverburgh, Northton, Harris.

NF 992898 LR: 18 (Map ref: 55)

Set in a picturesque location, the centre features a small display relating to the ornithologist W. MacGillivray.

Open all year.

Explanatory displays. WC. Picnic tables. Car park.

St Kilda or Hirta

('western isle' or 'shield shaped')

Location
OS Landranger map 18
Lies 41 miles W of North Uist at Griminish Point

How to Get There
By ferry (contact Stornoway TIC for organised tours tel: 01851 703088 or NTS on 01631 570000)

Basic Info
The group of islands consist of St Kilda or Hirta proper, which is three miles long and extremely hilly, rising to over 1400 feet. The island has spectacular cliffs rising up to 1000 feet straight out of the Atlantic.

Soay is a small island, about one mile long, to the west of Hirta.

Boreray is a small island four miles to the north east of Hirta, and is one mile long.

The islands are home to huge numbers of sea birds, including the largest gannetry in the world (60,000 pairs) as well as fulmars, puffins (some 300,000 pairs), guillemots, razorbills, kittiwakes and Manx shearwaters.

History
Hirta was home to an isolated community for many hundreds of years, although it does not appear to have been permanently inhabited until medieval times. Viking burials have been found here. St Kilda was part of the Lordship of the Isles, then a property of the MacLeods of

Boreray, St Kilda.

Dunvegan from 1498 until 1930. There were three chapels on St Kilda, dedicated to St Brendan, St Columba, and Christ Church, but little remains. There are also the remains of a beehive house, known as the 'Amazon's House'.

The islanders had a tough life, and survived by exploiting the thousands of sea birds which live on the islands. There are a large number of 'cleits', huts used for storing dried sea birds, fish, hay and turf. The islanders had a very democratic system, and decisions were taken by an island council, made up of all the menfolk. The present village was set out in the 1830s above village bay, but in the 1880s much of the population left for Australia, and the remaining inhabitants were finally evacuated in the 1930s because of hardship and storms which had cut off the islands for weeks.

The island was bequeathed to The National Trust for Scotland in 1957 and was designated as Scotland's first World Heritage Site in 1987. It is possible to visit the island. The Ministry of Defence established a base on Hirta for tracking missiles fired from the station on South Uist.

The Street, St Kilda.

Places of Interest

Taigh an t-Sithiche, St Kilda

Village Bay, E side of St Kilda.
NF 100994 LR: 18 (Map ref: 56)
Taigh an t-Sithiche ('house of the fairies') is the remains of a souterrain, consisting of an underground passageway some 25 feet long, with a short passage branching from the main one.

Tobar na Cille

Ruaival, SE side of St Kilda.
NF 098984 LR: 18 (Map ref: 57)
A spring here was known as Tobar na Cille or St Brendan's Well, and was said to have been used by the islanders to find a favourable wind to take them east to Harris. An enclosure is all that remains of an old chapel and burial ground, dedicated to St Brendan.

Tobar nam Buaidh

Gleann Mor, N side of St Kilda.
NA 086002 LR: 18 (Map ref: 58)
A spring, with a stone well house, is known as Tobar nam Buaidh (the 'well of virtue'), and water from the well was said to cure nervous diseases and deafness.

Map 4: North Uist and Benbecula

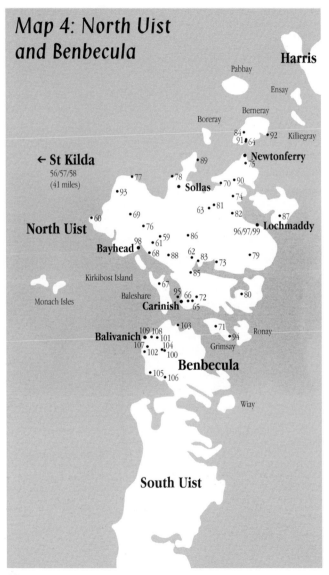

Harris

Pabbay

Ensay

Boreray

Berneray

84•
91•64
•92   Killiegray

← St Kilda
56/57/58
(41 miles)

•89

•77

•78

•70 •90

Sollas

•75

Newtonferry

•93

•74

63 •81

•82

•87

69•

•76

North Uist •60

96/97/99   **Lochmaddy**

98• •59 •86
•61

Bayhead •

•68 •88   62
•83 •73

•79

Kirkibost Island

•67

•85

Monach Isles

Baleshare

95
•66 •72

•80

Carinish   65

•103

•71

Ronay

Balivanich •
109 108
• •101

•94

107• •104
•102 •100

Grimsay

Benbecula

•105 •106

Wiay

South Uist

North Uist

('north abode'; Gaelic: Uist a' Tuath)

In Brief
Hills, moor, lochans and beaches. Duns. Chambered Cairns.

Location (see map 4, p 42)
OS Landranger maps 18, 22
SE of S tip of Harris
N of Benbecula
20 miles NW of Skye

Tourist Information Centre
Lochmaddy (tel: 01876 500321; fax: 01876 500321)
Open Easter-Oct
Stornoway, Lewis (tel: 01851 703088; fax: 01851 705244)
Open Jan-Dec

How to Get There
Ferry from Uig on Skye to Lochmaddy on North Uist (1 hr 50 mins; CalMac tel: 01470 542219 or 01876 500337)
Causeway from Benbecula
Causeway from Berneray
Also ferry from Otternish on North Uist to Leverburgh on Harris (50 mins; Cal Mac 01876 500337 or 01859 502444)

Basic Info
North Uist is one of the larger of the Hebrides, and covers an area of 115 square miles, being approximately eighteen miles long and fourteen miles wide at the most. The highest hill is

Baleshare, North Uist.

Thatched house, North Uist.

Eaval at 1138 feet to the south-east of the island. The north and west coasts have fine stretches of sand, including the beaches at Clachan Sands, Vallay Strand, Vallaquie Strand and Traigh Iar, Traigh Leanthann and between North Uist and Benbecula. The east of the island is indented with several sea lochs, and there are hundreds of lochans and islets. There is much good land, especially to the south and west, and the population was once over 5000, while now it is nearer 1800 – once again the island was cleared in the 19th century. The islanders are largely presbyterian and Gaelic speaking.

The largest settlement is Lochmaddy, but there are others at Newtonferry, Sollas, Bayhead and Carinish.

North Uist is joined to Benbecula by the North Ford Causeway, which was opened in 1960, making communication between the islands much easier and safer.

There is a youth hostel at Lochmaddy.

Wildlife
Large number of waders and sea birds at RSPB bird reserve at Balranald, which has a visitor centre.

History
North Uist has a wealth of prehistoric sites, including chambered cairns, duns, and standing stones and circles. Particularly notable are Barpa Langass, a fine chambered cairn; the stone circle at Pobull Fhinn; and several ruinous duns, including Dun an Sticar and Dun Torcuill. There are a large number of these duns in various stages of ruin, situated in small lochans and reached by causeways. Although these originate from the Iron Age, many appear to have still been in use in medieval times, and even into the 16th and 17th centuries.

North Uist was held by the Vikings, then the Lords of the Isles, then was granted to MacDonalds of Sleat in Skye from 1495 until 1855. There are apparently no castles on the island, but Dun an Sticar was used by the MacDonalds until the beginning of the 17th century. Teampull na Trionaid was an important ecclesiastical site and centre of learning. It may have been founded by Beathag, a daughter of Somerled, or by Amy MacRuari, from whom Clan Ranald are descended. There is also an old cross at Kilphedder.

The island had a thriving population at the turn of the 19th century, due to the good arable land and kelp industry. But when the latter collapsed, MacDonald of Sleat had much of the population cleared and replaced by sheep. This resulted in clashes between the islanders and police, some of them bloody as at Sollas. The MacDonalds sold the property in 1855.

Scolpaig Tower is a 19th-century folly built on the remains of a dun, and once used as a summer house.

Today

Crofting and fishing. Tourism. Knitwear and Tweed.

Berneray

Island ('Bjorn's Island') one mile north of Newtonferry on North Uist and joined to North Uist by a causeway. It is about 3.5 miles across at its longest, and about two miles wide. The island was a property of the MacLeods of Berneray, who had a stronghold here known as The Gunnery. A stone on Beinn a' Chlaidh is said to have the 'imprint' of a foot [NF 912806], and to have been an inauguration place of the Lords of the Isles. The island is the birthplace of 'Giant' MacAskill, who was 7'9" tall – there is a museum about him at Dunvegan on Skye.

The island is fertile and had a population of 500 in 1891, although this is now around 135, who make a living crofting and fishing. The west coast has a fine sandy beach running nearly the whole length of the island, while most folk live on the east of the island. There is a youth hostel.

Boreray

A small island three miles north of the north coast of North Uist and two miles west of Berneray. It is 1.5 miles long and one mile wide, and had good arable land – it supported a population of over 150 in 1861. It was a property of the MacLeans of Boreray, who were buried at Aird a' Mhorain on North Uist. One mile to the south-east is the **Lingay**, a tidal islet 1.5 miles west of Newtonferry.

Oransay

Small flat tidal island ('island of the ebb-tide') on the north coast of North Uist, one mile long and 0.5 miles wide.

Vallay

Tidal island north of Vallay Strand on the north shore of North Uist. It is about three miles long and 0.5 miles wide, and is mostly flat and fertile. There were said to have been three chapels on the island, although the remains of only two survive. The island also had the 'Brownie's Stone', where an offering of milk was left for the brownie (a fairy or gruagach).

Kirkibost Island

Tidal island two miles south of Bayhead on the southern shore of North Uist. The island is very flat, and is two miles long, and about 0.5 miles wide.

Grimsay

Island ('Grim's Island') to the south-eastern coast of North Uist, about three miles long and 1.5 miles wide. It is joined by a causeway to both North Uist and Benbecula. There are many islets nearby. The remains of an old chapel, dedicated to St Michael, survive, where the bodies of seamen washed up on the island were buried.

Ronay

Island ('Ronan's Isle') off the south-eastern tip of North Uist, just east of Grimsay. It is 2.5 miles long and two miles wide, and is hilly and steep, the land rising to over 600 feet. There are several islets nearby, including **Floddaymore** and **Floddaybeg** to the north-east.

Baleshare and Illeray

Tidal island ('east township') on south-west coast of North Uist, joined to North Uist by a causeway across the sands. It is three miles long and just under two miles wide, and is flat and fertile.

Heisker or Monach Islands

Group of islands and skerries, eight miles west of North Uist at Baleshare. The larger of the islands are about one mile long, and are quite flat, and there are large stretches of sandy beaches. The islands were connected to North Uist by a sand bar until the 16th century when it was washed away in a storm. This is one of the places where Lady Grange was imprisoned – she discovered her husband's Jacobite plotting and was held in the Hebrides until her death and is probably buried at Trumpan on Skye. The islands were populated until about 1900.

There is a lighthouse on **Shillay**, and the islands are a nature reserve with many sea birds and seals.

Barpa Langass, North Uist.

Places of Interest

Prehistoric

Airidhan an t-Sruthain Gairbh Cairn

Off A865, 3 miles NE of Bayhead, Guala na h-Imrich, North Uist.

NF 796693 LR: 18 (Map ref: 59)

The remains of a cairn, now about 65 feet in diameter and eight feet high, with the ruins of later buildings.

Aird an Runair Settlement

Off A965, 3 miles W of Bayhead, Aird an Runair, North Uist.

NF 697712 LR: 18 (Map ref: 60)

A prehistoric settlement, consisting of several round cells and midden material, was uncovered by tidal erosion of sand dunes. Pottery from here has been dated to the Iron Age.

An Carra, Beinn a' Charra

Off A865, 2 miles NE of Bayhead, Beinn a' Charra, North Uist.

NF 786691 LR: 18 (Map ref: 61)

Located east of the Committee Road is a tall standing stone, over nine feet high, which stands at an angle.

Barpa Langass

Off A867, 5 miles W of Lochmaddy, Ben Langass, North Uist.

NF 837657 LR: 18 (Map ref: 62)

Impressive chambered cairn rising thirteen feet or so above the moorland, dating from the Neolithic period. The entrance passage is fifteen feet long and leads from a forecourt into an oval burial chamber. The passage and the chamber are still covered, which is very unusual. Finds from excavation included burnt bone and sherds of pottery from the Bronze Age. Nearby is the well-preserved stone circle, called Pobull Fhinn.

Access at all times.

Parking.

Barpa nam Feannag

Off A865, 3 miles SE of Sollas, Bogach Maari, North Uist.

NF 857721 LR: 18 (Map ref: 63)

Meaning 'cairn of the hooded crow', the cairn is about 180 feet long and between 65 and 30 feet wide. It survives to a height of over eight feet, and the chamber has been disturbed. Several slabs may have been from a passage or chamber.

Beinn a' Chlaidh Stone

Off unlisted road, 0.5 miles SW of Borve, Beinn a' Chlaidh, Berneray.

NF 912806 LR: 18 (Map ref: 64)

A stone here, east of Loch Borve on a slope of Beinn a' Chlaidh, is said to bear the imprint of a foot, and was an inauguration place of the Lord of the Isles.

Caravat Barp

Off A865, 1 mile E of Carinish, Caravat, North Uist.

NF 837603 LR: 22 (Map ref: 65)

A chambered cairn, which is about 165 feet long by up to 85 feet wide. The cairn survives to a height of about six feet, and the chamber is indicated by several slabs. The cairn appears to have had a forecourt at the entrance end.

Carinish Stone Circle

On A865, 0.5 miles E of Carinish, North Uist.

NF 832602 LR: 22 (Map ref: 66)

The main road has been built through the middle of this stone circle. Seven stones survive on the north side of the road, with another two on the south.

Carnan nan Long Cairn

Off A865, 3 miles NW of Carinish, Illeray, North Uist.

NF 791637 LR: 18 (Map ref: 67)

A much-disturbed chambered cairn on the north-east tip of Illeray. It is 100 feet long by between 30 and 60 feet wide, and the cairn survives to a height of ten feet.

Clach Mhor a' Che

Off A865, 2 miles SE of Bayhead, Claddach Kyles, North Uist.

NF 770662 LR: 18 (Map ref: 68)

A standing stone, known as Clach Mhor a' Che, is nine feet high. It is said to mark the site of a battle.

Clettraval Chambered Cairn

Off A865, 2 miles N of Bayhead, South Clettraval, North Uist.

NF 749713 LR: 18 (Map ref: 69)

A Neolothic cairn which has been much reduced by robbing of stone. The slabs of the burial chamber and its entrance passageway can be traced, and the cairn had a forecourt. The kerb can be seen in places. The site was reused in the Iron Age, and there are remains of a wheel- or aisled house.

Druim na h-Uamha Souterrain

Off A865, 3 miles E of Sollas, Vallaquie, North Uist.

NF 865755   LR: 18   (Map ref: 70)

A souterrain or earth house, consisting of a curved underground passageway, which stretched for twenty feet and was five feet high with a higher domed roof at one end. The souterrain was found in 1861, at which time it was covered over, but since then most of the lintels have been robbed.

Dun Ban, Grimsay

Off A865, 4 miles SE of Carinish, Loch Hornary, Grimsay.

NF 870569   LR: 22   (Map ref: 71)

Situated on a small island at the east end of Loch Hornary are the ruins of a dun, the walls of which survive to a height of about seven feet. The entrance has a recess, and the submerged causeway can be traced.

Dun Ban, Loch Caravat

Off A865, 1.5 miles E of Carinish, North Uist.

NF 843608   LR: 22   (Map ref: 72)

On an island in a lochan Loch Caravat, Dun Ban – originally an Iron Age dun – was given mortared walls in medieval times, and had a hall block opposite the entrance. It probably dates from the 14th or 15th century, and it is said that the building was still roofed, with flat stones, in 1850.

Dun Nighean Righ Lochlainn, Breinish

Off A867, 4 miles SW of Lochmaddy, Breinish, North Uist.

NF 864640   LR: 18   (Map ref: 73)

A dun, on a small island, the walls of which survive to a height of six feet. The name means 'the dun of the daughter of the king of Norway'.

Dun Torcuill

Off A865, 3 miles NW of Lochmaddy, Loch an Duin, North Uist.

NF 888737   LR: 18   (Map ref: 74)

On a small island in the loch, connected to the mainland by a short causeway, is a dun or possible broch. The entrance, cells and gallery can be traced, and the walls survive to a height of about ten feet, although the inside of the building is choked with rubble and undergrowth.

Dun an Sticar

On B893, 0.5 miles S of Newtonferry, North Uist.

NF 898778   LR: 18   (Map ref: 75)

Although originally an Iron Age dun, Dun an Sticar was inhabited by Hugh MacDonald, one of the MacDonalds of Sleat and son of Hugh the Clerk, until 1602. He sheltered here after plotting to slaughter his kin, but was eventually captured to be starved to death in Duntulm Castle, on Trotternish, in Skye.

The massive walls of the dun had a gallery, part of which can be seen, and survive to a height of over ten feet. The entrance can be traced, and there are two splendid causeways out to a neighbouring islet, then another causeway out to the dun.
Parking nearby.

Fir Bhreige Standing Stones

Off A865, 1.5 miles NE of Bayhead, Toroghas, North Uist.

NF 770703   LR: 18   (Map ref: 76)

Two standing stones, known as Fir Bhreige, are situated about 40 yards apart on the south-east slope of the hill of Toroghas. The stones appear to have sunk into the peat, and are only a few feet high.

Foshigarry Prehistoric Settlement

Off A865, 4.5 miles W of Sollas, Foshigarry, North Uist.

NF 742764   LR: 18   (Map ref: 77)

The fragmentary remains of a settlement, dating from at least the Iron Age until 400 AD, consisting of the ruins of several roundhouses and a souterrain.

Leac nan Cailleachan Dubha

Off A865, 1.5 miles NW of Sollas, Cean Uachdarach, Vallay.

NF 791765   LR: 18   (Map ref: 78)

Located on the south-east coast of the island of Vallay are two substantial standing stones – one over five feet tall, the other a little smaller – about one foot apart. The stones were probably part of a chambered burial cairn.

Loch Hunder Dun

Off A867, 2 miles S of Lochmaddy, Loch Hunder, North Uist.

NF 905652   LR: 18   (Map ref: 79)

On an island in Loch Hunder are the ruins of an oval dun, the walls of which have at least one chamber. The island is connected to the mainland by a causeway, while another causeway leads to the adjacent island, then to the mainland.

There is another dun in the loch [NF 902653], Dun

Dun an Sticar, North Uist.

Ban, which also stands on a small island. The island is enclosed by two walls, the inner stronger than the outer. The remains of a water gate can be seen, and there are the ruins of several circular structures.

Loch a' Gheadais Dun

Off A865, 5 miles E of Carinish, Loch a' Gheadais, North Uist.

NF 914594 LR: 22 (Map ref: 80)

A dun on an island in Loch a' Gheadais, the walls of which survive to a height of six feet. A causeway connects the dun to the mainland, and there are the ruins of a small round building.

Maari Standing Stone

Off A865, 4.5 miles NW of Lochmaddy, Maari, North Uist.

NF 864729 LR: 18 (Map ref: 81)

On the eastern slopes of the hill of Maari, a standing stone, which is 7.5 feet long, stands at a sharp angle.

Na Fir Bhreige Standing Stones

Off A865, 2.5 miles NW of Lochmaddy, Blashaval, North Uist.

NF 888718 LR: 18 (Map ref: 82)

Standing on a ridge on the western slopes of the hill of Blashaval is a row of three low standing stones, none higher than three feet, called Na Fir Bhreige

'the false men', said to be three husbands from Skye who abandoned their wives and were turned to stone here by a witch.

Pobull Fhinn Stone Circle

Off A867, 5 miles W of Lochmaddy, Langass, North Uist.

NF 843650 LR: 18 (Map ref: 83)

The name of this stone circle refers to the warriors who followed Fionn mac Cumhaill – Finn MacCool. The circle, which is actually oval, is cut into the side of the hill, and consisted of about 48 stones, around 30 of which still remain, although some have fallen. The tallest stone is over seven feet high. The circle dates from between 3000 BC to about 1500 BC. **Access at all reasonable times.**

Sgalabraig Souterrain

Off unlisted road, 0.5 miles NW of Borve, Sgalabraig, Berneray.

NF 907815 LR: 18 (Map ref: 84)

A souterrain consists of a walled passage, fifteen feet long and four feet deep, with two lintels covering the passage. It was discovered in 1906, but stones were taken from here for building.

Pobull Fhinn Stone Circle, North Uist.

Sornach a' Phobuill Stone Circle

*Off B894, 6 miles SW of Lochmaddy, Loch a'
Phobuill, North Uist.*

NF 829630 LR: 18 (Map ref: 85)

A stone circle, oval in shape, now with fourteen
stones remaining, the tallest of which is about four
feet high.

Tigh Cloiche Cairn

*Off A865, 4.5 miles W of Lochmaddy, Marrogh,
North Uist.*

NF 833696 LR: 18 (Map ref: 86)

Standing on the south-east slopes of the hill of
Marrogh, Tigh Cloiche is a round chambered burial
cairn, 70 feet in diameter and fourteen feet high.
The passage to the chamber is almost intact, and
leads from a forecourt, but the central chamber has
been disturbed. Upright stones forming the kerb
can be seen.

Tigh Talamhant Souterrain

*Off A865, 2 miles NE of Lochmaddy, Loch
Hacklett, North Uist.*

NF 949712 LR: 18 (Map ref: 87)

On the west shore of Loch Hacklett, Tigh Talamhant
('house under the ground') consists of the ruinous
remains of a souterrain or earth house, the passage
of which was five feet high. There were apparently
three entrances.

Uneval Chambered Cairn

*Off A865, 3 miles E of Bayhead, S of Uneval,
North Uist.*

NF 800667 LR: 18 (Map ref: 88)

The remains of a Neolithic chambered cairn and
Iron Age house. Upright slabs survive from the cairn
although much of the stone has been robbed. Some
fragments of burnt bone, from an adult woman,
were found here during excavations, as well as pottery. A visit involves a long walk.

Historic and Heritage

Aird a' Mhorain Burial Ground

*Off A865, 2.5 miles N of Sollas, Aird a' Mhorain,
North Uist.*

NF 837787 LR: 18 (Map ref: 89)

On the eastern side of Aird a' Mhorain is a graveyard where the MacLeans of Boreray are buried, and
there was probably a chapel. A rock is decorated
with a two-foot-long cross.

Clach an t-Sagairt

*Off B893, 4 miles E of Sollas, Clachan Sands,
North Uist.*

NF 879760 LR: 18 (Map ref: 90)

A stone eight feet tall and eleven feet broad, with a
cross cut in one side. It is known as Clach an t-Sagairt

the 'stone of the priest', as well as Clach na h' Ulaidh 'stone of hidden treasure'. It may have marked one sanctuary boundary of St Columba's Chapel.

Cladh Maolrithe

Off unlisted road, 0.5 miles SW of Borve, Cladh Maolrithe, Berneray.

NF 912807 LR: 18 (Map ref: 91)

The probable site of a cashel or early Christian monastery, of which remains of the enclosing wall survive. Located in the old burial ground is a standing stone, known as Clach Mor, which is over eight feet tall. A chapel on the site is believed to have been dedicated to St Maelrubha.

There was another chapel on Berneray [NF 928826], dedicated to St Anselm, but nothing remains. A stone here, part of which is in the Museum of Scotland, was surrounded by coins, pins, needles and pebbles, offerings made at the shrine to the saint.

Gunnery of MacLeod

Off unlisted road, 1 mile E of Borve, Ludag Point, Berneray.

NF 933815 LR: 18 (Map ref: 92)

The Gunnery of MacLeod is said to have been the stronghold of the MacLeods of Berneray. At Borve is a stone shaped like a chair [NF 909816], and believed to have been a place of execution. North of the stone is a burial cairn and a standing stone.

Kilphedder Cross

Off A865, 5 miles W of Sollas, Kilphedder, North Uist.

NF 726744 LR: 18 (Map ref: 93)

A round-headed cross stands west of the road near the site of an old burial ground and chapel. The chapel was dedicated to St Peter.

St Michael's Chapel, Grimsay

Off A865, 5 miles SE of Carinish, Grimsay.

NF 882548 LR: 22 (Map ref: 94)

On a promontory on the south-east tip of Grimsay are the ruins of a chapel and burial ground. The chapel was dedicated to St Michael and probably founded by Amy MacRuari in the second half of the 14th century. The graveyard was used to bury the bodies of mariners found washed up by the tide.

Teampull na Trionaid

Off A865, Carinish, North Uist.

NF 816602 LR: 22 (Map ref: 95)

Teampull na Trionaid, 'the church of The Trinity', dates from the 13th or 14th century, and was one of the largest pre-Reformation churches in the Western Isles. It is believed to have been built on an older site by Beartrice, daughter of Somerled, about 1203; or Amy MacRuarie, first wife of John, Lord of the Isles. She was divorced by her husband so that he could marry Margaret, daughter of the future Robert II, and Amy was the progenitor of the Clan Ranald branch of the MacDonalds. The buildings are now ruinous, although a small adjoining chapel 'the chapel of Clan MacVicar' is better preserved.

Teampull na Trionaid was an important centre of learning in medieval times. In 1601, however, the buildings were used as a refuge by the MacDonalds from the MacLeods of Skye. The MacLeods were routed at the nearby battle of Carinish.

There was a holy well nearby [NF 814601], known as Tobar na Trionaid.

Access at all reasonable times.

Parking nearby.

Arts, Crafts and Industry

Island Crafts

On A865, Lochmaddy, North Uist; and Cnoc Ard, Grimsay.

LR: 18 (Map ref: 96)

At Island Crafts the emphasis is on island crafts – only Scottish crafts are sold. Also located at Cnoc

Ard on Grimsay: open evenings as well.

Open daily 10.30-17.15.

Sales area. Parking.

Tel: 01870 602418

Taigh Chearsabhagh Museum and Art Centre

Lochmaddy, North Uist.

NF 917683 LR: 18 (Map ref: 97)

Located in a building dating from around 1741 and

once an inn, Taigh Chearsabhagh is now home to a local museum about North Uist and photographic collection of some 2000 images, documenting local social history. There is also an art gallery, art and craft workshops, and sculpture trail, as well as a shop and cafe.

Open Feb-Dec, Mon-Sat 10.00-17.00; Jun-Sep, Fri until 20.00.

Explanatory displays. Gift shop. Tearoom. WC. Disabled access. Car and coach parking. Group concessions. £ (museum only).

Tel: 01876 500293   Fax: 01876 500293
Web: www.taigh-Chearsabhagh.org

Gardens, Animals and Miscellaneous

Uist Animal Visitor Centre

On A865, Kyles Road, Bayhead, North Uist. NF 748682 LR: 18 (Map ref: 98)

The centre has rare and domestic breeds of animals, birds of prey, poultry and game. Many of the animals can be fed and petted, and chicks can be seen hatching in glass-topped incubators.

Also available are Hebridean horse-drawn holidays (tel: 01478 612123).

Open Mon-Sat, 10.00-21.00; Sun, 12.00-18.00

Refreshments. Children's play area. Games area. Parking. Coaches are advised to book. Beach pony rides.

Tel: 01876 510223/706   Fax: 01876 510706/223

Uist Outdoor Centre

On A867, Cearn Disgaidh, Lochmaddy, North Uist.

LR: 18 (Map ref: 99)

The centre offers sea kayaking, sub-aqua diving, water sports, climbing and walking, wildlife watch, power boating, field studies and much more. Week-long courses and day-visitors catered for.

Open all year.

Accommodation available with disabled access. Range of activities available. Catering or self-catering.

Tel: 01876 500480   Fax: 01876 500480
Email: alyson@keiller.u-net.com   Web: www.uistoutdoorcentre.co.uk

Beach, nr Sollas, North Uist.

Benbecula

(Gaelic: Beinn a' Faoghla 'mountain of fords', pronounced 'Ben-na-Voola' in Gaelic)

Location (see map 4, p 42)
OS Landranger map 22
S of North Uist
12 miles W of Skye
N of South Uist

Tourist Information Centre
Stornoway, Lewis (tel: 01851 703088; fax: 01851 705244)
Open Jan-Dec

How to Get There
By causeway from South Uist or from North Uist
By air from Glasgow, Barra or Stornoway to Benbecula airfield (British Airways 0345 222111)

Basic Info
The island is sandwiched between North and South Uist, and is joined to its north and south neighbours by causeways. The island is about eight miles long and five miles wide, and the interior is filled with a mass of small lochans. The east coast is rougher and hillier with many inlets, sea lochs, bogs, moors and islands, while the west coast has fine sandy beaches. The highest hill is Rueval, which rises to over 400 feet. Stinky Bay is so called from rotting seaweed which sometimes accumulates here.

The population of about 1800 is a mixture of presbyterians to the north and catholics to the south. The largest settlement is at Balivanich, which is also the base of the Royal Artillery for the missile range of South Uist – there are up to 500 personnel based here. The offices of the Islands Council are also at Balivanich.

The island has a nine-hole golf course.

Wildlife
Sea birds and wild fowl.

History
The island has several prehistoric sites of some interest, including the chambered cairns near Rueval, the ruinous stone circles at Gramisdale, and the Iron Age duns Dun Buidhe and Dun Torcusay. A Pictish stone, now in the Museum of Scotland, was found near the small island of Sunamul to the north of the island, one of the few Pictish remains found in the Western Isles. The remains of aisled houses and a souterrain were discovered within Benbecula Airport.

Christianity was reputedly brought to the island by St Torrannan in the 6th century, and there is an old chapel, dedicated to St Columba, which is believed to be built on the site of St Torrannan's monastery. There was reputedly a nunnery at the aptly named Nunton, dating from the 14th century but suppressed during the Reformation. There are the remains of an old chapel.

The island was long held by the MacDonalds of Clan Ranald, then the MacDonalds of Sleat, who had a castle at Borve, but in the 17th century moved to Nunton. In 1839 the island was sold to the Gordons of Cluny, who themselves held the island until 1942. Bonnie Prince Charlie was sheltered in a cave here after defeat at Culloden in 1746, and was taken across to Skye, disguised as Flora MacDonald's maid Betty Burke.

The body of a mermaid, found around 1825, is said to be buried at the bay of Culla.

Today
Crofting and fishing. Royal Artillery Base. Tourism.

Wiay

Small island ('temple island') off the south-east coast of Benbecula, two miles long at most and about one mile wide. It is hilly and rises to over 300 feet. To the north of Wiay are the small **Keiravagh Islands**.

Flodda

Small island ('float isle') off the north coast of Benbecula and joined to the mainland by a causeway. The island is about one mile long. There are many other islets to the east of Benbecula.

Nunton, Benbecula.

Places of Interest

Prehistoric

Airidh na h-Aon Oidhche Cairn

Off A865, 3.5 miles SE of Balivanich, Loch Ba Una, Benbecula.
NF 817525   LR: 22   (Map ref: 100)
To the south of Loch Ba Una is a well-preserved chambered cairn, about 60 feet in diameter, and surviving to a height of eleven feet. The central chamber may be discernible in the centre of the cairn.

Dun Buidhe

Off A865 or B892, 1.5 miles E of Balivanich, Loch Dun Mhurchaidh, Benbecula.
NF 794546   LR: 22   (Map ref: 101)
Standing on a small island in Loch Dun Mhurchaidh is Dun Buidhe 'yellow dun', which was connected by a causeway via a second island to the mainland. The main part of the oval dun is very ruinous. A secondary wall, enclosing the island, is better preserved and rises to over seven feet high.
The island is said to have been reused by the Vikings.

Dun Torcusay

Off B892, 1.5 miles S of Balivanich, Garry-a-Siar, Benbecula.
NF 762531   LR: 22   (Map ref: 102)
A dun on an island in a small lochan Loch Torcusay. The walls survive to a height of about four feet, and there are the remains of a rectangular and two smaller chambers. The entrance can be traced.

Gramisdale Stone Circle

On A865, 3 miles E of Balivanich, Gramisdale, Benbecula.
NF 825561   LR: 22   (Map ref: 103)
Just east of the main road before the causeway to North Uist are the remains of a stone circle, consisting now of one upright stone, five-foot high, and several other fallen stones or stumps. There are the scant remains of another circle at NF 824552.

Stiaraval Cairn

Off A865, 3 miles SE of Balivanich, Stiaraval, Benbecula.
NF 812526   LR: 22   (Map ref: 104)
Not much remains of a chambered cairn, except upright slabs from the chamber and passageway, north of Loch na Clachan. It was probably about 60 feet in diameter, but now only survives to a height of four feet.

Historic and Heritage

Borve Castle

Off B892, 3.5 miles S of Balivanich, Benbecula.
NF 774506   LR: 22   (Map ref: 105)
Borve Castle is a strong ruined late 14th-century castle of the MacDonalds, possibly built by Amy MacRuari, first wife of John, Lord of the Isles. It was occupied until at least 1625, around which time the the MacDonalds moved to Nunton. The castle was burned down in the late 18th century.

Museum nan Eilean, Lionacleit

On B892, 4 miles S of Balivanich, Lionacleit, Benbecula.
NR 790497   LR: 22   (Map ref: 106)
Located within the large modern school, the museum and library has audio-visual and photographic material on aspects of the history and culture of the

Uists and Barra. A programme of varied exhibitions changes annually, and there are guided tours and lectures, as well as sports facilities and a swimming pool.
Open all year: Mon, Wed & Thu 9.00-16.00; Tue & Fri 9.00-20.00; Sat 11.00-16.00(shut 13.00-14.00).
Explanatory displays. Temporary exhibitions. Restaurant. WC. Disabled access. Car and coach parking.
Tel: 01870 602211   Fax: 01870 602817

Nunton

On B892, 1 mile S of Balivanich, Nunton, Benbecula.

NF 766538 LR: 22 (Map ref: 107)

An old ruinous chapel, dedicated to the Virgin Mary and dating from the 14th century, and associated burial ground. There is said to have been a nunnery here, which was suppressed at the Reformation.

Teampull Chaluim Chille

Off B892, E of Balivanich, Teampull Chaluim Chille, Benbecula.

NF 782549 LR: 22 (Map ref: 108)

A ruinous rectangular chapel, later extended, which was dedicated to St Columba. Part of the building may date from the 8th century or earlier: this may be the site of an early Christian monastery, founded by St Torrannan in the 6th century.

About 200 yards south of the chapel is a spring surrounded by a cairn of stones. The cairn is said to have been built of stones brought here as offerings by people who came to drink from the water.

Arts, Crafts and Industry

MacGillivrays

On B892, Balivanich, Benbecula.

NF 770555 LR: 22 (Map ref: 109)

MacGillivrays has a wide range of hand-woven Harris tweeds, hand-knitted sweaters, and local crafts, including Hebridean jewellery, souvenirs and new millennium product range.

Open all year.

Parking. Shop. World-wide mail order service – price list on request.

Tel: 01870 602525 Fax: 01870 602981

Loch Hermidale, South Uist (William Neill, Askernish, South Uist).

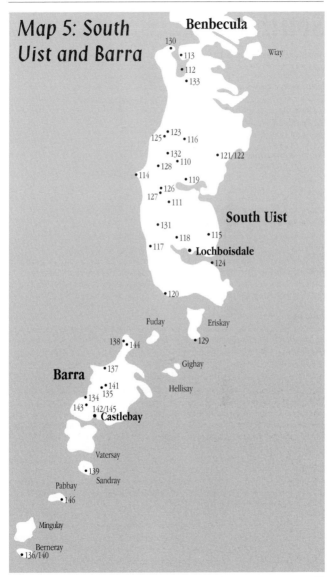

Map 5: South
Uist and Barra

Benbecula

Wiay

•130
•113
•112
•133

•123
125• •116
•132
•128 •110 •121/122
•114
•126 •119
127• •111

South Uist

•131
•118 •115
•117 • Lochboisdale
•124

•120

Fuday   Eriskay

138 •144
•129

Gighay

•137
Barra
•141
•134 135
143 • 142/145
• Castlebay   Hellisay

Vatersay

•139
Pabbay   Sandray

•146

Mingulay

Berneray
•136/140

South Uist

('south abode'; Gaelic: Uist a' Deas)

Location (see map 5, p 57)
OS Landranger map 22, 31
S of Benbecula
20 miles W of Skye
5 miles N of Eriskay and Barra

Tourist Information Centre
Lochboisdale (tel: 01878 700286; fax: 01878 700286)
Open Easter-Oct
Stornoway, Lewis (tel: 01851 703088; fax: 01851 705244)
Open Jan-Dec

How to Get There
By ferry from Oban on mainland to Castlebay on Barra, then on to/from Lochboisdale on South Uist (CalMac tel: 01631 566688 or 01871 810306 or 01878 700288).
Passenger ferry from Eoligarry on Barra to Ludag on South Uist and to Eriskay (Sound of Barra Ferry – tel: 01878 720265 between 9.00-13.00 and 01878 720238 after 14.00).
Vehicle ferry from Eriskay to Ludag on South Uist (Eriskay Car Ferry tel: 01878 720261)
Causeway from North Uist and Benbecula.

Basic Info
The island is 21 miles long and about six miles wide, covering 141 square miles. South Uist is joined to Benbecula by a causeway, which was first built in 1943, making access much easier: it was rebuilt in 1983. There are fantastic beaches down the west coast of the island, although many are used for military purposes (take heed of signs), while the east of the island is extremely hilly and even mountainous: Ben Mhor is the highest peak and rises to over 2000 feet, while Hecla is 1988 feet. The east is also indented with several sea lochs, and there are nearly 200 lochs and small lochans.

The largest settlements are Lochboisdale and Daliburgh, and the population is about 2300. The population is largely catholic, along with Barra to the south – while North Uist and Benbecula are presbyterian – and speaks Gaelic.

There is a golf course. Cycle hire.

Wildlife
Many birds can be seen at Loch Skipport and Loch Bee. Nature reserve at Loch Druidibeg, including greylag geese, corncrake, swans, ducks and other wild fowl.

History
There are a large number of duns situated in small lochans and reached by causeways. Although these originate from the Iron Age, many appear to have still been in use in medieval times, and even into the 16th and 17th centuries. There are also several wheel houses, also known as aisled houses, which appear to have been occupied between 200-300 AD.

Howmore, South Uist.

There were important ecclesiastical sites at Howmore and probably also at Kildonan. The north part of South Uist was a property of the Clan Ranald branch of the MacDonalds from the 1370s (who were descended from John, Lord of the Isles, and his first wife, Amy MacRuari) many of whom are buried at Howmore, then the MacDonalds of Sleat. The south was held by the MacNeils of Barra until 1621 when it passed to the Mackenzies of Kintail, although the MacNeils continued as tenants. Castles include Castle Calvay, off Eriskay; Caisteal Bheagram; and Ormacleit Castle, which was built in 1708 but was burnt out only seven years later. This is the 'newest' castle in Scotland. It is said that there was a battle near Snishival between the MacDonalds and a raiding party of MacLeods, from Skye, who were defeated.

The chief of Clan Ranald was killed fighting for the Jacobites at the battle of Sheriffmuir in 1715. Flora MacDonald was born at Milton on South Uist, and from here helped Bonnie Prince Charlie back over the Minch to Skye in 1746: he had sheltered in a small cave, known as the Prince's Cave [NF 834313], above Corodale Bay. The Prince had also sheltered in Caisteal Calvay. The previous year, Charlie had landed on Eriskay, but finding little support made for the mainland.

In 1838 the island, as well as Benbecula and Eriskay, was sold to the Gordons of Cluny, who cleared much of the population: at one time the population was well over 7000. There is an army missile station at the north of the island.

Today
Army missile range. Crofting and fishing for crabs and lobsters. Tourism.

Eriskay

Eriskay ('Eric's Island') lies one mile south of South Uist. It is three miles long and 1.5 miles wide, and the island is quite hilly, rising to 610 feet, although there is plenty of fertile land. The population of the island is about 200 souls, and there is a large catholic population. The island is reached by a vehicle ferry from Ludag on South Uist (Eriskay Car Ferry tel: 01878 720261) and passenger ferry from Ludag on South Uist and Eoligarry on Barra (Sound of Barra Ferry – tel: 01878 720265 between 9.00-13.00 and 01878 720238 after 14.00).

The island has its own breed of ponies.

It was here that Bonnie Prince Charlie first landed on 23 July 1745, during the Jacobite Rising of 1745-6, but he was disappointed with the lack of support, and quickly left for the mainland.

The S. S. *Politician* ran aground in 1941, carrying some 20,000 cases of whisky bound for America. The enterprising locals salvaged some of the cargo, which caused consternation amongst the authorities and a few of the islanders were imprisoned and fined, although it's hard to see what they had actually done wrong. *Whisky Galore!*, written by Compton Mackenzie and dramatising the events, was made into an Ealing Comedy in 1948. 'Am Politician' Lounge Bar is the only public house on the island.

Today the island has a thriving fishing, crofting and knitting community. Six-hole golf course. Boat hire.

Stack Islands

Stack Islands are a small group of islands to the south of Eriskay, and there is a small castle on the southernmost isle.

Calvay

Islet at the mouth of Loch Boisdale, two miles south-east of Lochboisdale village, with a small castle.

Eilean Iasgaich

Islets in Loch Boisdale, along with **Gasay**, **Pabbay**, and **Eilean Mor**.

Other islets on the east coast include **Stuley**; **Calvay**, in Loch Eynort; **Ornish**, **Shillay Mor** and **Luirsay** around Loch Skipport. Off the west coast at South Boisdale is **Orosay**.

Luatharan Glas (William Neill, Askernish).

Places of Interest

Prehistoric

An Cara, Loch an Athain

Off A865, 10 miles N of Lochboisdale, South Uist.

NF 770321 LR: 22 (Map ref: 110)

On the eastern slopes of Beinn Charra, 0.25 miles east of the road, is a tall standing stone, some seventeen feet high.

Barp Reineval

Off A865, 5.5 miles N of Lochboisdale, Reineval, South Uist.

NF 755260 LR: 22 (Map ref: 111)

Located on the north side of the hill of Reineval is a chambered burial cairn, about 70 feet in diameter and surviving to a height of twelve feet. The entrance passage can be traced.

Dun Mor, West Gerinish

On A865, 8 miles S of Balivanich, S of West Gerinish, South Uist.

NF 776415 LR: 22 (Map ref: 112)

On a small island in Loch an Duin Mhor are the ruins of a round dun, the walls of which survive to a height of ten feet. The entrance can be traced, and there was a causeway which joined the island to the mainland.

Dun Uiselan

Off A865, 5.5 miles S of Balivanich, Ollag, South Uist.

NF 778454 LR: 22 (Map ref: 113)

A dun, the walls of which survive to a height of eight feet, and a causeway from the island.

Dun Vulan

Off A865, 8.5 miles NW of Lochboisdale, Rubha Ardvule, South Uist.

NF 713297 LR: 22 (Map ref: 114)

A broch or dun with walls surviving to a height of about fourteen feet. There is a wall chamber and a stairway to a first-floor gallery, and the entrance can be identified. The site was occupied from the Bronze Age until at least 300 AD, and there is apparently a medieval building outside the broch wall. The headland the broch stands on, Rubha Ardvule, is said to be named after a Viking Princess called Vule.

Eligar Souterrain

Off A865, 2.5 miles NE of Lochboisdale, Eligar, South Uist.

NF 813228 LR: 31 (Map ref: 115)

A souterrain, in a remote location, consists of a passageway some 30 or so feet long, with the ruins of two cells.

Glac Hukarvat

Off A865, 11.5 miles N of Lochboisdale, Hukarvat, South Uist.

NF 779362 LR: 22 (Map ref: 116)

Set on the north-east slope of the hill of Haarsal, Glac Hukarvat is a chambered burial cairn with a forecourt, the mound surviving to a height of ten feet and diameter of about 65 feet.

Kilpheder Aisled (Wheel) House

Off B888, 3.5 miles W of Lochboisdale, Kilpheder, South Uist.

NF 734202 LR: 31 (Map ref: 117)

Known as Bruthach a Sithean, the 'brae of the fairy hill', the site consists of the well-preserved remains of an aisled wheel-house. The walls survive to a height of about seven feet. The house was probably abandoned about 200 AD.

The remains of other wheel-houses have been found west of Drimore [NF 758404] and [NF 756413], as well as at Uamh Iosal [NS 843333], where there are also souterrains.

Loch a' Bharp Cairn

Off A865, 2 miles NW of Lochboisdale, Loch a' Bharp, South Uist.

NF 777214 LR: 31 (Map ref: 118)

A chambered cairn, 90 feet in diameter, stands on the northern shore of an arm of Loch a' Bharp. The mound survives to a height of nineteen feet, although part of the cairn has been disturbed and robbed of stones.

North Locheynort Cairn

Off A865, 8 miles N of Lochboisdale, North Locheynort, South Uist.

NF 778297 LR: 22 (Map ref: 119)

A burial cairn, standing to a height of about ten feet, is on the north shore of Na Baighe Dubha.

Pollachar Standing Stone

On B888, 6 miles SW of Lochboisdale, Pollachar, South Uist.

NF 746145 LR: 31 (Map ref: 120)

A standing stone, six feet tall, with fine views across to Barra and Eriskay.

Uamh Ghrantriach Souterrain

Off A865, 12 miles N of Lochboisdale, Glen Usinish, South Uist.

NF 842334 LR: 22 (Map ref: 121)

In a remote location are the disturbed remains of a souterrain, which consists of two passageways and three round chambers. One of the passageways and a chamber are still roofed. There are two further souterrains nearby.

Uamh Iosal Souterrain

Off A865, 12 miles N of Lochboisdale, Glen Usinish, South Uist.

NF 843333 LR: 22 (Map ref: 122)

The ruins of an aisled wheel-house and a souterrain, which consist of the remains of a round building with cells arranged around the inside of the building. The walls survive to a height of about five feet. The souterrain was entered from the wheel-house, and a covered passageway led to a higher corbelled cell and a small chamber. Two souterrains also are located nearby, although all three are in a very remote location.

Historic and Heritage

Caisteal Bheagram

Off A865, 13 miles N of Lochboisdale, South Uist.

NF 761371 LR: 22 (Map ref: 123)

Standing on an islet in Loch an Eilean, Caisteal Bheagram is a ruined tower house, possibly dating from the 17th century, although the site was occupied by a dun or earlier castle before this. There was apparently a causeway out to the island. It was held by the MacDonalds of Clan Ranald.

Caisteal Calvay

2 miles SE of Lochboisdale, on rock on north coast of island of Calvay, South Uist.

NF 817182 LR: 31 (Map ref: 124)

Caisteal Calvay is a very ruined stronghold on a tidal islet. The lands were held by the MacNeils until around 1600. The castle was already ruined when Bonnie Prince Charlie sheltered here in 1746 after the defeat of his forces at the battle of Culloden.

Howmore Church and Chapels

Off A865, 11.5 miles N of Lochboisdale, Howmore, South Uist.

NF 758365 LR: 22 (Map ref: 125)

The complex at Howmore, once surrounded by marshes, consists of the ruinous remains of two churches and two chapels and associated burial ground. The area is enclosed by a stone bank, and there was probably an early Christian monastery here. This was an important centre of learning in medieval times, rivalling Iona.

The largest of the buildings 'Teampull Mor' – St Mary's or the Large Church – may date from the 13th century and was used as the parish church for South Uist, although not much now remains. The other buildings, all ruinous, on the site are Dugall's Chapel; St Dermot's Chapel, with an early Christian cross-marked grave slab, and dedicated to St Columba; and Clan Ranald's Chapel. By the 16th century, Howmore was the burial site for the Clan Ranald branch of the MacDonalds.

The village has interesting thatched cottages.

Kildonan Museum, Cafe and Crafts

Off A865, 7.5 miles NW of Lochboisdale, Kildonan, South Uist.

NF 742278 LR: 22 (Map ref: 126)

This was apparently once an important location, sited on the promontory and island in Loch Kildonan. It is said to have been an administrative centre such as Finlaggan on Islay, and may have been the seat of a bishop. The slight remains of a church and other buildings survive.

The new development houses a museum, exhibition, archives and local information centre, and there is a cafe, WC, and craft centre, which features spinning, weaving and knitting.

Open Mon-Sat, 10.00-17.00; Sun, 14.00-17.00.

Explanatory displays. Cafe. WC. Disabled access. Parking.

Tel: 01878 710343/700279

Milton

Off A865, 6 miles NW of Lochboisdale, Milton, South Uist.

NF 741269 LR: 22 (Map ref: 127)

This ruined cottage is where Flora MacDonald may have been born in 1722. Flora helped Bonnie Prince Charlie, who was disguised as her Irish maid Betty Burke, escape from Benbecula to Trotternish on Skye. There is a memorial cairn.

Ormacleit Castle

Off A865, 9.5 miles N of Lochboisdale, Ormacleit, South Uist.

NF 740319 LR: 22 (Map ref: 128)

One of the last castles built in Scotland, Ormacleit consists of a T-plan house of two storeys, and was completed in 1708. The castle was built as the residence of Ailean, Chief of Clan Ranald, a MacDonald. It was accidentally destroyed by fire in 1715, on the eve of the battle of Sheriffmuir during the Jacobite Rising, when the Clan Ranald chief was killed. It was never rebuilt, although part has recently been reoccupied.

Weaver's Castle

To S of island of Eriskay, 8 miles S of Lochboisdale, S tip of Stack Islands, Eilean Leathan.

NF 787072 LR: 31 (Map ref: 129)

Built on an almost inaccessible site on Eilean Leathan, Weaver's Castle or Stack consists of a small square ruinous tower. The castle is also known as Castle Stalker and Caisteal a' Bhrebider.

Arts, Crafts and Industry

Hebridean Jewellery

Off A865, Iochdar, N end of South Uist.

LR: 22 (Map ref: 130)

Celtic jewellery shop and workshop. Visitors can see five jewellers at work. Silver, gold and gemstones.

Open all year: Mon-Fri 9.00-17.30, Sat 9.30-17.30, closed Sun.

Gift shop. WC. Disabled access. Car and coach parking.

Tel: 01870 610288   Fax: 01870 610380

Studio Gallery

Off A865, 4 miles NW of Lochboisdale, Askernish, South Uist.

NF 738237 LR: 22 (Map ref: 131)

A gallery exhibiting wildlife and landscape paintings and prints.

Open all year.

Tel: 01878 700237

Uist Craft Workshop

Off A865, 9.5 miles N of Lochboisdale, Stoneybridge, South Uist.

NF 750330 LR: 22 (Map ref: 132)

A showroom and gift shop, housed among traditional Hebridean cottages. The workshop features Hebridean landscapes, cottages and wildlife as well as Celtic, Viking and Pictish style clocks, bookends

and chess sets. Range of hand-made wooden toys and puzzles as well as paintings and prints.

Open all year.

Showroom/gift shop. Parking.

Tel: 01870 620214   Fax: 01870 620214

Email: TAS@uist.demo.co.uk

Gardens, Animals and Miscellaneous

Our Lady of the Isles

Off A865, 8 miles S of Balivanich, South Uist.

NF 777408 LR: 22 (Map ref: 133)

On Rueval Hills – the 'hill of miracles' – is the statue of the Madonna and Child, erected in 1957 by the Catholic community with contributions from all over the world. The work of Hew Lorimer, the statue is 30 feet high. The inscription reads: 'Failte dhut a Mhoire', which is 'Hail Mary'.

Access at all times.

Parking nearby.

Barra

(from 'Saint Barr')

In Brief
St Barr. Castlebay. Beaches. Kiessimul Castle. Cille Bharra

Location (see map 5, p 57)
OS Landranger map 31
6 miles SW of the tip of South Uist

Tourist Information Centre
Castlebay (tel: 01871 810336; fax: 01871 810336)
Open Easter-Oct
Stornoway (Lewis) (tel: 01851 703088; fax: 01851 705244)
Open Jan-Dec

How to Get There
By ferry from Oban on mainland to Castlebay on Barra, then on to/from Lochboisdale on South Uist (5 hours; CalMac tel: 01631 566688 or 01871 810306 or 01878 700288).
Passenger ferry from Ludag on South Uist to Eoligarry on Barra and to Eriskay (Sound of Barra Ferry – tel: 01878 720265 between 9.00-13.00 and 01878 720238 after 14.00).
By air from Glasgow, Benbecula or Stornoway to Traigh Mor on Barra (British Airways tel: 0345 222111).

Basic Info
The island, sometimes called the 'Island of Flowers', is about eight miles long and about five miles broad, and covers about twenty square miles. The island is hilly, and Heaval is over 1200 feet high while Ben Tangaval is nearly 1100 feet. The island has several magnificent beaches, including Traigh Mor, which is also used as the island's airstrip, Traigh Scurrival and

Traigh Mor, Barra.

Traigh Eais, and Halaman Bay. Other parts of the island have high cliffs, although there is much good land.

Castlebay is the only settlement of any size. Barra has a population of 1400, most of whom are catholic, unusual in that most of the Outer Hebrides are presbyterian. There is a statue of the Madonna and Child high up on the slope of Heaval. There are also many Gaelic speakers, and the festival Feis Bharraigh is held here in July.

There is a nine-hole golf course. Boat trips to Mingulay and Eriskay. Cycle hire.

History

Barra has many prehistoric monuments, and the island was inhabited from the earliest times. Monuments include Dun Bharpa, a fine chambered cairn, and Dun Cuier, an Iron Age fort. The island has associations with St Barr, St Findbarr of Cork, who died in 623. St Barr is said to have converted the islanders to Christianity, and dissuaded them from cannibalism (!). There are three old chapels at Cille Bharra with carved gravestones.

The island was taken by Onund Wooden-Leg, a Viking, in 871, but was part of the Lordship of the Isles. It was long a property of the MacNeils of Barra, who were confirmed in possession by Alexander, Lord of the Isles, in 1427. The MacNeils had their castle on an islet in Castlebay, and a smaller tower in Loch Tangusdale.

Although the MacNeils were Jacobites, and fought at the battle of Killiecrankie in 1689 and in the Jacobite Rising in 1715, they were muted during the 1745 Rising and retained their lands. The MacNeils finally sold the island in 1838 because of debt, but the castle was bought back and restored, being completed in the 1970s. Much of the island was cleared in the 19th century, and there was once a thriving herring industry. The population of the island is now around 1400.

Today

Fishing and crofting. Tourism.

Fiaray

Islet off the north tip of Barra at Scurrival.

Fuday and Orosay

Small fertile island off the north of Barra, one mile east of Eoligarry, about one mile long and 0.5 miles wide. There are said to be Viking graves here. **Orosay** is smaller and lies to the north of Traigh Mor.

Hellisay and Gighay

Two small adjacent islands, three miles north-east of Barra.

Fuiay and Flodday

Two small islands, one mile east of Barra at North Bay.

Vatersay

An island ('glove island') just to the south of the south-west tip of Barra, which has been joined to Barra by a causeway since 1990. The island is about three miles long and 2.5 miles wide, but is nearly cut in two by bays, on its east and west coast, with large expanses of magnificent sandy beaches. The island is hilly, and rises to over 600 feet. It now has a population of about 70, many of who are Gaelic speaking.

Keissimul Castle, Castlebay, Barra.

The *Annie Jane*, a ship carrying immigrants from Liverpool to America, was shipwrecked off the island in 1853, and there is a monument [NL 630953] to commemorate the tragedy. Over 300 people were killed, and most of them were buried on Vatersay.

There is a small islet **Muldoanich** two miles to the east.

Sandray

An island ('sand island') one mile south of Vatersay. It is roughly round in shape, and has a diameter of about 1.5 miles. Much of the lower areas are covered in shifting sand dunes, but the island rises sharply to 800 feet. The ruins of a broch survive. There are small isles to the west: **Flodday**, which has a natural arch; and **Lingay**.

Pabbay

An island ('priest's island') two miles south-west of Sandray and 3.5 miles south of Vatersay. The island is about one mile long and 1.5 miles across at its greatest. The land rises to a height of over 500 feet. On the island is a Pictish symbol stone, with an incised cross, as well as several carved cross-slabs.

Mingulay

An island ten miles south-west of Barra and two miles south-west of Pabbay. Mingulay is about three miles long and two wide, is very hilly, rising to over 900 feet. There is a fine sandy beach on the east side at Mingulay Bay, but high cliffs elsewhere and the island is home to many seabirds. There is a natural arch, and the remains of a fort.

Berneray

Island ('Bjorn's island') just south of Mingulay, about 1.5 miles long and one mile wide, and rises to over 500 feet with impressive cliffs. The island has a prodigious number of seabirds, including kittiwakes, guillemots and puffins; and there are the remains of two forts. The former inhabitants of the island survived by exploiting the seabirds, although to acquire eggs and young birds involved deeds of great daring on the high cliffs.

Places of Interest

Prehistoric

Borve Standing Stones

Off A888, 2 miles N of Castlebay, Borve, Barra.
NF 653014 LR: 31 (Map ref: 134)

Two standing stones were located here, but one has fallen. The remaining stone is about 4.5 feet high. The stones are said to be associated with Viking burials, and human remains were found near here along with other artefacts including two bronze tortoise brooches, finger ring, and bronze pins.

Dun Bharpa Chambered Cairn

Off A888, 2.5 miles N of Castlebay, Craigston, Barra.
NF 671019 LR: 31 (Map ref: 135)

A well-preserved Neolithic chambered cairn, dating from about 3000 BC, with a number of large slabs of the kerb still in position. The cairn survives to a height of seventeen feet, and measures 85 feet in diameter. The cover-slab of the burial chamber is exposed near the top of the cairn.

Dun Briste

NW tip of Berneray.
NL 548806 LR: 31 (Map ref: 136)

The ruins of a fort, built on a promontory above high cliffs, with the landward side blocked by an impressive wall.

Dun Cuier

Off A888, 3 miles N of Castlebay, Allasdale, Barra.
NF 664034 LR: 31 (Map ref: 137)

A reasonably well-preserved dun, which was occupied until at least the 7th century.

Dun Scurrival

Off A888, 6 miles N of Castlebay, Eoligarry, Barra.
NF 695081 LR: 31 (Map ref: 138)

An oval dun, standing on a promontory above the sea. The walls survive to a height of over eight feet, and a gallery can be traced. There is also an outer wall.

Sandray

S side of Cairn Galtar, Sandray.
NL 638914 LR: 31 (Map ref: 139)

On the southern slopes of Cairn Galtar are the ruins of an oval dun and its outworks, the walls of which survive to a height of just under six feet.

An old chapel, dedicated to St Bride, is said to have stood on the island [NL 651919].

Sron an Duin Dun

On SW tip of Berneray, Barra Head Lighthouse.
NL 548802 LR: 31 (Map ref: 140)

A dun, built on a promontory, the wall of which survives to a height of about ten feet. The entrance passage, on the north-west side, had three lintel-slabs in place, and the remains of two galleries, one above the other, were visible. Some of the dun was destroyed with the building of the lighthouse.

Tigh Talamhanta, Barra

Off A888, 3 miles N of Castlebay, Tigh Talamhanta, Barra.
NF 677023 LR: 31 (Map ref: 141)

The remains of a wheel house and souterrain as well as later buildings. Tigh Talamhanta means the 'house under the ground'.

Historic and Heritage

Barra Heritage and Cultural Centre

On A888, Castlebay, Barra.
NL 663984 LR: 31 (Map ref: 142)

The centre is a new custom-built facility for exhibitions, mainly of local material: community arts and crafts; selection of items from archaeological excavations in Barra and other isles; extensive collection of old photographs including herring fishing, people, thatched houses and boats.

The centre also runs Dubharaidh, a restored traditional whitehouse type thatched cottage in a magnificent, secluded location, fifteen minutes walk from Craigston village, (which is three miles north-west of Castlebay). No cars at museum. Open May-Sep, Mon-Fri 11.00-17.00 – but check with centre (£).

Barra Heritage Centre open Apr-Sep, generally Mon-Fri 11.00-17.00, but check with centre.

Centre for exhibitions. Gifts and books. Cafe. WC. Disabled access. Parking. £.
Tel: 01871 810413 Fax: 01871 810413

Castle Sinclair

Off A888, 1.5 miles NW of Castlebay, Loch St Clair, Barra.

NL 648997 LR: 31 (Map ref: 143)

Castle Sinclair is a much-ruined tower house formerly of three storeys, probably a property of the MacNeils. There are traces of what may have been a causeway

Cille Bharra

Off A888, 6 miles N of Castlebay, Eoligarry, N end of Barra.

NF 704077 LR: 31 (Map ref: 144)

A ruinous medieval church, built about the 12th century and dedicated to St Barr. Two chapels also survive, one of which has been rerooted to provide shelter for several carved slabs from the churchyard, some which may have been used to mark the burials of the MacNeils of Barra. Other interesting slabs lie in the yard, while a fine carved stone of the 10th or 11th century – with a cross and runic inscription – is kept in the Museum of Scotland: a cast is displayed at Cille Bharra. The inscription reads: 'after Thorgerth, Steiner's daughter, this cross was raised'.

Access at all times.
Parking nearby.

Kiessimul Castle

Off A888, S of Castlebay, Barra.

NL 665979 LR: 31 (Map ref: 145)

Kiessimul Castle consists of a curtain wall shaped to fit the island on which it stands, enclosing a keep, hall, chapel and other ranges of buildings. Although Clan MacNeil claim descent from Neil of the Nine Hostages, High King of Ireland at the end of the 4th century, the first to settle in Scotland seems to have been Hugh, King of Aileachh and Prince of Argyll. His son, 21st in descent, was called Neil of the Castle, and built a stronghold here in 1030, or so it is claimed.

The clan were Jacobites, but only nominally supported Bonnie Prince Charlie in the Jacobite Risings, although even in 1750 an agent reported to the exiled Bonnie Prince Charlie that MacNeil of Barra would bring 150 men to a new rising in Scotland. The family was forced to sell the island in 1840,

but the castle was bought back in 1937, and restored in the 1950s and 60s.

Open Apr-Oct Mon, Wed & Sat afternoons – wind and tide permitting. Open at other times by appt.
Parking nearby. £.
Tel: 01871 810336/449

Pabbay

8 miles SW of Barra, E side of Pabbay.

NL 607875 LR: 31 (Map ref: 146)

In a burial ground are the ruins of a small rectangular chapel; and three cross-slabs, two of them upright. There is also a Class I Pictish stone, carved with a crescent and v-rod and flower symbol, as well as a later cross.

The Inner Hebrides

*Skye, Raasay, Small Isles, Coll, Tiree,
Mull, Iona, Slate Islands, Colonsay, Jura,
Islay, Gigha, Bute, Cumbrae and Arran*

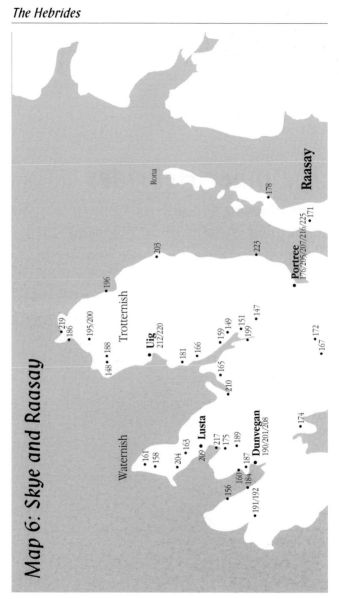

Map 6: Skye and Raasay

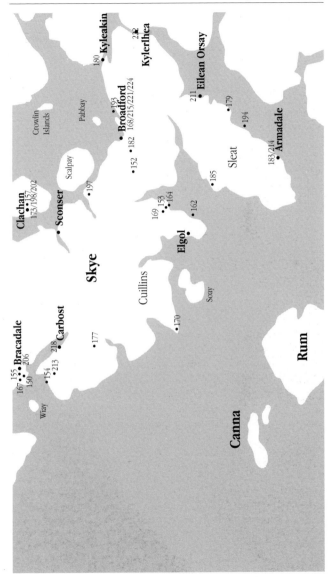

Kyleakin

222

Kylerhea

180

Eilean Orsay

211 • 179

194

Broadford

195 183/214 Armadale

168/215/221/224

Crowlin Islands

Pabbay

152 • 182

Scalpay

185

Sleat

Clachan 157

173/198/202 Sconser

197

169 153

164

162

Skye

Elgol

Cuillins

Scavy

Bracadale 155 206

Carbost 218

167 150 154 213

170

177

Way

Cuillins

Canna

Rum

Skye

(from Norse 'wing-shaped'; Gaelic 'An t-Eilean Sgitheanach' – the 'island of cloud or mist')

In Brief
Picturesque Cuillin Hills, Old Man of Storr and Quirang. Bonnie Prince Charlie. Brochs. Dunvegan Castle and Clan Donald Centre. Blackhouse museums. Flora MacDonald. Crofts. Clearances.

Location (see map 6, p 70-71)
OS Landranger maps 23, 32, 33, 39
Lies off the coast of mainland, W of Kyle of Lochalsh

Tourist Information Centres:
www.host.co.uk
Portree (tel: 01478 612137; fax 01478 612141)
Open Jan-Dec
Dunvegan (tel: 01470 521581; fax 01470 521582)
Open Jan-Dec
Broadford (tel: 01471 822361; fax: 01471 822141)
Open Apr-Oct
Uig (tel: 01470 542404; fax 01470 542404)
Open Apr-Oct
Kyle of Lochalsh (mainland) (tel: 01599 534276; fax: 01599 534808)
Open Apr-Oct
Mallaig (mainland) (tel: 01687 462170; fax: 01687 462064)
Open Apr-Oct

How to Get There
By toll bridge from mainland at Kyle of Lochalsh to Kyleakin on Skye
Ferry from Mallaig on mainland to Armadale on Skye (30 mins; CalMac tel: 01687 462403 or 01471 844248)
Ferry from Glenelg on mainland to Kylerhea on Skye (Mar-Oct; tel/fax: 01599 511302)
Also on services from Uig on Skye to Tarbert on Harris and Lochmaddy on North Uist (CalMac tel: 01475 650100)
Armadale on Skye to Canna, Eigg Rum and Eigg
Ferry from Sconser on Skye to Raasay (CalMac tel: 01475 650100)

Notes
Hill walking and climbing (in some places difficult). Cycling, pony trekking and watersports, including windsurfing and kayaking. Fishing available. Boat trips. There are three golf courses. Cars and bicycles can be hired. There are several tour operators, offering trips, tours and safaris around Skye. Many events, including Highland Folk Festival, Skye and Lochalsh Festival and Skye Folk Festival. Self-catering accommodation available at Neist Point Lighthouse.

Trotternish, Skye.

Basic Info

Skye is the second largest island of the Hebrides, after Lewis and Harris, being 60 miles long and between three and 25 miles wide, and covering an area of 535 square miles. The impressive saw-toothed Cuillin (pronounced 'Coolin') Hills dominate much of the island. There are twelve Munros in the range – peaks over 3000 feet – including Sgur Alasdair ('Alexander's peak', 3300 feet), Sgur a Greadhaich ('peak of torment', 3211 feet), Sgu nan Gillean ('the lad's peak', 3167 feet) and Bruach na Gillean ('brae of the forest', 3143 feet). Sleat (pronounced 'Slate'), to the south of the island and known as the garden of Skye, is very green, fertile and lush; while Trotternish, to the north, is rougher, with hills rising to 2500 feet, and has several unusual geologic formations, including the Old Man of Storr, a 160-feet-high pinnacle, and a series of pinnacles and crags at Storr rising to 2360 feet; and the Quirang, dominated by the structures of The Needle, The Prison and The Table. The island has a number of habitats and a large range of plants and wildlife. Glenbrittle is particularly picturesque, and the cliffs at Waterstein rise over 950 feet straight out of the sea.

The island has much fertile land and supports a large population, which was 9500 in 1974, but is now around 12,000. The biggest settlement and capital is Portree ('port of the king') – the name derives from the visit of James V in 1540. There are the remains of an old chapel on a tidal island in the bay, which was dedicated to St Columba.

Other settlements include Dunvegan, Kyleakin, Sligachan, Isleoransay, Elgol, Bracadale, Struan, Glendale and Uig.

Wildlife

Multitudes of birds, including corncrakes, warblers, finches, woodcock, spotted woodpeckers, grouse, sparrow hawks, golden eagles, buzzards and owls. Also ducks, geese, oystercatchers, terns, cormorants, guillemot, razorbill and kittiwake. Bats and adders. Red and roe deer, otters, toads and pine marten. Seals. Dolphins, porpoises and whales.

Cuillin mountains, Skye.

History

Skye was occupied from prehistoric times, and there is a fine range of monuments including numerous standing stones and burials cairns, including that at Rubh a' Dunain. The island has many brochs, duns and hill forts, some of them particularly well preserved, such as Dun Beag and Dun Ardtreck. There is a Pictish symbol stone, Clach Ard, at Tote, and other Pictish stones have been found here, one of which is in the museum at Dunvegan Castle.

St Columba is said to have visited the island in the 6th century, and Skye also has associations with St Maelrubha and St Moluag, early Christian missionaries. There are several ruinous chapels, and a cashel site – the site of an early Christian monastery – north of Uig.

The island was held by the Vikings from the 9th century, but after Norwegian defeat at the battle of Largs in 1263, the island became more and more under the influence of the kings of Scots. A high proportion of the place names on the island, however, are Norse, including Trotternish, Sleat, Waternish and Bracadale.

The island was held by the MacLeods, MacDonalds and MacKinnons. The MacLeods were based at Dunvegan to the north of the island, while the MacDonalds held Sleat and later Trotternish, and the MacKinnons were based at Dun Ringill and Caisteal Maol, holding the east of the island as well as Scalpay. The MacDonalds and MacLeods fought over control of parts of the island, and there were fortresses at Caisteal Camus, Dun Sciath, Caisteal Maol, Dun Uisdein and Duntulm. These battles, including a fight at Skeabost in 1539, led to the atrocity at Trumpan in 1578, when the MacLeod congregation had the church they were worshipping in burned down around them by the MacDonalds.

Bonnie Prince Charlie was sheltered on Skye in 1746 after the disaster at the battle of Culloden – he had a price of £30,000 on his head. He was brought to Trotternish from Benbecula, disguised as a maid 'Betty Burke', by Flora MacDonald. Flora sought help at Monkstadt House, and found Hanoverian troops, but the Prince was eventually sheltered at Kingsburgh, Flora's home – her house has gone but stood near the newer building. They parted in the building which is now the Royal Hotel, when he presented her with a lock of his hair. Flora, herself, was imprisoned in Dunstaffnage Castle, then the Tower of London. She was released and emigrated to America, but returned in 1779 and stayed at Flodigarry – her cottage now provides accommodation as part of the Flodigarry Hotel.

Charlie was taken to Portree, where he sailed for the nearby island of Raasay, but feeling unsafe then returned to Skye, again disguised as a servant. The Prince was helped by the MacKinnons, and sheltered in Strathaird, hiding in a cave south of Elgol, now known as 'Prince Charles's Cave'. From here was taken to Mallaig on the mainland on 4 July, and eventually fled Scotland in a French ship, never to return. The Prince is said to have given the chief of the MacKinnons the recipe for Drambuie, a whisky liqueur, although the original ingredients are said to have included cognac rather than whisky. MacKinnon may not have thought the recipe recompense for the years spent in prison as a result. By no means were all clans Jacobite, and MacDonald of Sleat and MacLeod of Dunvegan supported the Hanoverian government.

Incidentally, Johnson and Boswell met Flora MacDonald in 1773. She had emigrated to North Carolina, but after being paradoxically embroiled in the Wars of Independence on the Hanoverian side, returned to Skye, where she died. She died in 1790 and is buried at Kilmuir.

The population of Skye was 20,627 in 1821, but now is much smaller. Emigration from the island in the 19th century – not all of it forced by landlords – resulted in a drastic reduction in the population, following years of famine and the failure of the kelp industry. Abandoned settlements include those at Boreraig and Suisnish, where some of the most notorious clearances took place. In 1882 there were confrontations between local crofters and landowners, and police were brought in from Glasgow. A pitched battle resulted, the Battle of the Braes, and the sending of marines and gunboats to the island; there was a similar confrontation in Glendale. The strife resulted in the Napier Commission being established, which eventually resulted in the Crofter's Act of 1886. This established a fairer and more secure system of land tenure and rents, although things have only improved slowly.

Marble was quarried on Skye.

Many of the population of the island still speak Gaelic, particularly in the north of the island. There is a Gaelic college in Sleat – Sabhal Mor Ostaig.

Today
Crofting, forestry and fishing. Tourism and crafts. Light industry. Whisky distilling.

Scalpay
Lying off the north coast of Skye, the island ('isle shaped like boat') is oval in shape, over four miles at its widest and three miles at its least. The island is very hilly, and rises to just under 1000 feet. There are several forestry plantations. The island was a property of the MacKinnons, and the ruins of an old chapel, dedicated to St Francis, survive at Teampull Fraing [NG 629282]. The Sound of Scalpay abounds with oysters, and there is a small island **Longay** to the east of the island. Diving available.

Crowlin Islands
A small group of islands, the largest one mile long and rising to over 300 feet. The islands are situated east of Raasay and Scalpay, and west of Applecross peninsula.

Pabay

A small island ('priest's Isle') north of Skye at Broadford and east of Scalpay. There are the slight remains of an old chapel.

Soay

The island of Soay ('sow's island'), situated to the south of Skye, three miles west of Elgol. The island is about three miles long and about two miles at its widest, but is bisected by two bays.

Wiay

Small island ('temple isle') in Loch Bracadale to west of Skye. Other islets are **Harlosh Island**, **Tarner Island** and **Oronsay**.

Isay

Islet at mouth of Loch Dunvegan, which once had a 'considerable population'.

Ascrib Islands

Chain of small islands to north-west of Loch Snizort.

Eilean Trodday

Small island, with a lighthouse, one mile north of north tip of Trotternish and two miles north-east of Rubha Hunish.

Fladda-chuain

Islet, long but thin, three miles north-west of Rubha Hunish to the north of Trotternish. A chapel was dedicated to St Columba, and a monk called O'Gorgon – a contemporary of Columba – had a cell and is buried here.

Cuillins from Elgol, Skye.

Raasay and Rona

(Norse: 'roe deer island' or 'roe ridge island')
(Norse: 'rock surfaced isle')

In Brief
Wilderness. Unspoiled. Tranquil.

Location (see map 6, p 70-71)
OS Landranger map 24
Lies 1 mile off the N and E (Trotternish) coast of Skye
6 miles W of Applecross and Wester Ross
Rona is 0.5 miles N of the N tip of Raasay

Tourist Information Centres
Portree (tel: 01478 612137; fax 01478 612141)
Open Jan-Dec
Broadford (tel: 01471 822361; fax: 01471 822141)
Open Apr-Oct.

How to Get There
By ferry from Sconser on Skye to Suisnish on Raasay (15 mins; Cal Mac tel: 01475 650100 – times vary)

Notes
The East Coast walk is a challenging seven-mile walk: details from Outdoor Centre (see entry), through which windsurfing, canoeing, archery, climbing and orienteering are also available. Other walks available.

Basic Info
The island of Raasay is just over fourteen miles long and about 1.25 to four miles wide. The island is very hilly, the highest of the hills rising to 1450 feet at the peak of Dun Cann, and a third of the island is over 500 feet high. Parts of the island, however, are fertile and there are several wooded areas and forestry plantations, through which there are walks. Clachan and Inverarish are the largest settlements.

  The island of Rona is about 4.75 miles long and about one mile wide. It too is hilly, and rises to over 400 feet above sea level.

Wildlife
Many birds including golden eagles. Red deer, alpine hares, Raasay vole, otters, seals and porpoises.

History
The islands have surprisingly few listed prehistoric sites, although there is a dun at Dun Borodale and a cairn at Brae. Raasay was long a property of the MacLeods of Raasay, whose main fortress was at Brochel, then later at Kilmaluag, near the site of Raasay House. The ruins

Raasay and Skye from Applecross.

of an old church, dedicated to St Moluag, and burial ground survive at Clachan.

Bonnie Prince Charlie was sheltered on the island in 1746, before returning to Skye, and the MacLeods suffered for their support: Brochel and Kilmaluag are both said to have been torched. In 1843 the 12th and last chief became bankrupt, and the island was sold: in 1841 the population was 647. Much of Raasay was then cleared of people, and the population dwindled to 388 only 30 years later (and is now around 200) – Hallaig was cleared, and there is a cairn commemorating the former inhabitants: Sorley MacLean, who was born on Raasay, wrote about Hallaig in one of his poems. The island then had a succession of mostly unsuitable and uncaring landlords – although for a while iron ore was mined here – until 1979 when it was purchased by the government and the situation improved: Raasay House was opened as an outdoor centre.

The inhabitants of Rona are said to have worshipped in a cave on the east side of the island until the construction of the church. The cave had a stone pillar which served as a pulpit and there were rows of stones used as pews.

Eilean Fladday

Small tidal island ('flat island') off the west coast of Raasay at its northern tip. It is about one mile long – watch tides.

Eilean Tigh

A tidal islet ('isle of the house') at the northern tip of Raasay – watch tides.

Places of Interest

Prehistoric

Borve Standing Stones

Off A850, 3 miles NW of Portree, Borve, Skye.
NG 452480 LR: 23 (Map ref: 147)
Three standing stones, grouped by the unclassified road, which may have been part of a stone circle. The tallest is six feet high.

Carn Liath, Balgown

Off A855, 3 miles N of Uig, Balgown, Skye.
NG 372688 LR: 23 (Map ref: 148)
The robbed and disturbed remains of a burial cairn, which survives to a height of fourteen feet. The kerb can be traced in places.

Carn Liath, Kensaleyre

Off A856, 5.5 miles NW of Portree, Kensaleyre, Skye.
NG 420514 LR: 23 (Map ref: 149)
A prominent chambered burial cairn, some eighteen feet high and 80 feet in diameter. A cist was found here which contained human bones.

Carn Liath, Struanmore

Off A863, 0.5 miles SW of Bracadale, Struanmore, Skye.
NG 337376 LR: 23 (Map ref: 150)
Although robbed and reduced in height, the burial cairn is 90 feet in diameter and survives to a height of ten feet. Parts of the kerb can be traced, as can the entrance passage and possibly the chamber.

Clach Ard

Off B8036, 4.5 miles NW of Portree, Tote, Skye.
NG 421491 LR: 23 (Map ref: 151)
Set within railings, this is probably a standing stone which was reused by the Picts. The stone, which is about five feet high, is carved with a crescent and v-rod, double-disc and z-rod, and mirror and comb. At one time it was being used as a door lintel, and it is one of the few Pictish remains on Skye – or indeed the Hebrides.
Access at all times.
Parking nearby.

Clach na h-Annait

Off A881, 3.5 miles SW of Broadford, Kilbride, Skye.
NG 590203 LR: 32 (Map ref: 152)
Clach na h–Annait ('stone of the mother church')

is a standing stone which is eight-feet tall. It is said that a bell and stoup were found beneath the stone. Near the stone [NG 589202] is Tobar na h-Annait, a healing well, which is enclosed is a fairly modern building. The chapel of St Bridget is believed to have stood close by.

Cnoc nan Gobhar, Kilmarie

Off A881, 3 miles NE of Elgol, Kilmarie, Skye.
NG 553173 LR: 32 (Map ref: 153)
An impressive chambered burial cairn, between 70 and 60 feet in diameter, and rising to a height of fifteen feet.

Dun Ardtreck

Off B8009, 3.5 miles NW of Carbost, Portnalong, Skye.
NG 335358 LR: 32 (Map ref: 154)
Standing on a rocky crag above the sea, Dun Ardtreck consists of a dun with the remains of a wall, on the landward side, surviving to eight feet tall. The entrance is in the middle of the wall, and has a guard chamber.

Dun Beag

On A863, 8 miles S of Dunvegan, Struanmore, Skye.
HS NG 339386 LR: 32 (Map ref: 155)
Dun Beag ('small dun') is a well-preserved ruined broch on a small knoll. The entrance passage, an adjoining cell and mural stair rising about 20 steps all survive. The broch was occupied in the 18th century, and finds from here included pottery, an armlet of glass, a gold ring, bronze objects, coins and glass beads.
Open all year.
Parking.

Dun Boreraig

Off B884, 5 miles NW of Dunvegan, Dun Boreraig, Skye.
NG 194531 LR: 23 (Map ref: 156)
Standing on a rocky crag are the remains of a ruinous broch, which survives to a height of around nine feet, with an outwork.

Dun Borodale

Off unlisted road, 0.5 miles E of Clachan, N of Inverarish, Raasay.
NG 555364 LR: 24 (Map ref: 157)
In a forestry plantation is an oval Iron-Age dun and outwork in a strong position. The entrance with

Dun Beag, Skye.

cells can be traced, and the walls survive to a height of about eight feet.

Dun Borrafiach

Off B886, 4.5 miles N of Lusta, Dun Borrafiach, Skye.
NG 235637 LR: 23 *(Map ref: 158)*
A broch on a rocky crag, the walls of which survive to a height of nine feet. The entrance and an intra-mural gallery can be traced.

Dun Cruinn

Off B8036, 6 miles NW of Portree, Dun Cruinn, Skye.
NG 411518 LR: 23 *(Map ref: 159)*
Located on the summit of a rocky hill is Dun Cruinn, the ruins of a fort and dun with outlying defences. A defensive wall or rampart survives to a height of thirteen feet in one place. An oval dun is built on one part of the site, and the entrance can be traced.

Dun Fiadhairt

Off A850, 2.5 miles NW of Dunvegan, Fiadhairt, Skye.
NG 231504 LR: 23 *(Map ref: 160)*
Built on a rocky outcrop, Dun Fiadhairt consists of the ruins of an Iron Age broch. The wall survives to a height of five feet, and there are two entrances,

the main one between two walls with openings into guard cells. The broch is in relatively good condition.

Dun Gearymore

Off B886, 5 miles N of Lusta, Dun Gearymore, Skye.
NG 236649 LR: 23 *(Map ref: 161)*
The ruins of a broch, the remains of which survive to a height of about eight feet. The entrance can be traced, and there are a pair of cells within the wall, entered from within the broch.

Dun Grugaig

Off A881, 1.5 miles SE of Elgol, Glasnakille, Skye.
NG 535124 LR: 32 *(Map ref: 162)*
Standing on a small rocky outcrop above the sea, Dun Grugaig consists of a strong wall cutting off the promontory on the landward side. The wall, which survives to a height of thirteen feet above the inside level, has mural galleries and there are the treads of a stair. A massive lintel survives above the entrance, and the passageway is still roofed over.

Dun Hallin

Off B886, 2.5 miles N of Lusta, Hallin, Skye.
NG 256592 LR: 23 (Map ref: 163)

Standing on a ridge between Hallin and Gillen on the Waternish peninsula, Dun Hallin is a round Iron Age broch, ruinous and choked with debris. The entrance, guard cells and parts of the gallery walls can be traced; and the walls stand to a height of about twelve feet.

Dun Ringill

Off A881, 11 miles SW of Broadford, Kilmarie, Skye.
NG 562171 LR: 32 (Map ref: 164)

Dun Ringill consists of a dun, which was reused in medieval times. The wall has had a mural gallery, a cell, and an altered entrance. Within the dun are the foundations of two small medieval rectangular buildings. It was used by Clan MacKinnon before they moved to Dunakin or Castle Maol in the late 16th century, although the family eventually moved back to Kilmarie.

Dun Suladale

Off A850, 7.5 miles NW of Portree, Suladale, Skye.
NG 374526 LR: 23 (Map ref: 165)

Standing on a rocky outcrop is a relatively well-preserved broch, the ruins of which survive to a height of about nine feet, with a defensive outwork. The entrance and small chamber are visible, as is another oval cell or gallery.

Eyre Standing Stones

Off A856, 7 miles NW of Portree, Eyre, Skye.
NG 414524 LR: 23 (Map ref: 166)

A pair of standing stones, one story being that they were once used to support a massive cauldron of the old hero Fingal.

Knock Ullinish Souterrain

Off A863, 7 miles SE of Dunvegan, Knock Ullinish, Skye.
NG 333384 LR: 23 (Map ref: 167)

A disturbed souterrain, which now consists of an underground passageway running for about eighteen feet.

Liveras Cairn

On A854, Broadford, Liveras, Skye.
NG 642238 LR: 32 (Map ref: 168)

Standing by the side of the road are the remains of a chambered burial cairn with a cist: much robbed and disturbed. It is about 75 feet long by 55 feet wide, and survives to a height of thirteen feet.

Na Clachan Bhreige, Kilmarie

Off A881, 3.5 miles NE of Elgol, Kilmarie, Skye.
NG 543177 LR: 32 (Map ref: 169)

A setting of four standing stones, three upright and one fallen, known as Na Clachan Bhreige ('the false stones'). The stones are all over five feet tall.

Rubh' an Dunain Cairn and Dun

Off B8009, 4 miles S of Glenbrittle, Rubh' an Dunain, Skye.
NG 393163 LR: 32 (Map ref: 170)

A Neolithic chambered cairn, reused in the Bronze Age, consists of a round mound and concave forecourt. The entrance passage, from the forecourt, is still roofed with stone lintels, but the burial chamber is roofless. Remains were found of six different adults. Visit involves a long walk.

Nearby [NG 396160] are the ruins of a dun on a promontory. The wall rises to nine feet, and there are the remains of the entrance and galleries within the walls.

Storab's Grave, Raasay

On unlisted road, 3 miles N of Clachan, Brae, Raasay.
NG 561417 LR: 24 (Map ref: 171)

A cairn, prehistoric in origin, is said to mark the grave of Storab, a king of Norway killed while raiding Raasay.

Tungadale Souterrain

Off B885, 5 miles W of Portree, Glen Tungadale, Skye.
NG 408401 LR: 23 (Map ref: 172)

The remains of a ruinous souterrain, which now consists of a long underground passageway, stand in a forestry plantation, east of Loch Duagrich.

Uamh nan Ramh Souterrain

Off unlisted road, SE of Clachan, opposite old post office, Raasay.
NG 550364 LR: 24 (Map ref: 173)

The remains of a souterrain, formed from a natural fissure roofed over by large lintels. The name means 'cave of oars', as the souterrain was formerly used for storing boat oars.

Vatten Chambered Cairns

On A863, 3.5 miles SE of Dunvegan, Glen Heysdale, Skye.
NG 298441 LR: 23 (Map ref: 174)

Two impressive, little-disturbed and well-preserved

burial cairns. The more northerly is 100 feet in diameter and sixteen feet high, and the kerb can be traced; while the southerly cairn is 110 feet in diameter and eleven feet high, and has been robbed of stones. The kerb can also be seen.

Historic and Heritage

Annait, Skye

Off B886, 3.5 miles NE of Dunvegan, N of Fairy Bridge, Skye.
NG 272527 LR: 23 (Map ref: 175)
A triangular-shaped fort between the meeting of Bay River and a burn. A wall cut off the other side, which survives in places to a height of four feet. There are indications of huts or cells within the walls, as well as a rectangular building, probably a chapel. The fort was reused as an early Christian monastic site: the name means 'mother church'. The bodies of unbaptised children were buried here until about 1900. It is not easy to get to the site.

Aros Experience

On A850, Viewfield Road, Portree, Skye.
LR: 23 (Map ref: 176)
The audio-visual exhibition tells the story of Skye from 1700 until the present day, introducing the scenery of Skye. A purpose-built auditorium is the location for regular shows on Gaelic arts, including step dancing, singing and theatre. The auditorium is also used as a cinema and there are children's matinees.
Open daily: Apr-Sep, 9.00-21.00; Oct-Mar, 10.00-18.00.
Audio-visual exhibition. Gift and book shop. Restaurant and cafe. Creche, play area and forest walks. WC. Disabled access. Parking. Group concessions. £.
Tel: 01478 613649 Fax: 01478 613775
Email: aros@demon.co.uk

Borline Church and Cross

Off B8009, 3 miles S of Carbost, Eynort, Skye.
NG 375259 LR: 32 (Map ref: 177)
Along the shore from Eynort are the ruins of two churches in a graveyard, the smaller and older of which was dedicated to St Maelrubha. Outside the west end of the larger building are several fine carved slabs and part of a cross shaft.
Access at all reasonable times.
Parking.

Brochel Castle

Off unlisted road, 6.5 miles N of Clachan, Brochel, Raasay.
NG 585463 LR: 24 (Map ref: 178)
Perched on a high rock in a spectacular location, Brochel Castle is a small ruined fortress, built early in the 16th century by the MacLeods of Raasay. The last chief resident at Brochel was probably Iain Garbh around 1648, after which the family moved to Kilmaluag. The ruin is in a dangerous condition, but can be easily viewed from the exterior. Nearby are the remains of a small roofless and ruinous chapel.

Caisteal Camus

Off A851, 3.5 miles N of Armadale, Skye.
NG 671087 LR: 32 (Map ref: 179)
Standing in a picturesque location on a steep headland of the Sound of Sleat, Caisteal Camus – which is also known as Knock Castle – is a very ruinous stronghold of the MacLeods, then the MacDonalds of Sleat. The castle was said to be haunted by a 'Green Lady', a gruagach, a spirit who associated itself with the fortunes of their families. The castle is also said to have had a glaistig, who was particularly concerned with looking after cattle.

Caisteal Maol

Off A850, 0.5 miles E of Kyleakin, Skye.
NG 758264 LR: 33 (Map ref: 180)
Overlooking the old ferry crossing and the new bridge between Skye and the mainland at Kyle of Lochalsh, Caisteal Maol, 'the bare castle', is a very ruined 15th-century castle. According to tradition, the castle was built by a Norse princess called 'Saucy Mary' who was married to a MacKinnon chief. Their main income was from tolls on ships sailing through the Kyle. It is said that she was buried beneath a large cairn [NG 602234] on the top of Beinn na Caillaich (the 'mountain of the old woman').

In the middle ages the castle was known as Dunakin, and was a stronghold of the MacKinnons of Strath or Strathordil. In 1951 a hoard of coins was found hidden in a chink of masonry on the outer face of one of the walls.

Caisteal Uisdein

Off A856, 3 miles S of Uig, Caisteal Uisdein, Skye.
NG 381583 LR: 23 (Map ref: 181)
Caisteal Uisdein, 'Hugh's Castle', is a ruined rectangular 16th-century tower. Hugh MacDonald, the builder, was outlawed for piracy, his exploits extending even to the fishermen of Fife, although he

Colbost Croft Museum, Skye.

was later pardoned and made steward of Trotternish. However, he plotted to overthrow his MacDonald kin by slaughtering them at Castle Uisdein, but the plot was discovered, and he was eventually caught about 1602 and imprisoned in Duntulm Castle. He was given salted beef and no water, and when the pit where he had been buried was finally opened his skeleton was found with a broken pewter jug, which he had destroyed with his teeth. His skull and thigh bones were kept in a window of the parish church until they were buried in 1827.

Cill Chroisd

On A881, 2.5 miles SW of Broadford, Cill Chroisd, Skye.

NG 617207 LR: 32 (Map ref: 182)

Remains of a 16th-century rectangular chapel and graveyard, which has a burial ground of the MacKinnons. The name means 'Christ's church'.

Access at all reasonable times.

Parking.

Clan Donald Centre

Off A851, Armadale, Skye.

NG 640047 LR: 32 (Map ref: 183)

Armadale Castle was built in 1815 by the architect James Gillespie Graham for the MacDonalds of Sleat, then extended in 1855 by David Bryce, although there was an earlier house here. The MacDonalds had lived at Duntulm Castle – said to have been abandoned because of the ghosts; then Monkstadt House, both on Trotternish to the north of the island: Flora MacDonald brought Bonnie Prince Charlie to Monkstadt to shelter him from pursuit by Hanoverian troops in 1746.

Armadale Castle, now burnt out and ruined, houses the Clan MacDonald centre and 'The Museum of the Isles', with an exhibition and slide show covering 1300 years of history, in some of the outbuild-

ings. The presentation shows the story of the MacDonald clan and Lord of the Isles. Library and study centre offer genealogical research, and there is a countryside information service. Around the castle are 40 acres of woodland gardens and nature trails, as well as a walled kitchen garden.

Open Apr-Nov, daily 9.30-17.30, last entry 17.00; gardens open all year.

Guided tours. Explanatory displays. Gift shops. Licensed restaurant. Tearoom. Picnic area. WC. Disabled access. Induction loop in audio-visual theatre. Car and coach parking. Self-catering accommodation available all year. Group concessions. ££.

Tel: 01471 844305/227 Fax: 01471 844275

Email: office@cland.demon.co.uk Web: www.cland.demon.co.uk

Colbost Croft Museum

On B884, 4 miles W of Dunvegan, Colbost, Skye.

NG 215485 LR: 23 (Map ref: 184)

A museum in a blackhouse, containing 19th-century implements and furniture with a peat fire burning throughout the day. Replica of an illicit whisky still.

Open Apr-Oct, daily 10.00-18.30.

Explanatory displays. Car and coach parking. Group concessions. £.

Tel: 01470 521296

Email: Anniemac@annemacaskil.u-net.com

Dun Sgathaich

Off A851, 6 miles NW of Armadale, Tokavaig, Skye.

NG 595121 LR: 32 (Map ref: 185)

Standing on a rock with an enclosing wall, Dun Sgathaich is a ruined 14th-century castle, and has been a place of some strength. Meaning 'Dun of

Dunvegan Castle, Skye.

the Shadow', Dun Sgathaich is associated with Diarmid, a companion of Finn MacCool. The warrior queen Sgathaich trained men in the art of fighting, and Diarmid came here to be instructed by her. Another tradition is that the castle was built in a single night by a witch. Although the castle was originally held by the MacAskills, it passed to the MacLeods, then the MacDonalds. It was probably abandoned around 1618 when the family moved to Duntulm, although they later returned to Armadale (see Clan Donald Centre).

Duntulm Castle

Off A855, 6.5 miles N of Uig, Skye.
NG 410743 LR: 23 (Map ref: 186)
On a strong site, Duntulm Castle consists of a very ruined castle, once a strong and comfortable fortress and residence. Duntulm was originally an Iron Age broch or dun, later used by the Norsemen, then

held by the MacLeods, then the MacDonalds of Sleat.

Hugh MacDonald (also see Dun Uisdein and Dun an Sticar, North Uist) was imprisoned and starved to death in a dungeon here around 1700. His ghostly groans are said to then have been heard – there are several other ghost stories. The castle was abandoned around 1730 when the MacDonalds moved to Monkstadt House, then Armadale Castle in Sleat.

Shulista was held by the MacLean hereditary physicians to the MacDonalds, while Hunglader was the home of their pipers, the MacArthurs from Ulva.
View from exterior – care must be taken as dangerously ruined.
Parking Nearby.

Dunvegan Castle

Off A850, 1 mile N of Dunvegan, Skye.
NG 247491 LR: 23 (Map ref: 187)
Dunvegan Castle consists of a massive 14th-century keep, a 16th-century tower, the Fairy Tower, and a joining hall block from the 17th century. The Fairy Tower was built by Alasdair Crotach, whose fine tomb is at St Clement's Church at Rodel on Harris. The castle was completely remodelled and extended in the 19th century.

It was a property of the MacLeods from the 13th century. The castle is the home of the Fairy Flag, reputedly given to one of the chiefs by his fairy wife.

The flag allegedly gives victory to Clan MacLeod, whenever unfurled, said to have done so both at the battles of Glendale in 1490 and Trumpan, after the MacDonalds had slaughtered many of the MacLeods at the church there, in 1580. It was also said to make the marriage of the MacLeods fruitful, when draped on the nuptial bed, and to charm the herrings in the loch when unfurled.

Another interesting item is a drinking horn, Rory Mor's Horn, holding several pints, which the heir of the MacLeods had to empty in one go. There are many mementoes of Bonnie Prince Charlie and Flora MacDonald. Exhibition about Clan MacLeod and St Kilda, which the family held for centuries. A Pictish stone, with a crescent and v-rod and disc is in the museum here, and was used to cover a spring known as Tobar na Maor [NG 241465]. Another Pictish stone, which was found at Fiskavaig [NG 330340] is now in the Museum of Scotland.

Boat trips can be taken from the castle to a nearby seal colony, where the seals can be seen at close hand.

There was a MacCrimmon college of piping at Borreraig, who were renowned pipers to the MacLeod chiefs.

Open daily mid-Mar-end-Oct 10.00-17.30; Nov-mid-Mar, castle and gardens, 11.00-16.00; closed 25/26 & 31 Dec & 1 Jan; last entry 30 mins before closing.

Guides in each of the public rooms. Explanatory panels and displays. Audio-visual theatre. Gift shops. Restaurant. WC. Gardens. Boat trips to seal colony. Pedigree Highland cattle fold. Car and coach parking. Group/student/OAP concessions. Holiday cottages available. £££.
Tel: 01470 521206   Fax: 01470 521205
Email: info@dunvegancastle.com   Web: www.dunvegancastle.com

Eilean Chaluim Chille

Off A855, 3 miles N of Uig, Balgown, Skye.
NG 377689   LR: 23   (Map ref: 188)
On two former islands in the now drained loch are the remains of an early Christian monastery or cashel, known as Eilean Chaluim Chille, the 'island of St Columba'.

Fairy Bridge

On A850, 3 miles NE of Dunvegan, Skye.
NG 278512   LR: 23   (Map ref: 189)
A small bridge at the meeting of three roads, called the Fairy Bridge. It is said to be where the chief of

MacLeods parted from his fairy wife, by whom he had had a child. She reputedly gave him the Fairy Flag, which is preserved at Dunvegan.

Giant Angus MacAskill Museum

On A863, Dunvegan, Skye.
NG 255475   LR: 23   (Map ref: 190)
A museum about the tallest Scotsman and tallest true giant, who was born on the island of Boreray in the Sound of Harris in 1825. He stood 7'9 ", and died in St Anns, on Cape Breton Island, Nova Scotia in Canada, in 1863.

Open Apr-Oct, daily 9.30-18.00.
Explanatory displays. Car and coach parking. Group concessions. £.
Tel: 01470 521296
Email: Anniemac@annemacaskil.u-net.com

Glendale Toy Museum

Off B884, 7 miles W of Dunvegan, Glendale, Skye.
LR: 23   (Map ref: 191)
An award-winning toy museum, with a unique display of toys, games and dolls, as well as Meccano's biggest ever model, the Giant Blocksetting Crane. Also on display are early examples of Pinball and Shove Ha'penny.

Open all year, Mon-Sat 10.00-18.00.
Guided tours. Gift shop. WC. Disabled access. Car parking. Group concessions. £.
Tel: 01470 511240
Web: www.guides.co.uk/ scotskyetoymuseum.htm

Glendale Watermill

Off B884, 5 miles W of Dunvegan, Glendale, Skye.
NG 168498   LR: 23   (Map ref: 192)
A fine water mill, with wheel, in a picturesque location in the shore of Loch Pooltiel.

Kilashik

Off A850, 2.5 miles E of Broadford, Ashaig, Skye.

NG 687243 LR: 32 (Map ref: 193)

Not much remains of a chapel in a burial ground, known as Cill Askimilruby, the 'church of the ferry of St Maelrubha'. It was from here that St Maelrubha was said to sail across to his monastery on the Applecross peninsula. One story is that the saint's bell, hung on a nearby tree, would ring of its own accord every Sunday. Tobar Ashik is a holy well associated with the saint and issues a few feet above the shore.

Kilmore Old Parish Church

On A851, 2.5 miles NE of Armadale, Kilmore, Skye.

NG 658070 LR: 32 (Map ref: 194)

The rectangular overgrown shell of the old parish church, which dates from the 13th century. It was used until 1876, when the adjacent modern church was built. The MacDonalds of Sleat were buried here, and it is said that in the early 17th century men who had taken refuge after a battle were burnt alive in the church. Nearby is the stone of St Columba, where the saint is said to have blessed the land the church is built on.

Access at all reasonable times.

Kilmuir Church

Off A855, 4.5 miles N of Uig, Kilmuir, Skye.

NG 399719 LR: 23 (Map ref: 195)

There was a chapel here, dedicated to St Mary, but virtually nothing remains. In the burial ground, which was the burial place of the MacDonalds, is a carved grave slab for Charles MacArthur, a celebrated 17th-century piper to the MacDonalds. Flora MacDonald, who died in 1790, is buried here, and a Celtic cross marks her grave. A new church was built in 1810, but is also now ruinous.

Loch Siant Well

Off A855, 5.5 miles NE of Uig, Digg, Skye.

NG 471699 LR: 23 (Map ref: 196)

A spring here, which issues from a bank near Loch Siant, is enclosed by stones and was once said to have been the most celebrated well in Skye. Small offerings of rags, pins and coloured threads were left here, and it was believed to be a wishing well.

Luib Croft Museum

Off A850, 7 miles NW of Broadford, Luib, Skye.

NG 565278 LR: 32 (Map ref: 197)

The Luib Croft Museum displays living conditions in the early 20th century in an atmospheric blackhouse. A forthcoming exhibition is planned, covering Luib village from 1738 with photographs and maps.

Open Apr-Oct, daily 9.00-18.00.

Explanatory displays. Gift shop. WC. Disabled access. Car and coach parking. £.

Tel: 01471 822427

Raasay House

Off minor road, 2 miles N of East Suinish pier, Clachan, Raasay.

NG 546366 LR: 32 (Map ref: 198)

Raasay House – the Raasay Outdoor Centre (which is approved by the Adventure Activities Licensing Authority) – offers multi-activity holidays and day activities – tailored to the family, unaccompanied child, group or individual requirements – including courses in windsurfing, sailing, and kayaking as well as rock climbing, abseiling and orienteering. Mountain bike hire, archery and local knowledge of the surrounding sites of interest, historic and natural beauty spots are also available. A herit-

age museum (tel: 01478 660207) is located in the west wing, and has displays of artefacts from Raasay.

Nearby the house is the site of 16th-century tower house, called Kilmaluag Castle because of the proximity of St Moluag's church. The main residence of the MacLeods of Raasay was at Brochel Castle, but they moved here in the 17th century. This tower or a later residence was torched in 1745 after the Jacobite Rising, and replaced in 1747 by Raasay House, built by the 10th chief – Bonnie Prince Charlie was briefly sheltered on Raasay in 1746. The last traces of the castle were removed in 1846, and it was this year that the 12th and last chief of MacLeod had to sell the property.

In the garden is a Pictish stone [NG 547368], carrying a cross set inside a square above a tuning fork, crescent and v-rod. The stone was found during the building of a road.

Open Mar-Nov, Mon-Sat 9.00-19.00.

Outdoor sports tuition. Guided tours.
Explanatory displays. Gift shop. Restaurant and
cafe. Garden. WC. Disabled access. Car and
coach parking. Accommodation.
Tel: 01478 660266   Fax: 01478 660200
Email: raasay.house@virgin.net   Web:
www.freespace.virgin.net/raasay.house/

Skeabost Island

On A850, 5 miles NW of Portree, Skeabost, Skye.
NG 418485 LR: 23 (Map ref: 199)
A burial ground on an island in the river has the
remains of two chapels, although there were once
apparently six. The smaller of the surviving buildings is a ruinous rectangular structure, and was
possibly dedicated to St Columba. The larger
church is very fragmentary. Skeabost is believed to
have been the main Christian centre for Skye, and
there may have been an early Christian community here. There is a grave slab carved with the effigy of a warrior. It is believed that a church here
served as the Cathedral of the Isles until at least
1433.

Skye Museum of Island Life

On A855, 5 miles N of Uig, Kilmuir, Skye.
NG 394717 LR: 23 (Map ref: 200)
The museum shows the life of a crofting community from around the turn of the 19th century,
housed in a group of seven thatched buildings, including a blackhouse and smithy. Displays include
a wide range of agricultural implements and a
house with period furniture. Flora MacDonald is
buried in the nearby churchyard.

Open Easter-Oct, Mon-Sat 9.30-17.30.

Guided tours. Explanatory displays. Gift shop.
WC. Car and coach parking. Group cons. £.
Tel: 01470 552206   Fax: 01470 552206

St Mary's Chapel, Dunvegan

On A850, E of Dunvegan, Skye.
NG 256478 LR: 23 (Map ref: 201)
The ruins of St Mary's Chapel stand within a burial
ground, which has a memorial to the
MacCrimmons, pipers to the MacLeods of Dunvegan, and to the MacLeods themselves in the
church: a lintel is inscribed 'I ML 1694'. In the burial
ground are three carved grave slabs as well as other
old burial markers.

St Moluag's Chapel, Raasay

On unlisted road, Clachan, Raasay.
NG 548366 LR: 24 (Map ref: 202)
The ruinous remains of a 13th-century chapel, dedicated to St Moluag. There is a recess for a tomb in
one wall, and there is a burial vault of the MacLeods
of Raasay.

Access at all reasonable times.

Staffin Museum

On A855, 12 miles N of Portree, Elishader, Skye.
NG 502656 LR: 23 (Map ref: 203)
A collection of local fossils is housed in this small
stone-built museum, including species such as
Stegrosaur, Hadrosaur, Cetiocaurus and
Coelphysis, found in local Jurassic sediments. There
is also a large display of invertebrate fossils such as
ammonites and bivalves. The collection is recog-
nised as being of international importance due to
the inclusion of Scotland's first recorded dinosaur
fossils. Other displays include Bronze Age arrowheads and pottery, crofting implements and 19th-
century furniture.

Open Easter-Oct, Mon-Sat 9.30-18.00.

Parking. Parties welcome. £.
Tel: 01470 562321

Trumpan Church

Off B886, 3.5 miles NW of Lusta, Trumpan, Skye.
NG 225613 LR: 23 (Map ref: 204)
Trumpan Church, the ruins of a medieval church,
formerly with a thatched roof, was dedicated to St
Connan, and stands in an old burial ground. In the
graveyard is the Trial Stone, which has a small hole
near the top. The trial was carried out by blindfold-
ing the accused, who would be proved to be tell-
ing the truth if they succeeded in putting their finger in the hole at the first attempt. Lady Grange,
imprisoned by her husband as she had discovered
his Jacobite plotting, is believed to be buried in the
graveyard, and there are also two medieval carved
slabs.

The church is the scene of a massacre. A raiding party of MacDonalds came ashore here one Sunday about 1578. The congregation of MacLeods were at worship, and the MacDonalds set fire to the thatch and the congregation were burnt alive. Only one woman escaped. The MacLeods of Dunvegan, bringing with them the Fairy Flag, quickly arrived and the MacDonalds were all slain.

Open at all reasonable times.
Parking Nearby.

Arts, Crafts and Industry

An Tuireann Arts Centre

On B885, Struan Road, Portree, Skye.
LR: 23   (Map ref: 205)
A gallery for contemporary visual art and crafts, exhibitions and related educational events.
Open all year: summer, Mon-Tue 10.00-18.00; Wed-Sat 10.00-23.00; Sun 12.00-17.00; winter Mon-Fri 10.00-17.00.
Contemporary exhibitions for visual arts and crafts. Restaurant/cafe. WC. Disabled access. Induction loop. Car parking.
Tel: 01478 613306   Fax: 01478 613156
Email: norahcampbell@antuireann.demon.co.uk

Aurora Crafts

Off A863, 6 miles S of Dunvegan, 2 Ose, Struan, Skye.
LR: 23   (Map ref: 206)
A craft shop where lace, spinning, embroidery and other crafts are made on the premises. Demonstrations of lace-making most days.
Open Easter-mid Oct, daily 9.00-20.00.
Gift shop. Car parking.
Tel: 01470 572208

Castle Keep

Off A850, Unit 7B1, Portree Industrial Estate, 1 mile from Portree, Skye.
LR: 23   (Map ref: 207)
Castle Keep features a wide range of hand-forged swords, knives, dirks and Sgian Dubh, and a bladesmith makes the weaponry on site, using traditional methods. The workshop and showroom can be visited.
Open all year: Mon-Fri 10.00-16.30.
Explanatory displays. Gift shop. WC. Disabled access. Car parking.
Tel: 01478 612114
Email: robmiller86@hotmail.com
Web: WWW.CASTLEKEEP.CO.UK

Croft Studio

On A850, Portree Road, W of Dunvegan village, Skye.
LR: 23   (Map ref: 208)
The Croft Studio produces a range of designs inspired by Celtic manuscripts and the landscape of Skye, including water-colour paintings, silk paintings, wall hangings, cards, prints, pressed flower lampshades, wooden plaques, mirrors, cushions and jewellery. All work is original and produced on the premises by the Budge family.
Open all year Mon-Sat, 09.30-17.30; Sun, 10.00-16.30.
Sales area. Parking.
Tel: 01470 521383

Dandelion Designs and Images Gallery

On B886, 6 miles N of Dunvegan, Stein, Skye.
LR: 23   (Map ref: 209)
A craft workshop and gallery, making, displaying and selling distinctive hand-decorated wood-crafts, clocks, boxes and plaques, as well as original paintings, photographs, cards, jewellery, clothing, books

and postcards. Situated in a fine building, the Captains House, with magnificent views.

Open Easter-Oct, daily 11.00-17.00; winter by appt.

Gift shop. Gallery. Disabled access. Car and coach parking. Holiday flat available.

Tel: 01470 592218/223

Edinbane Pottery

On A850, 8 miles E of Dunvegan, Edinbane, Skye.

LR: 23 (Map ref: 210)

A pottery where work in progress can be seen in

the extensive workshop. A wide range of pieces, mostly wood-fired, are available in the showroom, including goblets, jugs, bowls and teapots.

Open Easter-Oct, daily 9.00-18.00.

Gift shop. Disabled access. Car and coach parking.

Tel: 01470 582234

Gaelic Whiskies – Whisky Exhibition

On A851, 8 miles S of Broadford, Eilean Iarmain, Skye.

NG 695125 LR: 32 (Map ref: 211)

Based at the highland estate offices of Fearann Eilean Iarmain, The Gaelic Whiskies was set up by Gaelic enthusiast Sir Iain Noble in 1976. Principle brands are the international award-winning Te Bheag blend and Poit Dhubh, a fine premium malt.

A must for a true whisky connoisseur. Small display of whisky-related artefacts. Outstanding views to Isle Ornsay, with its lighthouse, and the hills of the mainland beyond.

Open all year, Mon-Fri 9.00-17.30; Apr-Sep also Sat 10.30-14.30.

Free whisky tastings. Shop and exhibitions in gallery. Meals available in Hotel Eilean Iarmain next door.

Tel: 01471 833266 Fax: 01471 833260

Isle of Skye Brewing Company (Leann an Eilein) Ltd

On A856, adjacent to Pier, Uig, Skye.

NG 385635 LR: 23 (Map ref: 212)

The brewery produces several cask-conditioned real ales, most of which have won awards, including Red Cuillin, Black Cuillin and Young Pretender, Hebridean and Blaven. There are tours of the brewery, which only uses natural ingredients and Skye spring water. A wide range of Scottish bottled beers – including the above except Young Pretender – wines, and brewery souvenirs can be purchased.

Brewery and shop open Apr-Oct, Mon-Fri 10.00-18.00, Sun 12.30-18.00.

Guided tours by arrangement. Explanatory displays. Brewery shop. Disabled access. Car and coach parking. Group concessions. £.

Tel: 01470 542477 Fax: 01470 542488

Email: angus@skybrewery.demon.co.uk Web: www.skybrewery.demon.co.uk

Little Gallery

On B8009, 3 miles NW of Carbost, 7 Portnalong, Skye.

NG 348348 LR: 32 (Map ref: 213)

The gallery features works by Jean Thomas: etchings, water-colours and prints of the Cuillin mountains, landscapes and flora and fauna. There are also paintings by invited artists.

Open daily 10.00-18.00.

Parking. Shop.

Tel: 01478 640254 Fax: 01478 640254

Web: www.mtn.co.uk/skye-artist

Skye Batiks

Off A851, Armadale, Skye.

NG 637038 LR: 32 (Map ref: 214)

The award-winning shop features Celtic batik wall hangings and clothing, hand-loom cotton and tweed fisherman's smocks and much more, including gifts and souvenirs. There is another outlet at The Green in Portree (01471 613331).

Open daily all year.

Gift shop. Complimentary cup of coffee. Parking.
Tel: 01471 844396   Fax: 01471 844496
Email: info@skyebatiks.demon.co.uk   Web: www.skyebatiks.demon.co.uk

Skye Jewellery

Off A87, 8 miles W of Kyleakin, Broadford, Skye.
NG 644234   LR: 32   (Map ref: 215)

Skye Jewellery specialises in producing their own exclusive collection of gold and silver Celtic rings. This year a selection of jewellery to complement the rings has been introduced. The workshop can be viewed from the sales area. Skye marble jewellery and gifts are also produced.

Open April-Oct, Mon-Sat, 09.00-18.00; also Jul & Aug, Sun 12.00-16.00 (+ Easter, May Day & Whit Suns); open until 19.00 Jun-Aug.

Explanatory displays. Gift shop. Disabled access. WC nearby. Parking nearby.
Tel: 01471 822100   Fax: 01471 822100
Web: www.scoot.co.uk/skye_jewellery/

Skye Woollen Mill

Off A850, Dunvegan Road, Portree, Skye.
LR: 23   (Map ref: 216)

The weaving mill, originally used to produce yarn for Glaswegian carpet factories, features Isle of Skye tartan, knitwear and local gifts. Also a large selection of outwear and clothing.

Open all year: Jun-Sep 9.00-17.30; Oct-May 10.00-17.00; closed Christmas Day.

Explanatory displays. Gift shop. Coffee shop. WC. Disabled access. Car and coach parking.
Tel: 01478 612889

Skyeskyns

On B886, 5 miles NE of Dunvegan, 17 Loch Bay, Waternish, Skye.
LR: 23   (Map ref: 217)

Skyeskyns is the only traditional exhibition tannery in Scotland, showing how sheepskins are made using traditional methods. Demonstrations of rare tanning skills and hand-finishing are available, and lambs-wool rugs, leather goods and fleeces are for sale.

Open Apr-Oct, daily 10.00-18.00.

Guided tours. Explanatory displays. Gift shop. WC. Car and coach parking.

Tel: 01470 592237   Fax: 01470 592237
Email: clive@www.skyeskyns.demon.co.uk
Web: www.skyeskyns.demon.co.uk

Talisker Distillery

On B8009, 6 miles W of Sligachan, Carbost, Skye.
NG 378319   LR: 23   (Map ref: 218)

Beneath the impressive saw-toothed Cuillin mountains of Skye, the present distillery was founded in 1830. The distillery offers tours, but larger parties should book in advance: the approach road is not suitable for coaches. Adult admission includes a discount voucher redeemable in the well-stocked distillery shop towards the purchase of a 70cl bottle of malt whisky. Children under eight years of age are welcome but will not be admitted into the production area.

Open Apr-Jun & Oct, Mon-Fri 9.00-16.30; Jul-Sep, Mon-Sat 9.00-16.30; Nov-Mar, Mon-Fri 14.00-16.30; last tour at 14.00.

Guided tours. Explanatory displays. Gift shop. Picnic area. WC. Limited disabled access. Car parking. £.
Tel: 01478 640314   Fax: 01478 640401

Trotternish Art Gallery

On A855, 9 miles N of Uig, Kilmaluag, Skye.
NG 432742   LR: 23   (Map ref: 219)

A working retail gallery, set in a beautiful part of north Skye, featuring a wide selection of landscape originals, and mounted photographic work. Work in progress can be viewed.

Open Apr-Sep, daily 9.00-21.00; Oct-Mar, daily 9.00-17.00; closed Christmas day and Boxing Day.

Tel: 01470 552302

Uig Pottery

Off A87, Uig, Skye.
NG 385637   LR: 23   (Map ref: 220)

The Uig Pottery makes functional and unique individual pieces with landscape-inspired decorations expressive of Skye. Many of the pieces are hand thrown, and the workshop is open plan and the manufacturing work in process can be seen.

Open Apr-Oct, daily 9.00-18.00; Nov-Mar, Mon-Sat 9.00-17.00.

WC. Assisted disabled access. Car and coach parking.
Tel: 01470 542421   Fax: 01470 542421
Email: margaret@uigpottery.force9.co.uk
Web: www.uigpottery.co.uk

World of Wood

Off A850, Broadford, Skye.
LR: 32 (Map ref: 221)

The story of a tree from a seed, through planting, harvesting and saw milling, to the many wood-craft trades. Woodworking tools are on display, items of wood craft are for sale, and there is a small wood with native and introduced species of trees.

Open Apr-Oct, Mon-Sat.
Shop. Parking.
Tel: 01471 822831 Fax: 01471 822831

Gardens, Animals and Miscellaneous

Kylerhea Otter Haven

On A850, 8 miles S of Broadford, Kylerhea, Skye.
LR: 33 (Map ref: 222)

Kylerhea is a good place for otters – and they can often be seen from the hide. Specially constructed paths are designed to protect the habitat and the wildlife. As well as otters, there are all sorts of wild-life in this fine setting.

Open all year.
Explanatory displays. Disabled access. Car parking.
Tel: 01320 366322 Fax: 01320 366581
Web: www.forestry.gov.uk

Prince Charles's Cave

Off A855, 3.5 miles NE of Portree, Prince Charles's Cave, Skye.
NG 518482 LR: 23 (Map ref: 223)

In a remote location below cliffs is the cave where Bonnie Prince Charlie is said to have sheltered before being taken across to Raasay after the failure of the 1745 Jacobite Rising.

Skye Serpentarium Reptile World

On A850, 1 mile E of Broadford, Old Mill, Harrapool, Skye.
NG 660225 LR: 32 (Map ref: 224)

Skye Serpentarium is a unique award-winning reptile exhibition and breeding centre in a converted water mill. Reptiles on show include snakes, lizards, frogs and tortoises, in natural surroundings. This is also a refuge for neglected and illegally imported reptiles, and there are frequent informative snake-handling sessions.

Open Easter-Oct, Mon-Sat 10.00-17.00, Sun also in Jul, Aug & Bank Holidays; open winter by appt.
Guided tours for groups by arrangement. Explanatory displays. Gift shop. Car and coach parking. Group concessions. £.
Tel: 01471 822209/533 Fax: 01471 822209
Email: NIK@SNAKEBITE.COM
Web: HTTP://TRAVEL.TO/SERPENTARIUM

West Highland Heavy Horse Tours

From Aros Experience or Bayfield Road car park, Portree, Skye.
LR: 24 (Map ref: 225)

A traditional wooden horse-drawn cart, pulled by a Clydesdale and a Shire horse, can take visitors for an informative tour, which includes information on local history and folklore. Tours are also available on Raasay by prior arrangement – open June to September: phone 01478 660233 for details and discussion.

Operates Easter-Oct.
Car parking (Sconser). Max number ten persons. Group concessions. One way or return available. Tour lasts about 20 mins. Check £.
Tel: 01478 660233 Fax: 01478 660200
Web: www.host.co.uk

Small Isles: Rum, Eigg, Canna and Muck

In Brief
Picturesque islands. Nature Reserve. St Donan. Clearances.

Location (see map 7, below)
OS Landranger map 39
Lie about 12 miles from the W coast of mainland, S of Skye, and some 35 miles E of Barra

Tourist Information centre
Mallaig (mainland) (tel: 01687 462170; fax: 01687 462064)
Open Apr-Oct

How to Get There
By passenger ferry from Mallaig on mainland to Coroghon on Canna and Galmisdale on Eigg
as well as Por Mor on Muck and and Kinloch on Canna (CalMac tel: 01687 462043).
By passenger ferry from Arisaig on mainland to Kinloch on Rum (Charter tel: 01687 462043)
Inter-island ferries between Eigg, Muck, Canna and Rum.

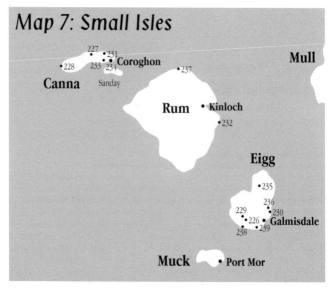

Map 7: Small Isles

Mull

Canna

Sanday

227
231
228 233 234 Coroghon
237

Rum • Kinloch
232

Eigg

235
236
229 230
226 Galmisdale
238 239

Muck • Port Mor

Basic Info

The Small Isles consist of Rum, Eigg, Canna and Sanday, and Muck

Rum

Rum ('hill ridge'?) is eight miles long and eight miles wide at most, and covers an area of sixteen square miles. It is located 7.5 miles west of Point of Sleat on Skye. It is the largest of the Small Isles, and provides an impressive aspect: the pinnacles of the Cuillins of Rum rise

Rum.

to a height of over 2600 feet. The climate is quite wet, and the island was once forested. It is still home to a large herd of red deer, as well as wild goats and ponies, and a colony of Manx shearwaters, which numbers some 120,000. There are also otters, seals, and sea eagles.

The island was settled from earliest times, but there are few remains of significance. Rum was a property of the Clan Ranald branch of the MacDonalds, but passed to the MacLeans of Coll. The island supported a population of over 400, but in 1826 it was cleared of all folk – who went to Nova Scotia – barring one family, and turned into one large sheep farm. In 1845 it was to be converted into a sporting estate, but it was sold in 1885 to John Bullough, a successful machinery manufacturer, and his son built the splendid Kinloch Castle. In 1957 the Nature Conservancy Council bought Rum and the whole island is now a nature reserve, and Kinloch Castle is run as a hotel.

Visitors wishing to stay overnight should contact the Reserve Office in advance – tel: 01687 462026.

Eigg

Eigg ('nick' or 'hollow'; the 'notched isle') is located five miles south-west of Point of Sleat on Skye and four miles south-east of Rum; and is 6.5 miles long and 4.5 miles wide at most. It is riven in the middle by a glen, which divides the mass of the Sgurr, which rises to a height of 1289 feet, from the rest of the island. Eigg is a fertile place, and once supported a large population.

There are several prehistoric sites on the island, including the fort at an impressive site on An Sgurr and at Rubha na Crannaig, which has also been suggested as the site of St Donan's monastery. Kildonan is the site of an old church and burial ground, and the saint is said to have been martyred and to be buried on the island.

Eigg was a property of the Clan Ranald branch of the MacDonalds, and in the cave, Uamh Fhraing, 200 souls were suffocated to death in 1577 during a clan fight with the MacLeods. In

Eigg.

1826 the island was sold to Hugh MacPherson, a professor of archaeology, and has gone through several hands until being bought by the local population. Inhabitants now number about 60, who mostly make a living crofting.

Canna and Sanday

Known as the 'garden of the Hebrides', Canna ('porpoise', 'whale' or possibly 'rabbit' island; or 'can or pot shaped') is located three miles north-west of Rum and nine miles south-west of Skye. Canna is 4.5 miles long and one mile wide at the most, and is connected to the small island of Sanday ('sand isle') to the south, itself about two miles long. The island has much good land, but is also rough and rocky to the east and rises to over 800 feet. The island has a large puffin colony, corncrakes and some rare butterflies. Dolphins, whales and basking sharks may be seen near Canna.

Canna.

The island has the remains of fortifications at Dun Channa at the extreme west end and Coroghon Castle at the east. Canna was an early Christian site, and there is a broken cross at A' Chill near the site of a church dedicated to St Columba. The island was a property of Clan Ranald until sold in 1820 to Hector Munro, who cleared much of the population. The islands changed hands until gifted to The National Trust for Scotland in 1981, who still own them: tel 01687 462466 for information. Pony trekking available.

Muck

An island ('island of pigs' or 'island of sea-pig or porpoise') three miles north-west of the mainland of Scotland at Sanna Point and three miles south-west of Eigg.

Muck is flat and relatively fertile, although it rises to 600 feet, and there are many species of seabirds including puffins, kittiwakes, fulmars, shearwaters as well as sea-eagles.

Muck was held by the Abbey of Iona, but passed to the MacLeans of Ardnamurchan, then to Clan Ranald, then was sold again and had several owners. Again much of the island was depopulated in the 19th century, the islanders emigrating to Nova Scotia: from 155 inhabitants in 1831 to 51 in 1891.

Places of Interest

Prehistoric

An Sgurr Fort

Off unlisted track, 2 miles NW of Galmisdale, An Sgurr, Eigg.

NM 461847 LR: 39 (Map ref: 226)

In a difficult and inaccessible location on a hill 400-feet high are the remains of a fort, which covers more than nine acres. A wall defends the only access, which survives at one place to nearly six feet high.

Beinn Tighe Souterrain

Off unlisted road, 2 miles W of Coroghon, Beinn Tighe, Canna.

NG 244062 LR: 39 (Map ref: 227)

The souterrain consists of two roofed underground passageways, one twenty feet long, the other ten feet. Modern breaks provide access through the roof, and they may be associated with the mound nearby.

Dun Channa

On W tip of Canna.

NG 206048 LR: 39 (Map ref: 228)

Built on a relatively inaccessible rocky stack, the landward side has been further strengthened by a wall, now much ruinous. There are foundations within the wall, which may be medieval in origin.

Loch nam Ban Mora Dun

Off unlisted track, 2 miles W of Galmisdale, Loch nam Ban Mora, Eigg.

NM 455852 LR: 39 (Map ref: 229)

On an island in the loch are the remains of a small dun, defended by a wall which survives to a height of four feet. The dun was traditionally occupied by abnormally large women (!).

Rubha na Crannaig Fort

Off unlisted track, 1 mile NE of Galmisdale, Rubha na Crannaig, Eigg.

NM 491848 LR: 39 (Map ref: 230)

Standing on a rocky crag on sea-girt promontory are the remains of a fort, triangular in shape, with a ruinous wall. This has been suggested as the site of the early monastery of St Donan.

Stone of Punishment, Canna

Off unlisted road, 0.5 miles NW of Coroghon pier, A' Chill, Canna.

NG 269055 LR: 39 (Map ref: 231)

A standing stone here, six feet tall, is known as the 'Stone of Punishment'.

Historic and Heritage

Bagh na h-Uamha Stone

Off unlisted track, 2 miles SE of Kinloch, Bagh na h-Uamha, Rum.

NM 421972 LR: 39 (Map ref: 232)

A cross-slab, with an incised cross, was found here on the beach and has been reerected. It dates from the 7th or 8th century.

Canna Cross

Off unlisted track, 0.5 miles W of Coroghon pier, A' Chill, Canna.

NG 269055 LR: 39 (Map ref: 233)

The broken cross is located in the old burial ground of St Columba's Church. The 8th- or 9th-century cross survives to a height of over six feet, but only one arm of the cross remains. Located against the outer part of the wall enclosing the modern graveyard is a stone with a cross incised on one face.

Coroghon Castle

On NE of island of Canna, on N side of Harbour.

NTS NG 288055 LR: 39 (Map ref: 234)

Not much remains of Coroghon Castle on the summit of a steep rock. It was a property of the Clan Ranald branch of the MacDonalds. The site is said to be haunted by the ghost of a woman imprisoned here by one of the MacDonald Lord of the Isles. **Ruin may be in a dangerous condition – view from exterior.**

Fivepennies Well

Off unlisted track, 3.5 miles N of Galmisdale, Camus Sgiotaig, Eigg.

NM 476901 LR: 39 (Map ref: 235)

A spring above Traigh na Biail (the 'singing sands') was known as Fivepennies Well, and was a healing well 'for a person's first disease and for the deformities of strangers to the island'.

Kildonnan, Eigg

Off unlisted road, 1 mile N of Galmisdale,
Kildonnan, Eigg.

NM 489853 LR: 39 *(Map ref: 236)*

In the burial ground of the ruinous church is the shaft of a 14th-century cross. The church was dedicated to St Donan who was martyred in Eigg in 617 and is believed to be buried here. The present ruinous church dates from the 16th century, and was built by John MacDonald, Captain of Clan Ranald. There are two cross-incised stones within the church, and four other slabs from here are preserved in the porch of Gramisdale House. Three nearby cairns were excavated in the 19th century, and Viking burials were discovered.

Kilmory, Rum

Off unlisted road, 3.5 miles NW of Kinloch,
Kilmory, Rum.

NG 361037 LR: 39 *(Map ref: 237)*

By the abandoned township is an old burial ground with a stone decorated with a saltire within a circle and a cross. The stone is very weathered.

St Catherine's Well

Off unlisted track, 1.5 miles W of Galmisdale,
Grulin, Eigg.

NM 457840 LR: 39 *(Map ref: 238)*

A spring on the south coast of Eigg was believed to be a healing well for all kinds of diseases, although it was reportedly good for 'the falling sickness'. Others, however, were afraid of drinking from the well as they were concerned they would then catch the disease themselves.

Gardens, Animals and Miscellaneous

Uamh Fhraing, Eigg

Off unlisted road, 0.5 miles SW of Galmisdale,
Uamh Fhraing, Eigg.

NM 475835 LR: 39 *(Map ref: 239)*

The cave, known as Uamh Fhraing ('Frances's cave') was the site of a cruel massacre in 1577. The MacDonalds from Eigg were sheltering here from a party of MacLeods, who had landed on the island intent on revenging a slight suffered by some of their kinsmen. The MacLeods blocked the entrance to the cave with brushwood, and then set fire to it – killing all those within, said to be 200 souls. In the 19th century the floor of the cave was said to be strewn with bones.

Canna.

Coll

In Brief
Beaches. Scenic and peaceful island. Spring flowers.

Location (see map 8, below)
OS Landranger map 46
Lies 11 miles W from the coast of Mull at Treshnish
2 miles NE of Tiree, its neighbouring island
19 miles NW of Iona

How to Get There
By ferry from Oban on mainland or Scarinish on Tiree to Arinagour on Coll (2 hrs 40 mins/55 mins; CalMac tel: 01631 566688)

Tourist Information Office
Oban (mainland) (tel: 01631 563122; fax: 01631 564273)
Open Jan-Dec.

Basic Info
Coll covers about 29 square miles, being some twelve miles long and between one and 3.5

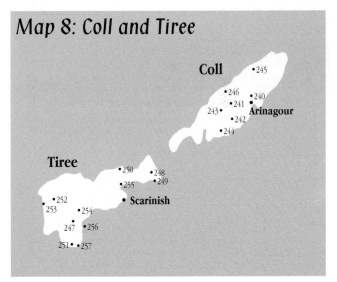

Map 8: Coll and Tiree

miles wide. It is fairly flat, although Ben Hogh rises to 340 feet, and the interior is rocky, particularly to the north of the island.

Notes
Isle of Coll Hotel, Arinagour (tel: 01879 230334; fax: 01879 230317)

Wildlife
Many birds – some 150 species – including corncrakes, razorbills, Arctic skuas and terns. Minke whales, porpoises and dolphins are sometimes seen off the island. Seals.

History
There are many prehistoric sites on the island, including the cairn at Druin an Airidh Fhada and another north of Arinagour, the standing stones at Totronald, and several Iron Age forts and duns, including Dun an Achaidh, which although very ruinous is the best preserved.

The island was held by the MacDonald Lords of the Isles, but on their forfeiture passed to

Coll.

the MacLeans of Coll, who held the property until 1865, although only after battles between the MacLeans, MacNeils and MacDonalds. There is a medieval castle at Breachacha, possibly built by the Lords of the Isles, with an 18th-century mansion close by. The island supported a population of 1162 in 1801, but by 1891 this had dropped to 522 – while there were between 6000-7000 sheep on the island and 1000 cattle – and now only about 150 people live on Coll. One of the abandoned townships is at Sorisdale.

Gunna
Island off the western tip of Coll, about one mile long.

Places of Interest

Prehistoric

Cnoc a' Bhadain

Off B8071, 0.5 miles N of Arinagour, Cnoc a' Bhadain, Coll.

NM 222581 LR: 46 (Map ref: 240)

Remains of a cairn, about 45 feet in diameter and surviving to a height of three feet. Much of the stone of the cairn has been robbed, but some of the kerb stones survive, as do two cists within the cairn.

Druim an Airidh Fhada Cairn

Off B8070, 2 miles W of Arinagour, Druim an Airidh Fhada, Coll.

NM 198565 LR: 46 (Map ref: 241)

The cairn here is a stony mound, about five feet high and 50 feet across, with boulders forming a kerb round the edge. The cairn is set on the top of a hillock with fine views.

Dun an Achaidh

Off B8070, 3 miles SW of Arinagour, SW of Acha Mill, Coll.

NM 183545 LR: 46 (Map ref: 242)

A dilapidated dun and outwork, standing on the top of a rocky ridge. The walls rise to a height of about three feet, and the entrance can be traced.

Totronald Standing Stones

Off B8070, 3.5 miles W of Arinagour, Totronald, Coll.

NM 167560 LR: 46 (Map ref: 243)

Set on the top of a ridge, two standing stones are known as Na Sgailaichen – the 'teller of tales' – and stand about 50 feet apart. One is six feet high, while the other is a little shorter.

Historic and Heritage

Breachacha Castle

Off B8070, 5 miles SW of Arinagour, Breachacha, Coll.

NM 159539 LR: 46 (Map ref: 244)

On the edge of the bay, Breachacha Castle, built in the 14th century. The island was given by Robert the Bruce to Angus Og MacDonald of the Isles, but changed hands between the MacDonalds, MacNeils and MacLeans. A new mansion was built nearby in 1750 for the MacLeans, and the castle became ruinous. Dr Johnston and Boswell visited in 1773. The property passed to the Stewarts of Glenbuchie in 1856, but the castle was bought and restored by a descendant of the MacLeans in 1965.

Killunaig

Off B8072, 3 miles N of Arinagour, Killunaig, Coll.

NM 221617 LR: 46 (Map ref: 245)

The ruins of a rectangular medieval church within a walled burial ground, dedicated to St Fynnoga of Coll. There are several 17th- and 18th-century grave slabs in the burial ground.

Gardens, Animals and Miscellaneous

Ben Hogh Rocking Stone

Off B8071, 2.5 miles W of Arinagour, Ben Hogh, Coll.

NM 181581 LR: 46 (Map ref: 246)

On the summit of Ben Hogh, the highest hill on Coll, is a natural formation of stones, with a boulder set upon three smaller stones – so that it can be rocked.

Tiree

(from Gaelic 'the land of Ith' or Tir-Iodh 'the land of corn').

In Brief
Beaches. Surfing. Unspoilt island. Flowers in spring.

Location (see map 8, p 97)
OS Landranger map 46
Lies 20 miles W from the coast of Mull at Treshnish
2 miles SW of Coll, its neighbouring island
19 miles NW of Iona

Tourist Information Office
Oban (mainland) (tel: 01631 563122; fax: 01631 564273)
Open Jan-Dec

How to Get There
By ferry from Oban on mainland or Arinagour on Coll to Scarinish on Tiree (3 hrs 40 mins/55 mins; CalMac tel: 01631 566688)
By air from Glasgow (British Airways tel: 0345 222111)

Basic Info
Tiree is a flat island and covers some 29 square miles, being about fourteen miles long and varying in thickness between 0.75 miles and six miles. It has many fine beaches, although its exposed position means it can be battered by gales. It does, however, have more hours of sunshine than any other part of the UK. The island is very fertile and is rich in plant life: some 500 species – which are particularly spectacular in the spring. The main settlement is at Scarinish.

Wildlife
Many birds – some 150 species – including corncrakes, razorbills, Arctic skuas and terns. Minke whales, porpoises and dolphins are sometimes seen off the island. Seals. Loch Bhasapoll has many wild geese and ducks.

History
There are many prehistoric sites on the island – including about 50 identified forts, duns and brochs. The finest is Dun Mor, Vaul – although finds from excavations here are kept at the Hunterian Museum in Glasgow. There was also an impressive cross at Kirkapol, dating from the 15th century, but this was taken to Inveraray Castle.

The island was held by the MacDonald Lords of the Isles, but on their forfeiture passed to the MacLeans, then the Campbell Earls and Dukes of Argyll. There was a castle on a former island in Loch an Eilean, on the site of which a factor's house was built (Island House). The island is very fertile, and at one time supported a population of 4450, but after famines and evictions it had dropped to 2700 in 1881. In 1886 the Duke of Argyll sent in police and soldiers from the mainland to clear folk off the land.

Tiree.

The Skerryvore Lighthouse, which is over 130 feet high, is situated 4.5 miles W of Tiree, and was completed in 1844. The lighthouse is now unmanned, and there is a museum in the Lightkeepers' houses at Hynish.

Today
Crofting and fishing; tourism – surfers.

Places of Interest

Prehistoric

Balinoe Standing Stone

Off B8066, 4.5 miles W of Scarinish, Balinoe, Tiree.

NL 973426 LR: 46 (Map ref: 247)

An impressive pointed standing stone, which reaches a height of nearly twelve feet.

Caolas Standing Stone

Off B8069, 3 miles NE of Scarinish, Caolas, Tiree.

NM 077483 LR: 46 (Map ref: 248)

A tall standing stone, about nine feet tall, which leans to one side.

Dun Mor a' Chaolais

Off B8069, 3 miles NE of Scarinish, Dun Mor a' Chaolais, Tiree.

NM 083476 LR: 46 (Map ref: 249)

The remains of a broch and its outworks on a rocky hillock. The walls survive to a height of about five feet, and galleries and the entrance can be traced.

Dun Mor, Vaul

Off B8069, 2.5 miles N of Scarinish, Vaul, Tiree.

NM 042492 LR: 46 (Map ref: 250)

A well-preserved broch and outworks, the walls of which survive to a height of about seven feet. A gallery ran up inside the wall, and a doorway gave access to a stair, which led up to the upper parts of the broch. The entrance has a small guard chamber, and there was a water tank in the floor. The broch site was occupied between about 500 BC to about 300 AD. The disarticulated skeleton of man was found within the broch, dating from the time of the Vikings.

Dun na Cleite

Off B8066, 6 miles SW of Scarinish, Hynish, Tiree.

NL 974385 LR: 46 (Map ref: 251)

Not much remains of a fort on a strong site on a cliff-top promontory. A complex of walls encircles the weak points of the summit and defend the approach. The walls stand to a height of about 3.5 feet, and the entrance can be traced.

Hough Stone Circles

Off B8065 or B8068, 6.5 miles W of Scarinish, Hough, Tiree.

NL 958451 LR: 46 (Map ref: 252)

The remains of two stone circles, which stand nearby each other. The first consists of only one upright six-foot stone, several fallen stones, and the stumps of others. The second circle consists of eleven fallen stones and the stump of another.

Traigh Ghrianal Cairn

Off B8065, 6.5 miles W of Scarinish, Greenhill, Tiree.

NL 939445 LR: 46 (Map ref: 253)

The remains of a cairn, eighteen feet in diameter and surviving to a height of about eleven feet.

Historic and Heritage

Castle Loch Heylipol

Off B8065, 3 miles W of Scarinish, Loch Heylipol, Tiree.

NL 986435 LR: 46 (Map ref: 254)

On a former island in the loch is the site of a strong castle of the MacDonalds. It was later held by the MacLeans, then the Campbell Earls and Dukes of Argyll, who had a causeway and factor's house built on the site in 1748. The factor, called MacLaren is said to have died before he could enter his new house. His ghost reputedly haunts the house, as does a 'Green Lady'.

Cladh Orain

Off B8069, 2 miles N of Scarinish, Kirkapol, Tiree.

NM 042472 LR: 46 (Map ref: 255)

In the small burial ground are the ruins of a rectangular chapel, formerly the old parish church, and five grave slabs decorated with crosses, and dating between the 14th and 16th centuries. The chapel, which dates from the 14th century, was dedicated to St Columba.

Old Parish Church, Sorobaidh

On B8066, 4 miles W of Scarinish, Sorobaidh, Tiree.

NL 984416 LR: 46 (Map ref: 256)

The site of the old parish church, dating from the 13th century, of Sorobaidh stands within a burial ground, but only foundations remain. There is an upright early Christian cross-slab and a broken cross-shaft. An inscription on the latter states that this cross was erected by Anna (MacLean), Prioress of Iona 1509-43. There are other early Christian and medieval carved stones in the burial ground. This was probably an important early Christian site.

Skerryvore Museum

On B8066, 5 miles SW of Scarinish, Hynish, Tiree.
NL 985392 LR: 46 (Map ref: 257)
The museum tells the story of the building of the Skerryvore Lighthouse, twelve miles to the southwest of Tiree. The lighthouse may be viewed by telescope.
Open all year, daily 9.00-18.00.
Parking. Not suitable for large parties.

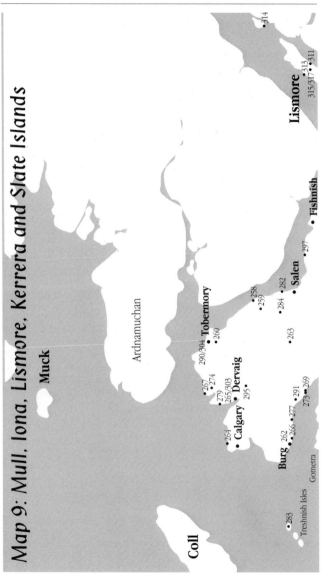

Map 9: Mull, Iona, Lismore, Kerrera and Slate Islands

Muck

Ardnamuchan

Tobermory

Lismore

314

315/317 • 313 • 311

Fishnish

297

Salen

282

284 •

259 •

258 •

263 •

260 •

290/304

Dervaig

Calgary

267 •
274 •
279 •
265/303
295 •
264 •

Burg

262
266 • 277 • 291
273 •• 269

283 •

Coll

Treshnish Isles

Gometra

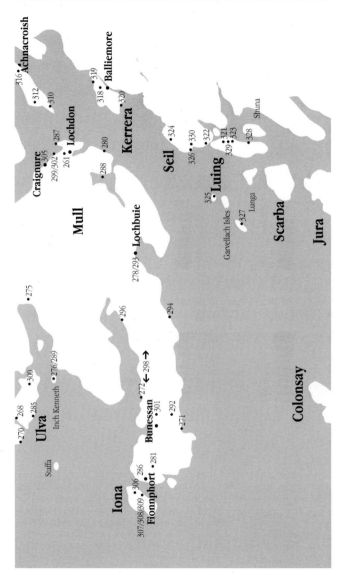

Mull

(probably 'bare hill' from Gaelic *maol*)

In Brief
Duart Castle. Tobermory. Glen Mor. Beaches. Lochbuie.

Location (see map 9, p 104-105)
OS Landranger map 47, 48, 49
Lies off the coast of Argyll, south of Ardnamurchan and Morvern
7 miles W of Oban

Tourist Information Centres
Craignure (tel: 01680 812377; fax: 01680 812497)
Open Jan to Dec
Tobermory (tel: 01688 302182; fax 01688 302145)
Open Apr to Oct

How to Get There
By ferry from Oban on mainland to Craignure on Mull (45 mins; CalMac tel: 01631 566688 or 01680 812343)
Also across Sound of Mull from Lochaline on mainland to Fishnish on Mull (15 mins; CalMac tel: 01631 566688 or 01680 812343)
Also from Kilchoan on mainland (Ardnamurchan) to Tobermory on Mull (35 mins; CalMac tel: 01631 566688 or 01680 812343), which also connects to Coll, Tiree and the outer isles.
Ulva can be reached from a passenger ferry from Mull (1 min; tel: 01688 500226).
Staffa can be visited: tel 01681 700373, 01681 700338 and 01688 400242: summer only.

Notes
Island Encounters offer wildlife and bird-watching expeditions, and there are boat trips to Staffa and the Treshnish Isles, leaving from Fionnphort and Iona, as well as to Coll and Muck. Walking, cycling, pony trekking and climbing. There are two golf courses. Sea and loch fishing – permits readily available – and diving.

  The Mull Experience offers a day trip to Mull, including ferry to Craignure, trip on the Mull Railway, chance to explore Torosay Castle, and a visit to Duart Castle (For info tel: 01680 812421).

Basic Info
One of the largest of the Hebrides – being the third largest after Lewis and Skye – Mull has a land area of 353 square miles, and is a picturesque and hilly place, which is very fertile and green in places, particularly the north, and wild and windswept in others. It is 30 miles long at its greatest point, and twenty miles at its widest. The island is dominated by the mountain of Ben More, which rises to 3169 feet, and has several other peaks over 2000 feet.

  Near Ardmeanach at Burg is MacCulloch's Tree, a remarkable fossil tree impression found in 1819, 40 feet high and five feet wide. There are fine sandy beaches to the south of the island, such as Ardalanish, Scoor and Uisken, as well as at Calgary to the west of Mull. There

Glen Mor, Mull.

are forest walks and cycle routes in Aros Park, Ardmore and Fishnish and Garmony (contact TICs or Forest Enterprise tel: 01680 300346).

Tobermory, a planned village of 1787 and built by the British Fisheries Society, is the largest settlement on the island and has attractive painted houses, each in a different colour. The name is from Tobar Mhoire – 'St Mary's Well' from the well and chapel above the village – and it has one of the finest harbours in the Hebrides, sheltered by **Calve Island**.

There are also villages at Salen; Bunessan; Fionnphort, gateway to Iona; Dervaig; Lochdon; and Craignure.

Adjacent to the island is Iona (see separate entry), the cradle of Scottish Christianity – ferry from Fionnphort on Ross of Mull. There was a pilgrim's way from Grass Point to Iona, the route marked by a series of standing stones. Other nearby islands include Ulva, Gometra, Inchkenneth, Staffa and – of course – Iona. Ulva and Gometra, incidentally, also have basaltic columns similar to those found on Staffa.

Wildlife

Many birds including golden eagles and white tailed sea eagles, and colonies of puffins and fulmars, as well as divers, razorbills, guillemots, peregrin falcons, owls, shags, skuas and merlin. Red and fallow deer, feral goats and polecats. Minke whales, dolphins and porpoise, and even killer whales and basking sharks have been seen off the Treshnish Isles. Common and Atlantic Grey seals.

History

There are many archaeological sites, ranging from chambered cairns and standing stones to vitrified forts, duns and brochs as well as several important castles.

Notable among the prehistoric remains is the stone circle at Lochbuie and a further complex of three groups of stones is located near Dervaig. An Iron Age dun, Dun Aisgain, near Burg, is particularly well preserved, and there are other Iron Age strongholds at Dun nan Gall and Dun na Fheurain. There are the remains of several interesting chapels, including those at Pennygown, Kilvickeon and on Inch Kenneth.

Guarding the Sound of Mull is Duart Castle, the splendid and daunting 13th-century fortress of the MacLeans. Aros Castle, near Salen, was once one of the most important places on the island, but is now very ruinous. Moy Castle, the empty tower of the MacLaines of Lochbuie, is in a magnificent setting at Lochbuie. There were other strongholds at Dun Ara, and at Eilean Amalaig in Loch Spelve, where the MacLeans marshalled their birlinns (galleys).

A fierce battle was fought in the 15th century, just north of Tobermory, between Angus, Lord of the Isles and the Earls of Huntly and Crawford, and the site is known as 'Bloody Bay'. One of the ships of the Spanish Armada, *Florenica*, was moored in Tobermory Bay and blown up here in 1588 after much plotting and deviousness, reputedly with £300,000 of gold bullion on board.

Many areas of Mull were cleared of people during the Clearances and later: there are several deserted townships, including Cille Mhuire, Kildavie, Shiaba and Tir Fhearagain. The herring industry was also very important, but this too has dwindled. The population of Mull was recorded as 10,612 in 1821, but by 1969 had dwindled to 2100. The population is now around 2900.

Today
Forestry, crofting, fishing, sheep farming, fish farming. Tourism (over 600,000 visitors annually).

Staffa
Staffa ('isle of Staves', from the rock formations) is small but very well known because of the hugely impressive hexagonal columns (which resulted from the slow cooling of lava) and the

Staffa.

magnificent Fingal's Cave, also known as An Uamh Ehinn – 'the musical cave'. The cave is over 270 feet deep and 66 feet high. The island's 71 acres are now uninhabited, but have been visited by Sir Walter Scott; Felix Mendelssohn, who wrote the Hebrides Overture after being inspired by the noise of the sea in Fingal's Cave; J M W Turner; William Wordsworth; Queen Victoria; Jules Verne; David Livingstone and Robert Louis Stevenson – to name but a few. The island can be visited, although landing is only possible in calm seas. Warm and water-proof clothing and sensible footwear may be advisable. The island has a large colony of puffins.

The island can be visited: tel: 01681 700373, 01681 700338 and 01688 400242: summer only.

Ulva

The nearby island of Ulva ('wolf-island' or 'Olaf's island') can be reached by passenger ferry from Ulva Ferry (1 min; tel: 01688 500226 – all year, Mon-Fri, also Sun, Jun-Aug). The island is very hilly – Beinn Chreagach is over 1000 feet high – and wildlife includes many birds, seals, deer and otters. There is a sandy beach to the south of the island.

Ulva was inhabited from the Mesolithic period, and finds from a cave include midden material, pottery, flint, bone implements and other items dating both from the Mesolithic and early Neolithic periods. The island was a property of the MacQuarries from 1473 or earlier until the 18th century. The MacQuarries had an old mansion near the present Ulva House, and also apparently a 'castle' at Dun Ban. Ulva was cleared of people in the 19th century: from 204 souls in 1851 to 46 in 1891 – there is an old burial ground at Cille Mhic Eoghainn – the population is now around 25.

The island once had a thriving kelp industry, and was also the home of the MacArthur's piping college, who were pipers to the MacDonalds at Duntulm on Trotternish, Skye. This island has been visited by Dr Johnson and Boswell, Sir Walter Scott and Beatrix Potter.

The islanders also make a living farming cattle and sheep, and fish and oyster farming, as well as tourism. There is a heritage centre on the island, as well as a reconstructed traditional thatched cottage and licensed tearoom. Signposted walks.

Note

Park on mainland, near Ulva ferry.

Gometra

The adjacent island of Gometra ('isle of Godman') is about two miles long by one wide – a bridge joins it to Ulva. This island also has basaltic columns and a series of terraces, and rises to a height of 800 feet.

Little Colonsay is a small isle about 0.5 miles south of Ulva.

Eorsa

This picturesque small island, in Loch na Keal two miles east of Ulva, was a property of the Abbey of Iona, but passed to the Campbell Duke of Argyll. It was described in 1549 as 'being fertile and full of corn'.

Inch Kenneth

Inch Kenneth (the 'island of Kenneth' – a monk from Iona who died in 600) is a small island one mile south of the east end of Ulva and just off the coast of Mull. It was a property of the nunnery of Iona, but passed to the MacLeans in 1547, and was visited by Dr Johnson and Boswell: Boswell is said to have been frightened by a ghost. A Viking hoard was found here, consisting of coins, rings and a silver chain, dating to about 1000 AD. The artefacts are in the Museum of Scotland and British Museum.

The island was once owned by the Redesdale family, parents of the Mitford girls.

Treshnish Islands

A group of islands, the Treshnish Islands ('headland peninsula') five miles north and west of Staffa and three miles west of the island of Mull. The most easterly of the islands, Cairnburghmore and Cairnburgbeg, had a castle; Fladda is flat (hence the name) and may have had an early Christian site with chapel and burial ground; the largest, Lunga, rises to 300 feet and is a bird sanctuary; while Bac Mor or Dutchman's Cap is said to resemble the latter. The islands can be visited by boat from Dervaig. Minke whales, dolphins and porpoise, and even killer whales and basking sharks have been seen off the islands, and there are colonies of seals and seabirds, including puffins and fulmars.

Earraid

Close to the south-east tip of the Ross of Mull, lies the small island of Earraid, which was used by Robert Louis Stevenson in his novel Kidnapped: Davie Balfour was shipwrecked here. He then crossed Mull back to the mainland.

Calve Island

Small island 0.5 miles east of Tobermory.

Calgary Sands, Mull.

Places of Interest

Prehistoric

An Sean Chaisteal

Off A848, 4 miles N of Salen, Ardnacross, Mull.
NM 551499 LR: 47 (Map ref: 258)
On cliffs above the shore of the Sound of Mull is a
ruinous broch, which survives as a stony mound
about seven feet in height. The entrance can be
traced, and there are some remains of a defensive
outwork.

Nearby is a chamber is a burial cairn[NM 550501],
some 55 feet in diameter and six feet high.

Ardnacross Cairns and Standing
Stones

Off A848, 3.5 miles N of Salen, Ardnacross, Mull.
NM 542492 LR: 47 (Map ref: 259)
Two cairns and two settings of standing stones are
located at Ardnacross. The better-preserved cairn
is some fifteen feet in diameter with a kerb of large
boulders, while the other is more fragmentary.
There is an eight foot standing stone, while two
other stones have fallen down.

Baliscate Standing Stones

*Off A848, 0.5 miles S of Tobermory, Baliscate,
Mull.*
NM 500541 LR: 47 (Map ref: 260)
A setting of three standing stones, only two of which
remain upright. The tallest is more than eight feet
high, while the other is over six.

Barr Leathan Standing Stone

*Off A849, 1.5 miles S of Craignure, Lochdon,
Mull.*
NM 726342 LR: 49 (Map ref: 261)
Standing on moorland to the west of the road and
north of Lochdon is a leaning standing stone, some
eight feet long.

Burg

*Off B8035 (then rough path), 7 miles W of
Tiroran, Mull.*
NTS NM 422262 LR: 48 (Map ref: 262)
Covering 1405 acres, this is a magnificent, wild and
remote part of Mull, volcanic eruptions forming the
stepped outline of the peninsula with its spectacular cliffs. The impression of a tree, MacCulloch's
Fossil Tree, some 50 million years old, can be
reached down a steep iron ladder down to the

Burg.

beach, although only at low tide.

Two large cairns [NM 428265] stand close to the
shore near Burg, 100 yards apart. They are both 40
feet in diameter, and survive to a height of over
five feet.
Open all year.
*Car parking at Tiroran – cars not permitted
any further. Dogs must be kept on leads and
cannot negotiate ladder.*
Tel: 01631 570000

Carrachan Standing Stones

Off A848, 4 miles W of Salen, NW of Tenga, Mull.
NM 504463 LR: 47 (Map ref: 263)
A setting of four standing stones on moorland
north-west of Tenga. The tallest stone is over seven
feet high.

Cillchriosd Standing Stone

*Off B8073, 3.5 miles W of Dervaig, Cillchriosd,
Mull.*
NM 377535 LR: 47 (Map ref: 264)
A tall standing stone, some 8.5 feet in height.

Dervaig Standing Stones

Off B8073, E of Dervaig, Mull.
NM 438517 LR: 47 (Map ref: 265)
Just east of the village of Dervaig are three groups
of standing stones.

The first [NM 438517] is just beyond the burial
ground at Kilmore, and three upright stones survive, while a fourth forms one side of a gateway.
These stones are about three feet high. Another
group, Cnoc Fada, survive just within the forestry

plantation [NM 439521], and consists of two upright stones of at least five, all of which would have been about eight feet tall. The third group of three stones, two of which are upright, is deep in the plantation at Maol Mor [NM 436531] and involves a long walk. The upright stones are both about seven feet tall.

Dun Aisgain

Off B8073, 4 miles S of Calgary, near Burg, Mull.
NM 377452 LR: 47 (Map ref: 266)
Set on a rocky crag, Dun Aisgain is a well-preserved round dun, with an outer wall closely following the knoll. The walls survive to a height of about nine feet, and the entrance passage, on the west side, has three lintels still in position.

Dun Ara

Off B882 or B8073, 5 miles W of Tobermory, Dun Ara, Mull.
NM 427577 LR: 47 (Map ref: 267)
Standing on a large outcrop of rock, Dun Ara consists of the ruinous remains of a wall enclosing the summit of the rock. Dun Ara was a stronghold of the MacKinnons, who held lands here from 1354 or earlier. The castle appears to have still been in use in the 17th century.

Dun Ban, Ulva

Off track, 3.5 miles W of Ulva House, Baligortan, Ulva.
NM 384416 LR: 47 (Map ref: 268)
Situated in the narrow channel between Ulva and its neighbouring island of Gometra, Dun Ban consists of a rectangular building standing on the summit of a small islet. The island was a property of the MacQuarries from 1473 or earlier until the 18th century, and they had an old mansion or castle [NM 442389] near the present Ulva House, the site now occupied by a farm steading.

Dun Choinichean

Off B8073, 8 miles W of Salen, N of Kilbrennan, Mull.
NM 441431 LR: 48 (Map ref: 269)
Standing on a rocky outcrop are the remains of a dun, the wall of which survives to a height of six feet. Although the dun is overgrown and choked with masonry, the entrance can be traced and there may be the vestige of a gallery.

Dun Eiphinn, Gometra

Off track, 5 miles W of Ulva House, 0.5 miles S of Gometra House, Gometra.
NM 358402 LR: 47 (Map ref: 270)
On a rocky hillock is Dun Eiphinn, an Iron Age fort or dun, which is protected by cliffs. A wall enclosed the top of the crag, and survives to a height of about 2.5 feet.

Dun an Fheurain

Off A849, 2 miles S of Bunessan, Ardalanish Bay, Mull.
NM 370187 LR: 48 (Map ref: 271)
Located on a craggy promontory, above the picturesque sandy bay, are the remains of Dun an Fheurain, a once strong Iron Age fort. The fort is protected by the steepness of the cliffs and by a series of ramparts and terraces. The ramparts survive to a height of over six feet.

Dun na Muirgheidh

Off A849, 2 miles NE of Bunessan, Knockan, Mull.
NM 413236 LR: 48 (Map ref: 272)
The ruins of a fort, standing on a rock promontory, cut off by four walls on the landward side. The massive walls survive to a height of five feet, and the entrance to the fort can be traced.

Dun nan Gall

Off B8073, 9 miles SW of Tobermory, Ballygown, Mull.
NM 433432 LR: 48 (Map ref: 273)
On a rocky promontory above the beach are the remains of a well-preserved Iron Age broch, the walls of which survive to a height of about six feet. The entrance, mural cell and a stair lobby can be seen.

Glengorm Standing Stones

Off B8073, 4 miles W of Tobermory, W of Glengorm Castle, Mull.
NM 435571 LR: 47 (Map ref: 274)
A group of three standing stones, all just over six feet high.

Gruline Standing Stones

On B8035, 3 miles SW of Salen, Gruline, Mull.
NM 543398 LR: 47 (Map ref: 275)
Standing by the road is an eight foot standing stone, while another stands some 200 yards to the southeast [NM 546396] in a field on the other side of the road.

Inchkenneth Cairn
On N end of island of Inch Kenneth, 1 mile W of Mull.
NM 443359   LR: 47   (Map ref: 276)
A grass-covered cairn, surviving to a height of over four feet and about 40 feet across. The remains of a cist can be seen on the top.

Kilninian Cairn
On B8073, 10 miles W of Salen, Kilninian, Mull.
NM 394454   LR: 48   (Map ref: 277)
By the road is a large burial cairn, 50 feet in diameter and over six feet high, and the kerb can be traced in places.

Lochbuie Stone Circle
Off A849, Lochbuie, 300 yards N of Lochbuie House, Mull.
NM 618251   LR: 49   (Map ref: 278)
An impressive stone circle in a pleasant location. The circle was originally of nine stones, eight of which remain, and the stones survive to a height of six feet.

There are four further standing stones outwith the circle. The first is some fifteen feet from the circle,

while another is 100 feet to the south west [NM 617251], and is ten feet tall. Another stone is 400 yards to the north [NM 616254], and is six feet tall, while yet another is 350 yards to the south west [NM 619251], but the top has been broken off.

Mingary Standing Stone
Off B8073, 2.5 miles NW of Dervaig, Mingary, Mull.
NM 414552   LR: 47   (Map ref: 279)
A standing stone, nine feet high. Nearby is at least one other fallen stone, and there is the stump of another.

Port Donain Cairns
Off A849, 4.5 miles S of Craignure, Port Donain, Mull.
NM 737292   LR: 49   (Map ref: 280)
Above the shore at the small bay of Port Donain is a chambered burial cairn, about 100 feet long and 35 wide, although it has been robbed and disturbed. The remains of a chamber, kerb and facade can be traced, and there are also the remains of a cist.

100 yards to the north-west is a smaller round cairn, 20 feet in diameter and surviving to a height of two feet. Part of the kerb can be seen, and nearby may be a fallen standing stone.

Pottie Standing Stone
Off A849, 1.5 miles E of Fionnphort, Pottie, Mull.
NM 325222   LR: 48   (Map ref: 281)
A large standing stone, some eight feet high.

Historic and Heritage

Aros Castle
Off A848, 8 miles SE of Tobermory, Aros, Mull.
NM 563450   LR: 47   (Map ref: 282)
Once one of the most important sites on Mull, Aros Castle consists of a ruined 13th-century hall house, and an overgrown courtyard. It was built by the MacDougalls of Lorn, but at the beginning of the 14th century passed to the MacDonald Lords of the Isles, then to the MacLeans of Duart, then the Campbells, although by then the castle was probably already ruinous. Aros lost importance to Tobermory, which has a more sheltered harbour.

Cairnburg Castle
Cairn na Burgh, Treshnish Isles, 2.5 miles from Mull.
NM 305447   LR: 47   (Map ref: 283)
The castle consists of a walled courtyard from at least as early as 1249, with work of a later date, including a barracks block and chapel, which are the best preserved parts. It was a property of the Mac-Dougalls of Lorn, then the MacDonald Lord of the Isles, then the MacLeans of Duart. MacLean of Duart had the chief of the MacLaines of Moy imprisoned here to prevent him producing an heir. MacLaines's only female companion was an old ugly woman, who he made pregnant. MacLaine himself was murdered, but the woman managed to escape and produced a son, who eventually recovered Moy. Many of the books and records rescued from

Iona were destroyed in a siege by Cromwell's forces in the 1650s. The castle was garrisoned during both the 1715 and 1745 Jacobite Risings.

Cill an Ailein, Glen Aros

Off A848, 2 miles NW of Salen, Glen Aros, Mull.

NM 546456   LR: 47   (Map ref: 284)

In a clearing in a forestry plantation, north of the Aros River, are the remains of a 13th-century chapel and burial ground, with a medieval grave slab. There are a number of other burial markers, dating from the 14th to the 18th century.

Cille Mhic Eoghainn

Off track, 3 miles W of Ulva House, S coast of Ulva.

NM 395389   LR: 47   (Map ref: 285)

An old burial ground, with the footings of what may have been a chapel. The chapel is believed to have been dedicated to Ernan, son of Eoghan, a nephew of St Columba. The oldest identifiable gravestone is 1765.

Columba Centre

On A849, Fionnphort, Mull.

NM 305235   LR: 48   (Map ref: 286)

The Columba Centre features an exhibition about the Celtic church, Iona and St Columba, the 6th-century saint, who founded a monastery on Iona and converted the Picts of the mainland. Displays include photographs, calligraphy, Chiro Stone, recreation of ancient landscape, and the model of a curragh. The centre also provides information on the local area.

Open May-Sep, Mon-Sat 10.00-17.00, Sun 11.00-17.00.

Explanatory displays. Gift shop. Refreshments. WC. Disabled access. Car and coach parking. Group concessions. ££. Groups by appt.

Tel: 01681 700660   Fax: 01898 840270

Email: iona_abbey@compuserve.com

Duart Castle

Off A849, 2 miles S of Craignure, Duart, Mull.

NM 749354   LR: 49   (Map ref: 287)

An extremely impressive and daunting fortress, Duart Castle consists of a large 12th-century curtain wall, enclosing a courtyard on a rocky knoll, with a strong 14th-century keep.

Duart Castle.

It was a property of the MacLeans of Duart. While fighting with the MacDonalds, the 6th chief Red Hector was killed at the battle of Harlaw in 1411, slaying and being slain by Sir Alexander Irvine of Drum.

Lachlan Cattanach, 11th Chief, became so unhappy with his Campbell wife that he had the poor woman chained to a rock in the Firth of Lorn to be drowned at high tide. However, she was rescued and taken to her father, the Campbell Earl of Argyll. As a result, MacLean was murdered in his bed in Edinburgh by Sir John Campbell of Cawdor.

In 1674 the castle and lands were acquired by the Campbell Earl of Argyll. The MacLeans remained staunch supporters of the Stewarts throughout the Jacobite Risings. Although garrisoned from time to time, the castle was not used as a residence, and became derelict and roofless. It was acquired in 1911 by Fitzroy MacLean, 26th Chief, who restored the castle.

The castle can be visited, and features the dungeons where officers from a Spanish galleon were imprisoned, and an exhibition of clan history. The castle can be reached from Oban in the motor launch *The Duchess*, which lands at the castle slipway. Entry to the grounds is free.

Open May-mid-Oct, daily 10.30-18.00.

Exhibition. Tea room and gift shop. WC. Picnic areas. Disabled access to tea room and gift shop. Car and coach parking. Group concessions. ££ (castle).

Tel: 01680 812309

Eilean Amalaig Castle

Off A849, 4.5 miles S of Craignure, Loch Spelve, Mull.

NM 708298 LR: 49 (Map ref: 288)

Site of castle of the MacLeans of nearby Duart on a tidal islet. It was at Loch Spelve that the MacLeans marshalled their birlinns or galleys and this is said to be 'the sacred island of the MacLeans'. At the end of the 16th century, Sir Lachlan MacLean was warned not to sail his galleys anticlockwise around the island or trouble would follow. He ignored this warning, and soon afterwards was killed in 1598 on Islay at the battle of Traigh Gruinart by the Mac-Donalds.

Inchkenneth Chapel

E side off island of Inch Kenneth, 1 mile W of Inchkenneth.

HS NM 437354 LR: 48 (Map ref: 289)

The fine ruinous rectangular church, which dates from the 13th century, was dedicated to St Cainnech of Aghaboe, a contemporary of St Columba. In the burial ground and protected within the chapel are several fine carved grave slabs, dating from the 14th and 15th centuries. There are also a number of 17th- and 18th-century table gravestones, and a 16th-century ring-headed cross of slate.

Access at all times.

Tel: 0131 668 8800

Isle of Mull Museum

On A848, Main Street, Tobermory, Mull.

LR: 47 (Map ref: 290)

A small museum with collections relating to the island's past, including objects, photographs and documents. A reference library is available.

Open Easter-Oct, Mon-Fri 10.00-16.00, Sat 10.00-13.00.

Explanatory displays. Disabled access. Parking nearby. Group concessions. £.

Tel: 01688 302208

Kilninian Chapel

On B8073, 10 miles W of Salen, Kilninian, Mull.

NM 397456 LR: 48 (Map ref: 291)

Kilninian, although built in 1755, stands on the site of an old chapel, possibly dedicated to St Ninian of Whithorn. There are medieval grave slabs, dating from the 14th century, housed in the vestry and within the burial ground.

Kilvickeon Church

Off A849, 2 miles SE of Bunessan, Kilvickeon, Mull.

NM 413196 LR: 48 (Map ref: 292)

Remains of a 13th-century parish church, which once had a Sheila na Gig, a somewhat suggestive female figure, although it is too worn to be discernible here. The church was probably dedicated to St Ernan, a nephew of Columba, and there is a 16th-century grave slab within the walls. The burial ground has 18th-century memorials.

Access at all reasonable times.

Parking.

Moy Castle

Off A849, 10 miles SW of Craignure, Mull.

NM 616247 LR: 49 (Map ref: 293)

In a beautiful situation on a rocky crag by the seashore, Moy Castle is a ruinous 15th-century tower house. The MacLaines owned the property, an unruly branch of the MacLeans. MacLean of Duart, desiring Lochbuie, captured one of the MacLaines, and confined him on the Treshnish isle of

Moy Castle.

Cairnburg to prevent him producing an heir. His only female companion was an old and ugly woman who, however, he contrived to make pregnant. MacLaine, himself, was murdered, but the woman managed to escape, and produced a son, who eventually regained the property.

Iain the Toothless, the chief, and his son and heir, Ewen of the Little Head, fought in 1538 over the latter's marriage settlement: apparently Ewen's wife was not satisfied with their house on a fortified island in Loch Squabain [NM 631307], and desired something more luxurious. Ewen was slain in the subsequent battle, his head being hewn off and his horse riding away for two miles with the decapitated body. A cairn [NM 649326?] was said to mark the spot where Ewen finally fell from his horse, but has apparently been destroyed. His ghost, the headless horseman, is said to been seen riding in Glen Mor when one of the MacLaines is about to die.

The castle was abandoned in 1752, and when Boswell and Johnson visited Lochbuie in 1773 they stayed in a small house nearby, which was in turn replaced by a large Georgian mansion. The MacLaines had a burial vault from 1864 at the old chapel [NM 626236], where there is also a number of 18th-century memorials, but sold the property in the 20th century, and

View from exterior.
Walk to castle.

Nuns' Cave, Carsaig

Off A849, 7.5 miles E of Bunessan, Carsaig, Mull.
NM 524204 LR: 48 (Map ref: 294)

On the footpath between the settlement at Carsaig and the Carsaig Arches is a cave, known as Uamh nan Cailleach or the 'nuns' cave', which has numerous carvings, including crosses from as early as the 6th century, masons' marks, a trident, and a sailing ship. It is said that nuns driven out of Iona at the time of the Reformation sheltered here, hence the name. A cave at Scoor [NM 418186] also has carvings.

Old Byre Heritage Centre

Off B8073, 1.5 miles S of Dervaig, Mull.
NM 434502 LR: 47 (Map ref: 295)
Originally a stone byre of a working farm, the building now houses a museum, tearoom and gift shop.

Twenty-five models chart the social history of Mull, and an audio-visual presentation features the flora, fauna and history of Mull from prehistoric times until the Clearances. Shows are half hourly, but are limited to 25 persons.

Open Easter-Oct, daily 10.30-18.30, last show at 17.30.
Explanatory displays. Gift shop. Tearoom. WC. Car parking. Coaches by prior arrangement. Group concessions. £.
Tel: 01688 400229

Pennycross

On A849, 7.5 miles E of Bunessan, Pennycross, Mull.
NM 506263 LR: 48 (Map ref: 296)
Pennycross was the home of the Beatons of Mull, who were renowned physicians in medieval times. The cross here, known as Crois an Ollaimh – the 'cross of the Beatons' – was erected in 1589 to commemorate members of the family.

Pennygown Chapel

Off A849, 2 miles E of Salen, Pennygown, Mull.
NM 604432 LR: 49 (Map ref: 297)
The shell of a rectangular 13th-century chapel stands within the old burial ground. Within the chapel is the base of a 16th-century carved crossshaft. Interesting burial ground, with two 17th-cen-

Pennygown Chapel.

tury slabs with effigies of a man and a woman, as well as 18th-century memorials.
Access at all reasonable times.
Parking.

Pilgrims Way to Iona

Barvas and Ross of Mull, Mull.
LR: 48 (Map ref: 298)
A series of standing stones is said to mark the old

pilgrim route from Grass Point [NM 748310] to Fionnphort as markers for pilgrims on their way to Iona. Stones which survive include:

- Six-foot standing stone at Uluvalt, W of A849 [NM 547300]
- Seven-foot standing stone at Rossal, S of A849 [NM 543282]
- Seven-foot standing stone at Taoslin, just S of A849 [NM 397224]
- 6.5-foot standing stone at Suie, N of A849 near cairn [NM 371218]
- 8.5-foot standing stone at Tirghoil, just N of A849 [NM 353224]
- Eight-foot standing stone at Achaban, just N of A849 [NM 313233]

There was a final standing stone at Catchean, near to Fionnphort, but this was destroyed by accident in 1863.

Torosay Castle

On A849, 1 mile SE of Craignure, Mull.
NM 729353 LR: 49 (Map ref: 299)
Torosay Castle is a fine castellated mansion of 1858, designed by David Bryce for the Campbells of Possel. It was sold to the Guthrie family in 1865, and remains with their descendants. The principal rooms of this stately home are open to the public. The twelve acres of gardens, laid out by Sir Robert Lorimer in 1899, include formal terraces, an Italian statue walk, Japanese garden, walled garden and woodland, and there are fine views. A working farm has pedigree Highland cattle.

There is a miniature steam railway from Craignure. Isle of Mull Weavers is also located here.

House open Easter-mid-Oct, daily 10.30-17.30; gardens open all year, daily 10.30-sunset.
Guided tours by arrangement. Gift shop. Tearoom. WC. Disabled access. Car and coach parking. Group concessions. ££.
Tel: 01680 812421 Fax: 01680 812470
Email: torosay@aol.com

Ulva Heritage Centre

Off B8073, 0.25 miles N of Ulva House, Ulva.
NM 443398 LR: 48 (Map ref: 300)
The heritage centre provides details of the walks, wildlife and historical remains on Ulva. There is a faithful reconstruction of traditional thatched cottage, which was still occupied in the 1930s.
Open all year.
Explanatory displays. Cafe. WC. Parking.
Tel: 01688 500241/264 Fax: 01688 500264

Arts, Crafts and Industry

Isle of Mull Angora Rabbit Farm

On A849, 1 mile E of Bunessan, Rebmor Croft, Mull.
NM 402228 LR: 48 (Map ref: 301)
A croft where about 30 Angora rabbits are bred for their hair, which is used for knitting yarns and clothing. The fluffy rabbits can be held and petted, and information is provided about their lives and habits. There are clipping (12.00) and spinning (15.00) demonstrations; and a treasure hunt every Sunday. The shop has a variety of Angora garments, fibre and knitting yarns.
Open Easter-Oct, Sun-Fri 11.00-17.00.
Explanatory displays. Guided tours available. Gift shop. Refreshments. WC. Picnic area. Nature trail. Children's play area. Viewpoint. Car parking. Group concessions. £.
Tel: 01681 700507

Isle of Mull Weavers

On A849, 1.5 miles S of Craignure, The Steading, Torosay Castle, Mull.
NM 729353 LR: 49 (Map ref: 302)
The award-winning centre has displays of traditional weaving on old dobby looms and loom-side demonstrations. The shop features a range of tweed, travel and floor rugs, and many other items made on the premises.
Open Feb-Easter, Mon-Sat 9.00-17.00; Easter-Oct, daily 9.00-17.00; Nov & Dec, Mon-Sat 9.00-17.00.
Guided tours. Explanatory displays. Gift shop. Disabled access. Car and coach parking.
Tel: 01680 812381

Mull Theatre

Off B8073, 8 miles NW of Tobermory, Dervaig, Mull.
NM 434517 LR: 47 (Map ref: 303)
Founded in 1966, this theatre seats 43 people, and according to the Guinness Book of Records is the smallest professional theatre in the UK. Features a season of repertory theatre, new work and touring shows.
Open Apr-Sep; tours in spring and winter.
Tel: 01688 400245(box office) Fax: tel 01688 400377 (admin)
Email: mulltheatre@tesco.net

Tobermory Distillery

Off A848, Tobermory, Mull.
NM 505551 LR: 47 (Map ref: 304)
Located in the pleasant town of Tobermory, with its painted houses, the distillery was established in 1798. The distillery produces the Tobermory Single Malt Scotch Whisky, and offers tours: there is a visitor centre and shop.

Open Easter-Oct, Mon-Fri 10.00-17.00. Other times by appt.

Guided tours. Explanatory displays. Gift shop (entrance fee discounted on certain goods). Limited disabled access. Car and coach parking. £.
Tel: 01688 302645 Fax: 01688 302643

Gardens, Animals and Miscellaneous

Mull & West Highland Narrow Gauge Railway

Off A849, Old Pier Station, Craignure, Mull.
NM 725369 LR: 49 (Map ref: 305)
The first passenger railway built on a Scottish island was opened in 1984, and links the Old Pier at Craignure with Torosay Castle, a stately home with twelve acres of gardens and walks – which is open to the public (see separate entry). Both steam and diesel trains operate on the narrow gauge line, which is just over one mile long – a 20-minute journey. There are extensive and dramatic woodland and mountain views, including Ben Nevis, the Glencoe hills and Ben Cruachan, and departure times normally coincide with the ferry from Craignure.
Provision to carry one person seated in wheelchair on trains.

Open Easter-mid Oct, daily 11.00-17.00. Check timetable for departure times with TICs or tel: 01680 812494.

Gift shop. Disabled access. Car and coach parking. Group and family concessions. £.
Tel: 01680 812494 Fax: 01680 300595
Web: www.zynet.co.uk/mull/rail

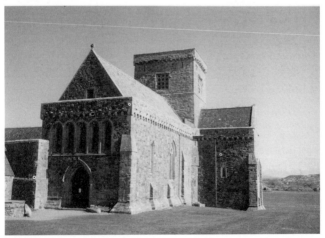

Iona Abbey.

Iona

(from Icolmkill: the island of St Columba)

In Brief
Cradle of Scottish Christianity. St Columba. Abbey. High Crosses. Peaceful island.

Location (see map 9, p 104-105)
OS Landranger map 48
Lies off the W coast of Mull

Tourist Information Centres
Craignure (Mull) (tel: 01680 812377; fax: 01680 812497)
Open Jan to Dec
Tobermory (Mull) (tel: 01688 302182; fax 01688 302145)
Open Apr to Oct

How to Get There
By ferry from Fionnphort on Mull to Iona– no cars on Iona (15 mins; CalMac tel: 01681 700559)

Notes
There are horse-drawn carriage tours of the island (tel: 01681 704230 – phone after 18.00).

Basic Info
Iona is 3.5 miles long by about 1.5 miles wide, and is a green and pleasant place, with a third of the island being good land while the rest is rough pasture. There are several fine sandy beaches on both sides of the island, and the views from Iona are spectacular. The only settlement is Baile Mor.

History
There are few prehistoric sites on the island, but the scant remains of an Iron Age fort survive [NM 265245]. The island was visited by St Columba in 563, and he founded a Christian monastery here, on the site of which is Iona Abbey.

The island was a property of the MacDonald Lords of the Isles, but passed to the MacLeans at the end of the 15th century then to the Campbell Earls of Argyll, along with much of Mull. Most of the island was gifted to The National Trust for Scotland in 1979, although the Abbey and other historic sites are owned by the Iona Cathedral Trustees.

The island is very fertile, and at one time supported a population of over 500, but nowadays it has dropped to about 90.

Places of Interest

Historic and Heritage

Iona Abbey

Off A849, Iona.

NM 287245 LR: 48 (Map ref: 306)

Situated on the beautiful and peaceful island of Iona, this is where St Columba came to form a monastic community, and converted the Picts of mainland Scotland to Christianity. He died in 597, and Columba's shrine, within the Abbey buildings, dates from the 9th century.

The abbey was abandoned after raids by the Vikings, but reestablished by Queen Margaret, in the 11th century. Some of the surviving abbey buildings date from the early 13th century after it had been refounded as a Benedictine establishment in 1203 by Reginald, son of Somerled, Lord of the Isles, and it was dedicated to the Virgin Mary. The buildings fell into disrepair after the Reformation. The abbey church and cloister were rebuilt from 1910 for the Iona Community, and it is possible to stay at the Abbey.

The magnificent St Martin's Cross and St John's Cross – the latter a replica – stand just outside the church, and the museum houses a splendid collection of sculptured stones and crosses, one of the largest collections of early Christian carved stones in Europe. Between the abbey and the nunnery is MacLean's Cross, a fine 15th-century carved stone cross.

Many of the early Kings of Scots are buried in 'Reilig Odhrain' – the 'Street of the Dead' – as well as kings of Ireland, France and Norway: 48 Scottish, 8 Norwegian and 4 Irish kings. The 11th-century chapel of St Oran also

survives. The nearby Augustinian nunnery of St Mary was founded in 1208, also by Reginald, and is a fine consolidated ruin.

Open at all times – ferry from Fionnphort (£), no cars on Iona. Walk to abbey.

Day tours from Oban in summer. Guided tours. Explanatory displays. Gift shop. Tearoom. WC. Car and coach parking at Fionnphort. £ (ferry). Week long programmes for guests.

Tel: 01681 700404

Fax: 01898 840270

Email: iona_abbey@ compuserve.com

Iona Heritage Centre

Off unlisted road, the Old Manse, Iona.

NTS LR: 48 (Map ref: 307)

Located in the Old Telford Manse, the museum has displays illustrating the lives of

St John's Cross, Iona.

the islanders over the past 200 years.

Open Apr-Oct, Mon-Sat 10.30-16.30.

Explanatory displays. Gift shop. Tea room. Picnic area. Garden. WC. Disabled access. Car and coach parking (Fionnphort).

Tel: 01681 700576

Arts, Crafts and Industry

Iona Pottery and Gallery

Off unlisted road, Iona.

LR: 48   (Map ref: 308)

A working pottery where work in progress can be viewed. Displays include both thrown and hand-built decorative stoneware. There are also landscape paintings, etchings and edition prints by various modern artists, as well as 19th- and 20th-century paintings and etchings.

Open Apr-Oct, Mon-Sat 9.00-17.00.

Gift shop. Disabled access. Car and coach parking (Fionnphort).

Tel: 01681 700439   Fax: 01681 700328

Mhiann Arts

Off unlisted road, the Village, Iona.

LR: 48   (Map ref: 309)

This is the fourth generation of Macdonald weavers to occupy Tigh-na-Beart, which means the 'house of the loom'. Working in the same weaving room, contemporary woven sculpture and wall hangings are produced. Also on display is a range of Celtic silverware.

Open Apr-Oct.

Parking (Fionnphort). Sales area.

Tel: 01681 700652   Fax: 01681 700652

Email: mhianarts@mhiannartsiona.freeserve.co.uk

Mhiann Arts.

Lismore

(Gaelic 'great garden')

In Brief
Scenic island. Bishop of the Isles.

Location (see map 9, p 104-105)
OS Landranger map 49
Lies off the W coast of Argyll, NW of Oban and W of Appin

How to Get There
By vehicle ferry from Oban on mainland to Achnacroish on Lismore (50 mins; Cal Mac tel: 01631 566688)
By passenger ferry from Port Appin to N tip of island

Tourist Information Office
Oban (mainland) (tel: 01631 563122; fax: 01631 564273)
Open Jan-Dec

Basic Info
The island is 10.5 miles long and about 1.5 miles wide at its widest. The island is very lush and

Lismore.

fertile, hence the name, and at one time had many trees and supported a large population. Achnacroish is the only village.

History

The island was inhabited since prehistoric times, and prehistoric sites include Tirefour Broch and Dun Chruban. The island was long a property of the Stewarts of Appin, but in the 16th century was acquired by the Campbells. Lady's Rock, between the southern-most tip of Lismore and Mull, was where MacLean of Duart stranded his Campbell wife so that she would drown. She was rescued, however, and MacLean was murdered in revenge by the Campbells.

From 1236, Lismore was the location of the cathedral of the isles, and part of the church survives and is still used as the parish church. It was probably built on the site of an old Celtic monastery. There was a castle at Achadun, a property of the bishops of the isles.

The island is rich in lime, and it was exploited and exported to the mainland for centuries, although the once numerous trees were burnt to extract the lime. In 1831 the population was 1497, but many of the folk emigrated and by 1885 there were 600 inhabitants, and the population is now under 150.

Today

Crofting and farming. Tourism.

Bernera Island

The island ('Bjorn's isle') is tidal and lies off the west coast.

Shuna Island

Island off coast at Portnacroish, with the remains of a castle.

Eriska

Small island ('Eric's Isle') in the mouth of Loch Crerar.

Pladda and Eilean Dubh

Islets ('flat' and 'black isle') off south coast of Lismore.

Places of Interest

Prehistoric

Dun Chruban

Off B8045, 5.5 miles SW of Achnacroish, Dalnarrow, Lismore.
NM 793360 LR: 49 (Map ref: 310)
An Iron Age dun, standing on a crag and defended by cliffs, is oval in plan. The walls survive to a height of eleven feet or so, and the position of the entrance can be seen.

Tirefour Broch

Off B8045, 2 miles NE of Achnacroish, Lismore.
NM 867429 LR: 49 (Map ref: 311)
Standing on a rocky outcrop, Tirefour is a well-preserved broch. The wall rises to over ten feet for most of its length, and in one place survives to a height of sixteen feet. The inside of the broch is partly filled with debris, but a doorway in one interior face survives. The entrance and the remains of an intramural gallery can be seen, and outside the broch are two ruinous outworks defending the approach.
Open all year.

Historic and Heritage

Achadun Castle

Off B8045, 4 miles SW of Achnacroish, Lismore.
NM 804392 LR: 49 (Map ref: 312)

Sited on the top of a ridge, Achadun is a ruinous 13th-century castle. It was held by the Bishops of Argyll until about 1510, when they moved to Saddell in Kintyre, and part of their cathedral, now considerably altered, is still used as a parish church.

Castle Coeffin

Off B8045, 1.5 miles N of Achnacroish, Lismore.
NM 853437 LR: 49 (Map ref: 313)

Standing on a rock, Castle Coeffin is a much ruined and overgrown 13th-century hall house and courtyard of the MacDougalls of Lorn. It passed in the second half of the 15th century to the Campbells of Glenorchy, but was probably abandoned by the 17th century. The Campbells held the island until the 18th century.

The castle is said to be named after the son, Caifen, of a Norse king, who lived here. His sister, Beothail, died of a broken heart after her betrothed was killed. Her spirit was said to haunt the castle, and did not find peace until she was buried beside her love in Norway.

Castle Shuna

S side of Shuna Island, Appin.
NM 915482 LR: 49 (Map ref: 314)

Castle Shuna is a ruined 16th-century tower house, and was built by the Stewarts of Appin: it is said never to have been completed.

Cathedral of St Moluag, Lismore

Off B8045, 1.5 miles N of Achnacroish, Clachan, Lismore.
NM 860434 LR: 49 (Map ref: 315)

The church, much reduced in size and now the parish church, was once used as the Cathedral of Argyll and the Isles. Only the 14th-century choir of the original building still stands, although foundations of the nave and tower remain – the original building was 137 feet long. The church was dedicated to St Moluag, an Irish saint, and the bishopric was transferred here in 1236. The choir was roofless by 1679, but was restored in 1749 – at which time the walls were lowered by as much as ten feet. Several carved slabs, dating from medieval times, survive in the burial ground.

St Moluag founded a Christian community in the 560s, and is said to have converted parts of Pictland to Christianity. His relics are believed to have been kept here.

Parish church.
Disabled access. Parking nearby.

Cill an t-Suidhe

Off B8045, 0.5 miles W of Achnacroish, Killean, Lismore.
NM 848415 LR: 49 (Map ref: 316)

A round enclosure, which has the remains of a ditch, is believed to have been the remains of an early Christian burial site. There is said have been an old chapel at Killean, dedicated to St John.

Clachan Cross

On B8045, 1.5 miles N of Achnacroish, Clachan, Lismore.
NM 860433 LR: 49 (Map ref: 317)

The base of a cross shaft survives by the road, and an old chapel probably stood nearby.

Kerrera

('copse-water land')

In Brief
Unspoilt landscape. Cattle. Site of death of Alexander II.

Location (see map 9, p 104-105)
OS Landranger map 49
Lies off the W coast of Argyll, W of Oban

Tourist Information Office
Oban (mainland) (tel: 01631 563122; fax: 01631 564273)
Open Jan-Dec

How to Get There
By passenger ferry mainland S of Oban to middle of island (tel: 01631 563665)

Notes
No cars – cycle or walk. Pony trekking, fishing trips and boat hire available. Detailed maps available from ferry. There is a tea garden and bothy at Lower Gylen.

Basic Info
The island is just over four miles long and about 1.75 miles wide at its widest. Although hilly in places, rising to over 600 feet, there is also good land. The island shelters Oban Bay,

Kerrera.

making it a very safe anchorage, and has two harbours itself at Ardantrive Bay and Horse Shoe Bay. There is a sandy beach at Slatrach.

Wildlife
Many birds. Otters. Seals. Wild goats.

History
The island was inhabited since prehistoric times, and there are several cairns and cists, as well as an early Christian settlement or cashel at Rubh a' Bhearnaig. Kerrera was held by the Vikings – Alexander II of Scots took a fever and died here at Dalrigh near Horse Shoe Bay in 1249 while on an expedition to take the area, and King Hakon of Norway held court here before going on to defeat at the battle of Largs in 1263. The island was a property of the MacDougalls, who had a castle at Gylen, 'castle of fountains', and is still held by the same family.

The island was used as a stopping off place for moving cattle from Mull to the mainland: the beasts were ferried across to Barr nam Boc, then driven to the north of the island where there were forced to swim across to Oban.

The island once supported a population of nearly 200, but it has since dwindled.

Places of Interest

Prehistoric

Slaterich Cists
Off footpath, 0.5 miles N of Balliemore, N of Slaterich, Kerrera.
NM 820296 LR: 49   (Map ref: 318)
Two cists with a capstone. The cists contained a beaker, food vessel and some quartz pebbles, which are now in the Museum of Scotland in Edinburgh.

Historic and Heritage

Cladh a' Bhearnaig
Off unlisted road, 2 miles NE of Balliemore, Rubh a' Bhearnaig, N tip of Kerrera.
NM 842312 LR: 49   (Map ref: 319)
The site of an early medieval monastery or cashel, consisting of a round enclosure divided in two by a wall. The foundations of several buildings survive within the enclosure.

Gylen Castle
Off unlisted track, 2 miles SW of Balliemore, Gylen, S side of Kerrera.
NM 805265 LR: 49   (Map ref: 320)
On a rocky promontory jutting into the sea, Gylen or Gylen Castle – the 'castle of fountains' – is a ruinous 16th-century L-plan tower house. Gylen was a property of the MacDougalls. An earlier castle here was where Alexander II died during an expedition to recover the Western Isles in the mid 13th century, although Dalrigh near Horse Shoe Bay is given as an alternative site. The castle was captured and burnt by a Covenanter army, led by General David Leslie, in 1647. The Brooch of Lorn, a brooch torn from Robert the Bruce's cloak, was also stolen, and not returned by the Campbells of Inverawe until the 19th century.

Slate Islands: Seil, Luing, Shuna and Scarba

In Brief
Slate. Scenic islands. Bridge over the Atlantic. Garvellachs.

Location (see map 9, p 104-105)
OS Landranger map 55
Lie of the W coast of Argyll, N of Jura, S of Mull

Tourist Information Office
Oban (mainland) (tel: 01631 563122; fax: 01631 564273)
Open Jan-Dec

How to Get There
By bridge to Seil by Clachan Bridge (single-arched bridge, built in 1782)
By ferry from Cuan on Seil to Luing (Argyll and Bute Council tel: 01631 562125)
By boat from Toberonochy to Garvellach isles
By passenger ferry from Seil to Easdale

Seil Island.

Seil

(Seil from 'Isle of Seil', a personal name)

Basic Info

Joined to the mainland by the so-called 'bridge over the Atlantic', which was designed by the architect Thomas Telford and built in 1782. The island is just over four miles long and some two miles wide at its widest. The west of the island is quite hilly and rises to over 800 feet. To the south-east of Seil is the small island of Easdale ('horse fell').

History

The island was a property of the MacDougalls, who had a castle at Ardfad, but later passed to the Campbells of Breadalbane. There is a fine ruinous chapel at Kilbrandon. Slate (for roofs) was quarried here from the 16th century, and the settlements of Balvicar and Ellanbeich grew up around the industry – although better slate is said to have come from the nearby isle of **Easdale**.

Another nearby island, **Torsa**, is also one of the 'slate' islands, and has a castle at its northern end, Caisteal nan Con. It was a property of the MacDougalls but passed to the MacLeans.

One mile to the west of Seil is the small **Insh Island**.

Luing

(Luing from 'a ship', pronounced 'Ling')

Basic Info

The island is just over six miles long and about 1.5 miles wide at most. The highest point is at Cnoc Dhomhnuill at just over 300 feet.

History

Prehistoric remains include Iron Age fortifications and the fine ruinous dun at Leccamore. The ruinous medieval chapel at Kilchattan has 16th-century gravestones. The island was a property of the MacDougalls, but later passed to the Campbells of Breadalbane. Slate was quarried here, started at Cullipool and Toberonochy in 1749 and continued until 1965. The island is known for the cattle that bear its name, a breed developed in the 1960s.

A small islet **Belnahua** lies off the west coast.

Shuna

The island is just over two miles long and about one mile wide at most. Unlike its neighbouring islands, Shuna has little slate and has many trees and woods on the rolling landscape. There are a number of cairns on the island, one said to be the grave of an ancient chieftain.

Lunga

The island ('ship isle' or 'long isle') is just over one mile long and about one mile wide at most, and is another of the 'slate' islands. This island is picturesque and hilly, and rises to over 1000 feet. The tidal current between Shuna and Scarba is said to be every bit as treacherous as the whirlpool of Corryvreckan. There are a group of small islands just north of Lunga, including **Fiola Meadhonach**, **Rubha Fiola**, **Eilean Dubh Mor** and **Eilean Dubh Beag**.

Scarba

Another of the Slate Islands, Scarba ('isle of cormorants') lies 0.5 miles north of the northern tip of Jura and about one mile west of Luing. The island is some three miles long and 2.5 miles wide. The west side of Scarba is very hilly and rough, and rises to just under 1500 feet, while the east side has better land as well as woodland. To the south of the island is the Gulf of Corryvreckan and the famous whirlpool. It is best seen between flood and half-flood, with a westerly or southerly wind – care should be taken if in a boat. There are the remains of an old chapel at Kilmory, but the island is now abandoned.

Garvellachs

A group of fertile islands ('rough islands') to the west of Luing and Lunga, held by the MacDougalls, MacDonalds, then the MacLeans. Places of interest include Dun Chonnuill, an ancient fort and 13th-century castle; and the monastery on **Eileach an Naoimh**, possibly first founded by St Brendan in 545, then refounded by St Columba later in the 6th century – his mother, Eithne, is believed to be buried here.

Places of Interest

Prehistoric

Ballycastle Dun
Off unlisted road, 1 mile SE of Cullipool, Ardinamir, Luing.
NM 753121 LR: 55 (Map ref: 321)
Standing on a rock outcrop on a ridge is an impressive oval dun, with walls surviving to a height of over six feet. The entrance can be traced, but the inside is filled with rubble.

Dun Mucaig
Off B8003, 1.5 miles SW of Balvicar, Seil.
NM 751154 LR: 55 (Map ref: 322)
Standing on an outcrop of rock is a dun with outer walls standing to a height of about five feet, while inside the dun they stand to about seven. The entrance is well preserved, the inside filled with rubble, and there are some traces of outworks.

Leccamore Dun
Off unlisted road, 1.5 miles N of Toberonochy, Luing.
NM 750107 LR: 55 (Map ref: 323)
Built on the top of a ridge, this is a well-preserved Iron Age dun, which consists of an enclosing wall with outlying ditches. There are two entrances, one with cells on both sides of the passage, and the remains of a flight of steps which may have once given access to the upper part of the dun. The walls stand to a height of ten feet. There are many cup marks on one of the slabs in the entrance. There have been other structures within the dun, and during excavations finds included some worked antler, stone implements, bronze and a fragment of an iron blade.
Seek permission from farmer at Leccamore.

Historic and Heritage

Ardfad Castle
Off B844, 2 miles NE of Easdale, Ardfad, Seil.
NM 769194 LR: 55 (Map ref: 324)
Not much survives of a 16th-century Z-plan castle: the building was said to be well preserved in 1915. It was a property of the MacDougalls of Ardencaple.

Caisteal nan Con
On NE of island of Torsa.
NM 765136 LR: 55 (Map ref: 325)
On a rocky crag on the small island of Torsa, Caisteal nan Con – the 'castle of dogs' – consists of the ruins of a simple castle of the 15th century. It was a property of the Campbells, then the MacDougalls of Rarey, but later passed to the MacLeans.

Dun Chonnuill
On SE side of Dun Chonnuill island, Garvellachs.
NM 680125 LR: 55 (Map ref: 325)
Dun Chonnuill is a ruined 13th-century castle, although the site was fortified from prehistoric times. On another crag to the north are the remains of a triangular dun, and at its foot are the foundations of more buildings. It was probably a property of the MacDougalls, although one story is that a MacLauchlan from Ireland took and fortified the island in the 14th century. It was later held by the MacDonalds, then the MacLeans.

Easdale Folk Museum
Off B844, Easdale island, Easdale (Seil).
NM 740170 LR: 55 (Map ref: 326)
A fine pictorial collection showing the industrial and domestic life of the Slate Islands in the 19th century, including records of slate quarries, the volunteers, Friendly Societies, education and public health. Fine views of the Firth of Lorn can be had from the hilltop, and there is a scenic walk to the sea-filled slate quarries, which were devastated by the great storm of November 1881.
Open Apr-Oct, daily 10.30-17.30.
Explanatory displays. Tearoom and bar nearby. WC. Car and coach parking on Seil (no cars on island). Group concessions on application. £. On-call ferry to island.
Tel: 01852 300370 Fax: 01852 300370

Eileach an Naoimh
N of Jura, one of the Garvellach islands.
HS NM 640097 LR: 55 (Map ref: 327)
On the picturesque island are the ruins of beehive cells from an early Christian community, first founded by St Brendan of Clonfert in 542. There are also the ruins of two churches within an enclosure, two burial grounds, as well as other buildings. Other features of early date include a small underground cell and the traditional burial place of Eithne, St Columba's mother, which is marked

by a round setting of stones. One small slab is decorated with an early cross, and it is said that when the grave was opened the remains of a woman were discovered. There is also a spring, known as Tobar Chaluim Chille, the 'well of St Columba'.

The island can be reached by hired boat from Toberonochy, Luing, weather permitting.

Access at all times – subject to weather.

Tel: 0131 668 8800

Kilchattan

On unlisted road, 0.25 miles NW of Toberonochy, Kilchattan, Luing.

NM 744090 LR: 55 (Map ref: 328)

The ruins of a small rectangular chapel, probably dating from the 12th century and dedicated to St Cathan. The church was abandoned about 1735, and there are some old gravestones in the burial ground.

Access at all reasonable times.

Tobar na Suil

Off unlisted road, 1.5 miles N of Toberonochy, Luing.

NM 753114 LR: 55 (Map ref: 329)

A spring here emerges into a small hollow, said to resemble an eyeball, and water from the well was used to cure eye disease. The well is reported as still being used – offerings were found under an adjacent stone – at least as late as the 1970s.

Gardens, Animals and Miscellaneous

An Cala Garden

On B844, Easdale, Seil.

NM 745175 LR: 55 (Map ref: 330)

The garden, designed by Mawson in the 1930s, features meandering streams, winding paths, formal terraces and lawns. A fifteen-foot-high wall protects the plants from winter gales, and much of the original planting still survives.

Open daily Apr-Oct 10.00-18.00.

Parking. Refreshments in village. Plants for sale (later in season). WC. £.

Tel: 01852 300237   Fax: 01852 300237

Map 10: Islay, Jura, Colonsay and Gigha

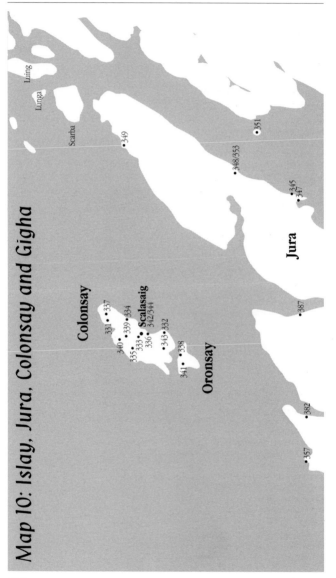

Luing

Lunga

Scarba

•349

•351

•348/353

•345
•347

Jura

Colonsay

Scalasaig

•331 •337
•339 •334
340• 333• 312/344
335• 336•
•343 •332
341 •338

•387

Oronsay

•382

•357

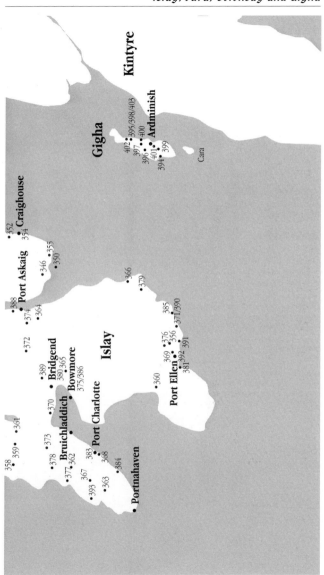

Kintyre

Gigha

Ardminish

402
395/398/403
397
400
396
401
394 399
Cara

Craighouse
352
354

Port Askaig
346
355
350

388
374
364

366
379

372

Bridgend
389
380 365
385
371/390
376
356
369 391
381 392

Islay

Bowmore
375/386

359 361
358

373
370

378 362
377 367
383
368
393 363
384

Bruichladdich

Port Charlotte

360

Port Ellen

Portnahaven

Colonsay and Oronsay

Colonsay (St Columba's isle)
Oronsay (St Oran's isle, a disciple of St Columba, or 'tidal island')

In Brief
Beach. Priory.

Location (see map 10, p 132-133)
OS Landranger map 61
12 miles S of the Ross of Mull
9 miles W of Jura

Tourist Information Office
Oban (mainland) (tel: 01631 563122; fax: 01631 564273)
Open Jan-Dec

How to Get There
By ferry from Oban on mainland to Scalasaig on Colonsay (2.25 hrs; CalMac 01631 566688;
Sun, Wed & Fri); also to/from Port Askaig on Islay to Scalasaig on Colonsay (35 mins; CalMac
01631 566688)
Oronsay accessed by tidal causeway from Colonsay – check tides locally

Notes
No caravans. Cycles can be hired. Eighteen-hole golf course. Oyster farm. Fishing available.
Colonsay Hotel (tel: 01951 200316; fax: 01951 200353). 500 species of local flora.

Basic Info
Colonsay is just over eight miles from north to south, with a maximum width of three miles.
Kiloran Bay has one of the finest unspoilt beaches in the Hebrides, while there are also other

Colonsay.

fine stretches of sand on both Colonsay and Oronsay. Scalasaig and Kiloran are the only settlements.

Oronsay lies immediately to the south of Colonsay is three miles long and two miles wide, and joined to Colonsay by a tidal causeway.

Wildlife

More than 150 species of birds, including golden eagles, sea-eagles, falcons, shearwaters, great northern and red-throated divers, merlin, swans, geese, and choughs. Seals, large otter population and wild goats.

History

The islands are rich in archaeological and historical remains, from the standing stones known as Fingal's Limpet Hammers to the burial cairns at Scalasaig and Milbuie. Dun Eibhinn is an Iron Age fort which was occupied by the MacDuffies in medieval times, as was a stronghold on Loch an Sgoltaire. There are several interesting carved stones on the islands, and Viking burials have been discovered here.

St Oran and St Columba are said to have stopped here on their way to finally settling on Iona: there is a well called Tobar Oran at Colonsay House. The island passed from the MacDuffies to the MacDonalds in the 17th century, then to the Campbell Duke of Argyll, then to the MacNeils in 1701. They removed to Colonsay House, built in 1722 and enlarged in the 19th century, which has fine gardens.

Oronsay has Mesolithic shell mounds, dating from before 4000 BC. Dun Domhnuill is a fine Iron Age fort. The island is also the site of a ruinous Augustinian priory, of which substantial

Oronsay Priory.

remains survive. It was founded by the Lords of the Isles, and produced carved grave slabs and stone crosses until 1500. The fine Oronsay Cross survives, a late medieval cross which is 12-feet high, as do the remains of another cross and about 30 carved grave slabs.

Today

Limited tourism.

Places of Interest

Prehistoric

Clach na Gruagach Standing Stone

Off A870, 4 miles NE of Scalasaig, Balnahard, Colonsay.
NR 415997   LR: 61   (Map ref: 331)
A five-foot unshaped boulder, known as Clach na Gruagach – the 'stone of the fairy woman' – has a small cup in the top. Milk was left in the dip for the gruagach or fairy.

Dun Cholla

Off A869, 2.5 miles S of Scalasaig, Dun Cholla, Colonsay.
NR 377913   LR: 61   (Map ref: 332)
Remains of a fort, protected on three sides by cliffs and on the last by a now ruinous wall with an entrance.

Dun Eibhinn

Off A870, NW of Scalasaig, Dun Eibhinn, Colonsay.
NR 382944   LR: 61   (Map ref: 333)
A well-preserved dun, the 'fort of Eyvind', from a Viking name. The enclosing wall and entrance can be traced, and there have been buildings within the fort. The dun was apparently used by the MacDuffies in medieval times.

Dunan nan Nighean

Off A870, 2.5 miles NE of Scalasaig, Colonsay.
NR 415976   LR: 61   (Map ref: 334)
Built on a small crag in a remote location are the ruins of a dun, the entrance of which still has three lintel stones in place. The dun is choked with rubble.

Fingal's Limpet Hammers Standing Stones

Off A870, 1.5 miles NW of Scalasaig, Lower Kilchattan, Colonsay.
NR 367949   LR: 61   (Map ref: 335)
Two prominent standing stones, one over ten feet high while the other is nearly nine feet. The stones are the remains of a circle, and are known as Fingal's Limpet Hammers after the ancient hero.

Milbuie Cairn

Off A869, 0.75 miles S of Scalasaig, Milbuie, Colonsay.
NR 387929   LR: 61   (Map ref: 336)
The remains of a round cairn, with kerb stones visible. In the centre of the cairn is probably a cist.

Historic and Heritage

Cill Chaitriona

Off A870, 4 miles N of Scalasaig, Balnahard, Colonsay.
NR 421998   LR: 61   (Map ref: 337)
Not much remains of a small rectangular chapel, which stands in a burial ground with an enclosing bank and four burial cairns. A cross is built into the wall of the burial ground wall. It is about four feet high, and is said to date from as early as the 7th century. Clach a' Pheanais [NR 421999], the 'Stone of Penance' is said to be where punishment was carried out after confession.

Cloch-thuill Stone

Off A869, 1 mile E & N of priory, Oronsay.
NR 365896   LR: 61   (Map ref: 338)
Cloch-thuill – the 'hole stone' – consists of a hole through an opening in the rock, formed behind a small column of rock in the face of a low cliff. It is traditionally associated with the curing of consumption, involving a benediction and an offering of food.

Colonsay House Gardens

Off A871, 2 miles N of Scalasaig, Kiloran, Colonsay.
NR 395968   LR: 61   (Map ref: 339)
A well-known rhododendron garden of twenty acres, adjacent to Colonsay House. The house dates from 1722, was extended in the 19th century, and is home of Lord Strathcona. In the woods surrounding the house, rocks, streams and contours of land have been used to create a natural woodland garden. There are various, more formal, walled gardens surrounding the house, including a fine terraced area where refreshments are served. Many tender and rare shrubs grow here because of the mildness of the weather. In the garden is Tobar Oran, a round covered well with steps leading down to the water; and beside the well is St Oran's Cross, which is carved with the face of a man and dates from early Christian times. The house was built on the site of Kiloran, an early Christian chapel which

was dedicated to St Oran. The 'big house' on Colonsay is said to have had a brownie (fairy or gruagach), which also acted as a herdsman.

Open Apr-Sep: Wed, 12.00-17.00; Fri, 15.00-17.30.

Lunches and afternoon teas. Shop selling local produce and crafts. Picnic area. Parking. Self-catering accommodation available in Colonsay House (and island cottages).

Tel: 01951 200211 Fax: 01951 200369

Web: www.colonsay.org.uk

Loch an Sgoltaire Castle

Off A870, 2.5 miles N of Scalasaig, Loch an Sgoltaire, Colonsay.

NR 386972 LR: 61 (Map ref: 340)

On an island in Loch an Sgoltaire are the considerable remains of a castle. It appears to have been much rebuilt in the 19th century, when a summer house was added. The castle was still used or was refortified in 1615 when the MacDonalds were trying to reassert themselves – unsuccessfully – and was used as a place of refuge in 1701.

Oronsay Priory

Off unlisted road, W side of Oronsay.

NR 349889 LR: 61 (Map ref: 341)

Oronsay Priory was founded in the 14th century by John, Lord of the Isles, and was a house of Augustinian canons. Substantial parts of the church, cloister and domestic buildings survive. The Oronsay Cross is a fine late-medieval carved cross. On one side is the figure of Christ being crucified, and there is a pattern of foliage on both sides, as well as the inscription: 'this is the cross of Colinus, son of Cristinus MacDuffie'. There are over 30 fine carved grave slabs preserved in the Prior's House.

Open all year – on tidal island: access by foot or post-bus is regulated by tides.

Tobar nan Gaeth Deas

Off A870, Scalasaig, Colonsay.

NR 391939 LR: 61 (Map ref: 342)

A spring here was called the 'well of the south wind'. The well was used by fishermen and other seafarers to ask for a south (favourable) wind in return for small offerings.

Arts, Crafts and Industry

The Barn

Off A869, 2 miles SW of Scalasaig, Garvard, Colonsay.

NR 367914 LR: 61 (Map ref: 343)

Studio and gallery, exhibiting oils and water-colours. Also features spinning and weaving, as well as T-shirt painting workshops for all ages. Advisable to phone and book workshops.

Working studio open to visitors – tel to check.

Parking.

Tel: 01951 200344

Email: lucymc@globalnet.co.uk

The Gallery, Colonsay and Oronsay Heritage Trust

On A871 or A870, Scalasaig, Colonsay.

NR 394942 LR: 61 (Map ref: 344)

A gallery featuring a number of exhibitions during the season, mostly work by local artists. There is also a heritage centre.

Opening times on notice board outside gallery.

Jura

(from Norse 'dyr-ey' – 'deer island' or 'Doirad's island')

In Brief

Wilderness. Red deer. George Orwell.

Location (see map 10, p 132-133)

OS Landranger map 61
4 miles from W coast of Argyll at northern end
Just N of Islay

Tourist Information Centre

Bowmore (tel: 01496 810254; fax: 01496 810363)
Open Jan-Dec

How to Get There

By ferry from Port Askaig on Islay to Feolin on Jura (5 mins; Argyll and Bute Council tel: 01496 840681)

Notes

Climbing and walks – guide available from TIC in Bowmore, Islay. Fishing available on lochs and burns. There is a sheltered anchorage at Craighouse.

Basic Info

The fourth largest island in the Hebrides, Jura is one of the last great wildernesses in the British Isles, and is dominated by the rounded peaks of the Paps ('breasts') of Jura and the other mountains down the length of the island. It is 28 miles from north to south and eight miles wide, although at Tarbert it thins to only about one mile across. It is not nearly as fertile as Islay, its southern neighbour – the western side of the island is rugged, while the south-east is more gentle. The other topographical feature associated with Jura is the famous whirlpool of Corryvreckan – Corrie Bhreacan: the 'cauldron of Breckan', off the north tip of Jura and south of the island of Scarba. It is best seen a westerly or southerly wind. Care should be taken if in a boat: George Orwell nearly drowned here.

The only settlement of any 'size' is Craighouse, which has a shop, hotel and distillery.

Wildlife

Large population (around 5000) of red deer. Otters are numerous, as well as seals and wild goats. Profusion of birds, over 100 species including snipe, golden eagle and osprey.

History

Scattered archaeological remains show that Jura was inhabited in prehistoric times, starting with Mesolithic sites. There is a Neolithic burial cairn south of Strone farm, and there are seven sites with standing stones on the south-east of the island. There are several Iron Age duns and forts, of which the most interesting is An Dunan on Lowlandman's Bay.

There was a battle on Jura in 768 between the Scots from Ireland and the Britons, but the island was held by the Vikings until the 13th century. Like Islay, Jura was held by the king of

Man but Somerled drove out the Norsemen and claimed the area for himself. The island passed to Reginald, Somerled's son, then to Donald, his son: it is from him the MacDonalds were descended. The MacDonalds became the Lords of the Isles, and along with the strongholds on Islay, had a castle and prison on the small island of Am Fraoch Eilean, just off the coast of Jura. It was from here that they were said to extort monies from shipping using the Sound. The Lords of the Isles were destroyed in a campaign by James IV, but the MacDonalds of Dunyvaig retained the lands. The island, however – along with Islay – later passed to the Campbells.

Paps of Jura.

The north of the island was held by the MacLeans, based at Aros Castle, and in 1620 the Campbells complained to the government that they were being raided by the MacLeans. This came to battle in 1647 when a force of Campbells routed the MacLeans at Glen Garrisdale. The Campbells held most of the island except for Ardlussa, which was sold by the MacLeans to the MacNeils of Colonsay in 1737, but sold the lands in parts: by 1938 they had sold everything. Much of the island is now used for 'sporting' estates, when deer are shot, although they may not see it as being quite so sporting.

George Orwell wrote his novel *1984* at Barnhill at the northern end of Jura during the summer months from 1946-9. The house is not open to the public.

The population of Jura has dwindled over the last 150 years, from around 1300 in the middle of the 19th century to less than 200 today.

Today
Farming. Fishing. Whisky distillery at Craighouse. Tourism.

Am Fraoch Eilean
Islet off south coast of Jura, with an old castle.

Brosdale Island
Islet off south coast of Jura.

Small Isles
Group of islets on south-east coast of Jura, north-east of Craighouse.

Places of Interest

Prehistoric

An Dunan, Lowlandman's Bay
Off A846, 4.5 miles NE of Craighouse,
Lowlandman's Bay, Jura.
NR 578730 LR: 61 (Map ref: 345)
Standing on an isolated rocky point above the sea
are remains of an Iron Age fort, reached up a flight
of crumbling stone steps. The walls can be traced
in places.
Long walk to site.

Camus an Staca Standing Stone
Off A846, 3 miles SE of Feolin Ferry, Jura.
NR 464648 LR: 61 (Map ref: 346)
A prominent standing stone, about eleven feet high,
which can be seen from the A846.

Knockrome Standing Stones
Off A846, 3 miles N of Craighouse, Knockrome,
Jura.
NR 547715 LR: 61 (Map ref: 347)
There are four standing stones, near to Knockrome.
The first two are on the south side of the road before coming to Knockrome, on either side of a track
which leads down to the beach. They are said to
mark the burial place of the ashes of two giants –
or at least Danes – Dih and Rah, and it is believed
to be lucky to pass between them. One story is that
Jura got its name from combining their names. A
third stone is near the bend of the road, while the
fourth stone is beyond Knockrome at Ardfernal,
and is about four feet high.

Tarbert Standing Stones
Off A846, 11 miles N of Craighouse, Tarbert,
Jura.
NR 605823 LR: 61 (Map ref: 348)
The first stone is by the roadside at the turn down
the track to Tarbert, and stands to a height of eight
feet. The second 'Carraigh Chaluim Bhainn' is in
the graveyard, and has crosses carved on both sides.
This is known as the standing stone of Calum the
fair, probably a reference to St Columba.

Standing Stone, Tarbert, Jura.

Historic and Heritage

Aros Castle
Glengarrisdale, on NW of Jura.
NR 645968 LR: 61 (Map ref: 349)
A castle here was a property of the MacLeans, who
held the north of Jura from 1330, although the ex-
act location of the stronghold is not clear. In 1620
the Campbells, to whom the southern part of the
island had passed from the MacDonalds, com-
plained that they were being harassed by the
MacLeans. This came to battle in 1647, and at Glen
Garrisdale a force of Campbells surprised the
MacLeans and slew many of them. By 1690, a John
Campbell was Governor of the castle, and took
action against any MacLeans who had not taken the
Oath of Allegiance to William and Mary.

Claig Castle
Off A846, 4 miles SE of Feolin Ferry, S of Am
Fraoch Eilean, Jura.
NR 472627 LR: 61 (Map ref: 350)
Little remains of the 13th-century Claig Castle, a
property of the MacDonalds, still in use in 1549. It
is said to have been used as a prison as well as a
stronghold. The story goes that the MacDonalds
used Claig to extort money from passing ships.

Eilean Mor, South Knapdale

2 miles W of the mainland at Kilmory, Eilean Mor.

NR 665755   LR: 61   (Map ref: 351)

Standing on an island are several sites associated with St Cormac. The remains of a chapel [NR 666752] with a barrel-vaulted chancel survive, although the building was being used as an inn around 1600. The chapel was dedicated to St Cormac about 640, although it appears to date from the 13th century. There is a stone effigy of a priest preserved in the chapel. St Cormac is reputedly buried on the island, a broken and weathered cross marking the spot [NR 667753]. The cross is decorated with interlace patterns and representations of animals and people. A cave Uamh nam Fear [NR 666750] is also associated with the saint, and one of the walls has an early Christian cross.

Kilearnadil Burial Ground

Off A846, 1 mile N of Craighouse, Kilearnadil, Jura.

NR 524687   LR: 61   (Map ref: 352)

The burial ground here contains some interesting gravestones as well as the Campbell mausoleum. The former village of Kilearnadil was decimated by plague.

Access at all reasonable times.
Parking

Kilmhoire Chapel

Off A846, 11 miles N of Craighouse, Tarbert, Jura.

NR 609822   LR: 61   (Map ref: 353)

Only foundations remain of a chapel, but the burial ground contains some interesting grave stones as well as standing stone, Carraigh Chaluim Bhainn, the 'standing stone of Calum the fair', apparently a reference to St Columba.

Access at all reasonable times.

Arts, Crafts and Industry

Isle of Jura Distillery

On A846, Craighouse, Jura.

NR 526669   LR: 61   (Map ref: 354)

On the wild and picturesque island of Jura, the original distillery was built in 1810, close to where illegal distilling had occurred for 300 years. The distillery was built by the Campbells and could pro-

duce 720 gallons of whisky a week. It was leased to James Ferguson in 1875, and completely rebuilt in 1884. When the lease expired, the Campbells tried to increase the rent – but Ferguson dismantled the distillery and sold the machinery. The present distillery was built in 1963, extended in 1971, and belongs to JBB (Greater Europe) Plc. The water comes from Loch a' Bhaile Mhargaidh – 'Market Loch'. The 10-Year-Old Single Malt is a light, slightly smoky, sweet-flavoured whisky.

Open by appointment only.

Open by appt.
Guided tours. Car parking.
Tel: 01496 820240   Fax: 01496 820344

Gardens, Animals and Miscellaneous

Jura House Walled Garden

On A846, 5 miles SE of Feolin Ferry, Ardfin, Jura.

NR 486636   LR: 61   (Map ref: 355)

Jura House Walled Garden has interesting woodland and cliff walks with local historical interest and wildlife and flowers. The walled organic garden has a wide variety of unusual plants and shrubs, suited to the protected west coast climate, including a large Australasian collection. The house is not open to the public.

Open all year, daily 9.00-17.00.
Explanatory boards. Tea tent in season. Picnic area. WC. Car and coach parking. £.
Tel: 01496 820315

Islay

(pronounced 'eye-la' – Norse: from 'Ile's island')

In Brief
Whisky. Lord of the Isles. Finlaggan. Kildalton Cross. Chapels. Birds.

Location (see map 10, p 132-133)
OS Landranger map 60
20 miles from W coast of Argyll
23 miles N of Northern Ireland

Tourist Information Centre
Bowmore (tel: 01496 810254; fax: 01496 810363)
Open Jan-Dec
www.islay.co.uk

How to Get There
By ferry from Kennacraig on mainland to Port Askaig and to Port Ellen on Islay (2 hrs; CalMac tel: 01880 730253 or 01496 840620 or 01496 302209); also from Scalasaig on Colonsay to/from Port Askaig on Islay (35 mins; CalMac 01631 566688)
By air twice daily from Glasgow to Glenegedale (tel: Glasgow Airport 0141 887 1111 or Islay Airport 01496 302022)
By vehicle ferry from Jura to Port Askaig on Islay (5 mins; Argyll and Bute Council tel: 01496 840681)

Notes
Walking and climbing. Bird watching. Loch or river fishing and sea angling available. Pony trekking, surfing, wind-surfing, sailing (there are good waters in Lochindaal, Port Ellen and the Sound of Islay) and diving – there are many wrecks round the island. Golf course. Cycle hire.

Basic Info
The most southerly of the Hebrides, Islay, also known as 'Queen of the Hebrides' is one of the largest of Scottish islands. It is 25 miles from north to south and nineteen miles from west to east, and covers 246 square miles. A wide range of habitats is found on the island: from mountainous moorland to sheltered woodland, from fertile farmland to low peat moor and high cliffs.

Islay has several interesting and picturesque villages, most of them planned, including Bowmore, dating from 1768 with its round church (no corners for the devil to hide in); Port Charlotte, an attractive village of 1828; Portnahaven; Port Wemyss and Port Ellen. Other villages include Ballygrant, Bridgend, Port Askaig and Bunnahabhain. The population is about 4000 people.

There are fine beaches in many places, including Traigh Mhachir and Saligo Bay, near Kilchoman – although currents can make bathing dangerous – and Big Strand to the south.

Bowmore, Islay.

Wildlife

Islay plays host to large populations of migrating geese from early October until the end of April, including barnacle geese, scaup and white-fronted geese. A huge variety and number of other birds (over 250 species have been recorded), and there is a sanctuary at the RSPB Reserve at Loch Gruinart (visitor centre featuring guided walks and events throughout the year tel: 01496 850505). Other wildlife includes seals, wild goats, otters and deer. Dolphins.

History

Due to Islay's location, warm climate and fertile land, it was inhabited from the earliest times. There are many remains of these early settlers, including the standing stones at Ballinaby and Coultoon; the broch of Dun Bhoraraic and fort of Dun Nosebridge.

The island was held by the Norsemen between 800 and 1156, and many of the place names date from their occupation. The island is said to be named after 'Ile', a Viking princess who died here.

Islay has the remains of many chapels, burial grounds and other monuments, including the fine cross at Kildalton, another and ruined chapel at Kilnave, and yet another cross at Kilchoman.Islay was the administrative centre of the Lords of the Isles, after the Hebrides had been wrested by Somerled from the Vikings and the king of Man in the 12th century. The Lords military power was based at Dunyvaig, while the administrative base was at Finlaggan, and they also had a small stronghold at Loch Gorm. James IV led a campaign against the Lords in 1493, and their power was crushed. Most of the lands were retained by the MacDonalds, but the Rhinns were given, with much argument, to the MacLeans of Duart. This dispute came to battle at Traigh Gruinart in 1598 and the MacLeans were routed and Lachlan MacLean of Duart, their chief, was slain. The MacDonalds did not profit from the victory, however, and the lands passed to the Campbells of Cawdor in the reign of James VI. The MacDonalds did all in their power to retain their property, and seized the island in 1615.

But it was to no avail, and the Campbells held the island.

In May 1847, during the Clearances, the *Exmouth*, which was carrying immigrants to America, was wrecked on the north-west coast and 266 folk were drowned. Two American troop carriers were also sunk, torpedoed by the Germans in 1918 with the loss of 266 lives. There is a memorial on the Oa peninsula.

There are several interesting lighthouses, including on the Rhinns of Islay at the small isle of Orsay, and those at Ruvaal, MacArthur's Head and Loch Indaal, which are all from the middle of the 19th century.

On the Oa are the deserted townships of Tokamal and Grasdal, inhabited until the end of the 19th century, but now deserted, as is Lurabus, above Carraig Fhada farm.

Kilchoman Cross, Islay.

Today

Large number of whisky distilleries: Bowmore, Caol Ila, Port Ellen, Bunnahabhain, Bruichladdich, Laphroaig, Lagavulin and Ardbeg. Cattle and sheep rearing, fishing, cheese-making and tourism (over 50,000 visitors annually).

Texa

The islet of Texa lies 0.5 miles south of Laphroaig on the south coast of Islay. The island has the remains of a chapel. There were several sculptured stones here, dating from the 14th to 16th centuries, which are now in the Museum of Islay Life.

Orsay and Eilean Mhic Coinnich

Two islets close to Portnahaven on the Rhinns of Islay. There are the remains of a chapel on **Orsay,** and there is an impressive lighthouse, which dates from 1824. The chapel was dedicated to St Orain. Cross-slab fragments found here, dating from about 7th century, are in the Museum of Islay Life.

Nave Island

Small island just off the coast at Ardnave Point to the north of Islay, again with the remains of a chapel, which was altered in the 18th century with the insertion of a chimney for kelp workers.

Places of Interest

Prehistoric

Achnancarranan Standing Stones

Off A846, 1.5 miles NE of Port Ellen, Achnancarranan, Islay.

NR 389461 LR: 60   (Map ref: 356)

Two standing stones, as well as a third fallen stone. The taller stone survives to a height of nine feet, while the second, some twenty feet away, is about a foot shorter.

Alt nan Ba

Off B8018, 6 miles NW of Bruichladdich, Alt nan Ba, Islay.

NR 218712 LR: 60   (Map ref: 357)

A low promontory is defended by a series of walls on the landward side. The best-preserved survives to a height of over six feet and the entrance can be traced, three feet high and with a few lintels still in place. Also on the promontory is a roofed beehive cell, and other ruins. The site would appear to be an early Christian monastery in the remains of an earlier fort.

Ballinaby Standing Stones

Off B8018, 4.5 miles NW of Bruichladdich, Ballinaby, Islay.

NR 219672 LR: 60   (Map ref: 358)

One of the most impressive standing stones in western Scotland. The stone is in a prominent position and despite its thinness can be seen from considerable distances. The stone is about sixteen-feet tall. A second stone, 200 yards to the north, is six feet high. By foot from Ballinaby farm.

Carnduncan

On B8018, 4 miles N of Bruichladdich, Carnduncan, Islay.

NR 240672 LR: 60   (Map ref: 359)

A round burial cairn, fifty feet in diameter and over five feet in height, which has been little disturbed. The kerb can be traced.

Carraigh Bhan

Off A846, 3 miles NW of Port Ellen, Carraigh Bhan, Islay.

NR 328478 LR: 60   (Map ref: 360)

A large standing stone, which stands to a height of 7.5 feet, is said to mark the grave of King Godred Crovan, the Norse King of Man.

Clach Mhic-'Illean

On B8017, 4 miles N of Bruichladdich, Aoradh, Islay.

NR 274674 LR: 60   (Map ref: 361)

A small stone here is said to mark the burial place of Lachlan MacLean of Duart, who was killed at the battle of Traigh Gruinart in 1598.

Cnoc Nan Guaillean Standing Stone

Off A847, 3 miles NW of Port Charlotte, Cnoc Nan Guaillean, Islay.

NR 224604 LR: 60   (Map ref: 362)

Standing stone, which is nine feet high.

Coultoon Stone Circle

Off A847, 4 miles NE of Portnahaven, Coultoon, Islay.

NR 196570 LR: 60   (Map ref: 363)

Remains of a small stone circle in a fine location, dating from around 1000 BC. The circle was apparently never completed and, although there are sockets for the upright stones, many were never put in place.

Dun Bhoraraic

Off A846, 2.5 miles SW of Port Askaig, Lossit Farm, Islay.

NR 417658 LR: 60   (Map ref: 364)

Standing on a small hill, Dun Bhoraraic consists of the remains of a broch, the walls of which are over twelve-feet thick. The remains of a guard cell defending the entrance and a mural chamber can be traced. It was used by the MacDonalds in medieval times.

Permission must be sought from Dunlossit Estate.

Dun Nosebridge

Off A846, 2.5 miles SE of Bridgend, Cluanach, Islay.

NR 372603 LR: 60   (Map ref: 365)

The large and impressive fort of Dun Nosebridge dates from the Iron Age. It is protected by a series of well-preserved ramparts and a wall, tiered one above the next. The fort is roughly rectangular in shape, and the entrances through the ramparts can be traced.

Dun Trudernish

Off A846, 7.5 miles NE of Port Ellen, Trudernish, Islay.

NR 468526 LR: 60 (Map ref: 366)

A fort, standing on a rocky promontory, was defended on the landward side by three walls. One wall survives to a height of about eight feet, and is vitrified in places. The entrance can be discerned. A second wall stands to a height of around six feet, while the outermost wall is more ruinous.

Gleann Droighneach Standing Stone

Off A847, 3 miles W of Port Charlotte, Gleann Droighneach, Islay.

NR 211594 LR: 60 (Map ref: 367)

A standing stone, which is about nine feet high.

Port Charlotte Cairn

On A847, 0.5 miles SW of Port Charlotte, Islay.

NR 248576 LR: 60 (Map ref: 368)

A robbed and disturbed chambered burial cairn, close to the road, with the remains of the chambers. Finds from here, including pottery, flints, arrowheads and a knife, are kept in the Museum of Islay Life.

Port Ellen Standing Stone

Off A846, NE of Port Ellen, Islay.

NR 372456 LR: 60 (Map ref: 369)

A tall but thin standing stone, thirteen feet high, is said to mark the site of an old battle.

Uiskentuie Standing Stone

On A847, 2.5 miles W of Bridgend, Uiskentuie, Islay.

NR 294634 LR: 61 (Map ref: 370)

A ten foot high standing stone.

Historic and Heritage

Dunyvaig Castle

Off A846, 2 miles E of Port Ellen, Lagavulin, Islay.

NR 406455 LR: 60 (Map ref: 371)

Dunyvaig Castle consists of the remains of a small 15th-century keep on top of a rock, with a small inner and larger outer courtyard of the 13th century. It was held by MacDonald Lords of the Isles, who had their main stronghold at Finlaggan. The Lord of the Isles was forfeited by James IV in 1493, and the castle passed to the MacIans of Ardnamurchan. The property was given to the Campbells in 1543, then leased back, but in 1598 the last MacDonald of Dunyvaig defeated the MacLeans of Duart at the battle at Traigh Gruinart in 1598. However, he was ordered to surrender the castle, then forfeited in 1608. The castle was besieged and taken by 'Old' Colkitto in 1647. After a siege by a Covenanter army under David Leslie, it was forced to surrender when the water supply failed, and old Colkitto was hanged from the walls. The Campbells

Dunyvaig Castle, Islay.

of Cawdor occupied the castle until about 1677, but demolished it soon afterwards, and moved to Islay House.

Access at all reasonable times.

Parking nearby.

Finlaggan

Off A846, 3 miles W of Port Askaig, Loch Finlaggan, Islay.

NR 388681 LR: 60 (Map ref: 372)

Finlaggan was a very important site in medieval times, but not much remains except foundations on two islands. Traces have recently been found of a 15th-century keep on the smaller or council island. The ruins of a chapel, dedicated to St Finlaggan a contemporary of St Columba, and many other buildings stand on the larger island, Eilean Mor. There are several carved gravestones, thought to commemorate relatives of the Lords of the Isles, who were themselves buried on Iona.

There was a kingdom of the Isles, subject to Norway, from about 900. In the 12th century, Somerled, of mixed Norse and Celtic blood, ousted the Norsemen from much of western Scotland and took control of their territories, although they remained as vassals of the King of Man. He was assassinated at Renfrew in 1164 when at war with Malcolm IV, King of Scots. Somerled was succeeded by his sons Reginald in Kintyre and Islay, Dugald in Lorn, Mull and Jura, and Angus in Bute, Arran and North Argyll.

The whole area became part of the kingdom of Scots in 1266 after the battle of Largs in 1263. Angus Og MacDonald (Young Angus) was the grandson of Donald, a son of Reginald: hence MacDonald the family name. Angus was a friend and supporter of Robert the Bruce, and died at Finlaggan in 1328: his son, John of Islay, was the first to use the title 'Lord of the Isles'. The independence of the Lords, however, and their power and influence, caused constant trouble for the kings of Scots. A campaign by the 2nd Lord led to the bloody battle of Harlaw in 1411, and the 3rd Lord was twice imprisoned by James I. In 1461 John, 4th Lord of the Isles and Earl of Ross, signed the treaty of Westminster-Ardtornish by which he, the Earl of Douglas, and Edward IV of England agreed to divide Scotland between them. James IV eventually destroyed the power of the Lords in a campaign in 1493, and had John imprisoned until his death in 1503. Attempts were made to restore the Lordship, but these were ultimately unsuccessful, although a

branch of the MacDonalds held the lands until the beginning of the 17th century, when they passed to the Campbells.

There is a visitor centre near the island, with archaeological finds, and a model of how Finlaggan would have looked during the lordship.

Open Apr: Tue, Thu & Sun 14.30-17.00; May-Sep: Mon-Tue 10/00-13.00 & 14.30-17.00, Wed-Fri 14.30-17.00, Sun 14.30-17.00, closed Sat; Oct: Tue, Thu & Sun 14.00-16.00.

Visitor centre. Parking nearby.

Tel: 01496 810629 Fax: 01496 810856
Email: LynMags@aol.com Web: www.islay.com

Gorm Castle

Off B8018, 3 miles NW of Bruichladdich, Loch Gorm, Islay.

NR 235655 LR: 60 (Map ref: 373)

Site of 15th-century castle of the MacDonalds, once a place of some strength, on a small island in the loch. It passed to the MacLeans, and is said to have been besieged in 1578 by the MacDonalds, and used by the MacLeans before going on to defeat at the battle of Traigh Gruinart in 1598. The castle was refortified, or still in use, in 1615 when Sir James MacDonald fought against the Campbells on Islay and Kintyre. The castle was garrisoned by the Campbells until the 1640s.

Keills Cross Shaft

Off A846, 1 mile SW of Port Askaig, Keills, Islay.

NR 417687 LR: 60 (Map ref: 374)

A medieval cross shaft, which survives to a height of about six feet. There are the ruins of an old chapel nearby, dedicated to St Columba.

Kilarrow (Bowmore) Parish Church

On A846, Main Street, Bowmore, Islay.

LR: 60 (Map ref: 375)

The church was built by the Campbells of Shawfield in 1767, and is unusual in being round: no corners for the devil to hide in. The church can hold 500 souls.

Open daily all year.

Parking nearby.

Kilbride Chapel

Off A846, 1.5 miles NE of Port Ellen, Kilbride, Islay.

NR 384465 LR: 60 (Map ref: 376)

The remains of a rectangular chapel, dedicated to St Bride. Nearby is Tobar an t-Sagairt, the 'well of the priest', south of the burial ground, and there is also a standing stone [NR 384466], which is over eleven feet high.

Kilchiaran Chapel

Off A847, 3 miles NW of Port Charlotte, Kilchiaran, Islay.

NR 204602 LR: 60 (Map ref: 377)

The chapel, dedicated to St Claran, dates from medieval times, and there are several carved grave slabs and the base of a cross shaft. One story is that St Columba landed here after leaving Ireland (as he also did on Colonsay), but he soon continued his journey north to Iona.

Access at all reasonable times.

Parking nearby.

Kilchoman Cross

Off B8018, 3 miles NW of Bruichladdich, Kilchoman, Islay.

NR 214631 LR: 60 (Map ref: 378)

In the burial ground is a fine eight-foot-high disc-headed cross, which was carved about 1500. In the base are cups and a stone. Wishes are said to be granted if the stone is turned in the holes in the correct order – towards the sun. There are several carved grave slabs, and a stone known as the Sanctuary Cross.

Access at all reasonable times.

Parking nearby.

Kildalton Cross and Chapel

Off A846, 7 miles NE of Port Ellen, Kildalton, Islay.

NR 458508 LR: 60 (Map ref: 379)

The finest surviving intact cross in Scotland, dating from the 8th century, and the ringed cross was carved from a single slab. The remains of a Viking ritual killing are said to have been found beneath the cross when it was excavated in 1890; and there may have been an early Christian community here. The small ruined chapel, dedicated to St John the Beloved, dates from the 12th or 13th century. It houses several carved grave slabs, several with effigies of warriors, and there are more in the churchyard, dating from the 15th-17th centuries. The 15th-century Thief's Cross is nearby.

Open all year.

Parking nearby.

Tel: 0131 668 8800

Killarrow Graveyard

On A846, Bridgend, Killarrow, Islay.

NR 335625 LR: 60 (Map ref: 380)

The burial ground has many fine carved slabs, including one dating from the 14th or 15th century, with the effigy of a clergyman. There was a settlement here, but it was moved to Bowmore as it was thought by the owners of Islay House to be too near their property.

Access at all times.

Parking nearby.

Kilnaughton

Off A846, 1 mile W of Port Ellen, Kilnaughton, Islay.

NR 344452 LR: 60 (Map ref: 381)

The ruins of a chapel, dating from the 15th century and dedicated to St Mechtan, who died in 679. In the burial ground are a number of old grave markers, including four medieval sculpted slabs.

Kildalton Cross, Islay.

Kilnave Chapel and Cross

Off B8017, 6 miles N of Bridgend, Kilnave, Islay.
NR 285715 LR: 60 (Map ref: 382)

The ruinous chapel is the scene of a massacre. A party of MacLeans fled here after the battle of Traigh Gruinart in 1598. The building was thatched and set alight, and all the fugitives perished except one man. By the chapel is the once fine but now broken and very weathered cross, which dates from about 750.

Access at all reasonable times.
Parking nearby.

Museum of Islay Life

Off A847, Port Charlotte, Islay.
NR 253587 LR: 60 (Map ref: 383)

Housed in an old church, this award-winning museum was opened in 1977 and covers all areas of island life. Displays include an important collection of carved stones, dating from the 6th to 16th centuries, as well as miniature reconstructions of prehistoric sites. There are also room exhibits, largely from Victorian times, and another item of interest is an illicit whisky still. There is a library and extensive archives.

Open Easter-Oct, Mon-Sat 10.00-16.30, Sun 14.00-16.30.

Explanatory displays. Sales area. WC. Disabled access (steps). Car and coach parking. £.
Tel: 01496 850358 Fax: 01496 850358

Nerabus Chapel and Burial Ground

Off A847, 3 miles S of Port Charlotte, Nerabus, Islay.
NB 225549 LR: 60 (Map ref: 384)

Fine carved medieval grave slabs, some dating from the 14th and 15th centuries, survive in the graveyard, along with the ruins of a small chapel. Parts of a cross also remain.

Access at all reasonable times.

Arts, Crafts and Industry

Ardbeg Distillery

On A846, 2.5 miles E of Port Ellen, Ardbeg, Islay.
NR 416462 LR: 60 (Map ref: 385)

The distillery was founded in 1815, and the whitewashed buildings are situated on the picturesque southern coast of Islay. The visitor centre is housed in the distillery's original kiln and malt barn, which has displays of old artefacts from the distillery and features tales from the past. The shop has a wide range of Ardbeg malt whiskies and gifts. The tour charge is redeemable on any purchase over £15.00.

Open all year, Mon-Fri 10.00-16.00, Jun-Aug also Sat & Sun 10.00-17.00; last full tour 15.30; also by appt.

Guided tours. Gift shop. Old Kiln Coffee shop. WC. Limited disabled access. Maximum ten per group. Pre-booking advisable for larger groups. Parking. £.
Tel: 01496 302244 Fax: 01496 302040

Bowmore Distillery

Off A846, School Street, Bowmore, Islay.
NR 311599 LR: 60 (Map ref: 386)

Bowmore (pronounced 'beau -more') Distillery is one of the oldest in Scotland, and was licensed in 1779. It uses the traditional method of producing its own floor-malted barley. Bowmore offers guided tours and a video presentation explaining the process of whisky making. The admission charge is redeemable in the shop, which stocks a full range of Bowmore Islay single malt Scotch whiskies. The tour includes a dram.

Across the entrance yard, a former warehouse, gifted to the local community, is now a swimming pool heated by waste energy from the distillery.

Open May-Sep, Mon-Fri: guided tours at 10.30, 11.30, 14.00 & 15.00, Sat 10.30, closed Sun; Oct-Apr, Mon-Fri 10.30 and 14.00.

Guided tours. Explanatory displays. Gift shop. Visitors receive a dram of whisky. Disabled access: walkways ramped for wheelchairs & WC. Car and coach parking. Group concessions. £. Booking advisable for groups.
Tel: 01496 810671 Fax: 01496 810757
Web: www.morrisonbowmore.co.uk

Bunnahabhain Distillery

Off A846, 3.5 miles N of Port Askaig, Bunnahabhain, Islay.
NR 418732 LR: 60 (Map ref: 387)

Bunnahabhain is Gaelic for 'mouth of the river' and is pronounced 'Boon-na-ha-ven'. It is the most northerly of Islay's distilleries, in a peaceful and picturesque location on the Sound of Islay. Visitors are welcome and are given a guided tour of the distillery. Individuals and groups are welcome, and the tour includes a dram of the Bunnahabhain

12-Year-Old Islay Malt Scotch Whisky.

Open all year except closed Christmas and New Year, Mon-Fri 10.00-16.00 – distillery tours by appt only.

Guided tours by arrangement. Gift shop. WC. Car and coach parking. Accommodation available in cottages.

Tel: 01496 840646 Fax: 01496 840248

Caol Ila Distillery

Off A846, N of Port Askaig, Caol Ila (signposted), Islay.

NR 428701 LR: 60 (Map ref: 388)

Caol Ila (pronounced 'Caal-eela') Distillery stands in a picturesque setting at the foot of a steep hill, with a small pier, overlooking the Sound of Islay and Paps of Jura, and local wildlife includes seals and otters. It was built in 1846 and even had its own steam ship, *The Pibroch*, which transported the whisky to Glasgow. A visit involves a personal tour, and the shop has a wide range of blended whiskies and well as the Caol Ila Malt Whisky. The adult admission includes a redeemable voucher towards the purchase of a 70cl bottle of malt whisky. Children under eight years of age are welcome but are not encouraged to take the tour.

Open all year, Mon-Fri by appt; at various times of the year the distillery is not in production although visitors are welcome and tours are provided.

Visitor centre. Guided tours by arrangement. Gift shop. WC. Car parking. £ but includes redeemable voucher. Children under eight years are welcome but are not encouraged to take the tour.

Tel: 01496 840207 Fax: 01496 302763

Islay Woollen Mill

Off A846, 1 mile NE of Bridgend, Islay.

NR 352632 LR: 60 (Map ref: 389)

An early Victorian mill, containing a tweed and woollen factory, which produces tartan.

Open Apr-Sep, Mon-Fri 10.00-17.00, Sat 10.00-16.00; Jan-Mar, Mon-Fri 10.00-17.00, Sat 13.00-16.00; closed Christmas day and New Year's day; other times by appt.

Guided tours. Explanatory displays. Gift shop. Picnic area. WC. Car and coach parking.

Tel: 01496 810563 Fax: 01496 810677
Email: islaywoollenmill@btinternet.cpm

Lagavulin Distillery

On A846, 2 miles E of Port Ellen, Lagavulin, Islay.

NR 405456 LR: 60 (Map ref: 390)

Near the ruins of Dunyvaig Castle, Lagavulin (pronounced 'Lagga-voolin') Distillery, was established

Lagavulin Distillery, Islay.

in 1816. Tours and tastings can be taken by appointment, and the adult charge includes a discount voucher redeemable at the distillery against a 70cl bottle of malt whisky. Tours are by appointment only; please telephone in advance.

Open Apr-Oct, Mon-Fri. Tours at 10.00, 11.30 & 14.30 and are by appt only.

Guided tours. Explanatory displays. Gift shop. WC. Car and coach parking. £. Children under the age of eight are welcome but are not encouraged to take the tour.

Tel: 01496 302400   Fax: 01496 302733

Laphroaig Distillery

Off A846, 1 mile E of Port Ellen, Laphroaig, Islay. NR 387452 LR: 60 (Map ref: 391)

Located in a scenic bay with otters and swans, the original distillery at Laphroaig (pronounced 'La-froyg' and meaning 'the beautiful hollow by the broad bay') was founded in 1815 and is housed in white-washed buildings. The distillery still uses its own floor maltings: the malted barley is dried over a peat fire. Tours of the distillery are available by appointment, and there is a shop.

Open all year, Mon-Thu: tours 10.30 & 14.00 by appt only; closed Jul & first two weeks in Aug.

Guided tours. Gift shop. WC. Disabled access. Car and coach parking.

Tel: 01496 302418   Fax: 01496 302496
Email: 106523.565@compuserve.com   Web: www.laphroaig.com

Port Ellen Pottery

Off A846, Tighcargaman, Port Ellen, Islay. LR: 60 (Map ref: 392)

A small local pottery with all items made on the premises.

Open daily, 10.30 until late.

Very small workshop. Not suitable for coach parties or large groups. Accommodation available.

Tel: 01496 302345   Fax: 01496 302345

Tormisdale Croft Crafts

Off A847, 4 miles NE of Portnahaven, Tormisdale, Islay. LR: 60 (Map ref: 393)

Tormisdale Croft Crafts features wool – from rare breed sheep – being hand spun and the natural dyed wools made into original design knitwear.

Other crafts include stirkmaking, patchwork, bird boxes, silk painting and paintings.

Open daily all year.

Parking. Assisted disabled access.

Tel: 01496 860239

Gigha

'Gee-a' (Norse: gja-ey 'cleft island' or 'God island' or 'good island')

In Brief
Unspoilt island. Gardens.

Location (see map 10, p 132-133)
OS Landranger map 62
3 miles W of Kintyre

Tourist Information Centre
Campbeltown TIC (mainland)
Tel: 01586 552056; fax: 01586 553291
Open Jan-Dec

How to Get There
By ferry from Tayinloan in Kintyre to Ardminish on Gigha (20 mins; Cal Mac tel: 01880 730253)

Notes
Gigha Hotel/The Boathouse, Ardminish (tel 01583 505254; fax 01583 505244). No caravans.
There is a nine-hole golf course. Fishing available. Anchorage for yachts.

Basic Info
Gigha is six miles long and two miles across at its widest. The land is fertile, although the west coast is rough and rocky. The island now has a population of around 200, although in 1801 there were over 500 inhabitants. The highest hill, Creag Bhan, rises to 330 feet, and there are

Gigha.

splendid views to Kintyre, Islay, Jura, and even Ireland on a clear day. There are also fine sandy beaches at Druimyeon Bay and Ardminish Bay.

Wildlife
Numerous species of birds. Otters and seals.

History
There are many prehistoric sites, including cairns, standing stones, forts and duns. A Viking grave was found in 1849 at East Tarbert Bay. There are fine carved grave slabs in the old burial ground at Kilchattan, including an ogham stone, which dates from as early as the 7th century. The Norse king Hakon held court on the island in 1263 before going on to defeat at the battle of Largs.

The island was long a property of the Lords of the Isles, but passed to the MacNeils of Taynish, who held it until 1780 when it was sold to the MacNeils of Colonsay. It has changed hands several times since then. Achamore House has fine gardens, which have been developed since 1944.

Today
Farming. Cheese. Fishing. Tourism.

Cara

The small island of Cara lies 0.5 miles south of the south tip of Gigha. It is about one mile long, but less than 0.5 miles across, and rises to about 150 feet. The island was a property of the MacDonalds of Largie, and a ruinous old chapel, dedicated to St Fionnlugh, is said to be the site of an early Christian monastery. The island is said to have had a brownie. **Gigulum** Island lies off the south-east coast of Gigha.

Places of Interest

Prehistoric

Ardlamey Cairn
Off unlisted road, 1 mile SW of Ardminish, Ardlamey, Gigha.
NR 631482   LR: 62   (Map ref: 394)
A burial cairn, probably from the Bronze Age, standing on a small headland south of Ardlamey. The diameter of the cairn is over fifty feet, and it survives to a height of about four feet. There is a cist in the cairn, and some kerb stones can be seen.

Druid's Stone, East Tarbert Bay
On unlisted road, 2 miles N of Ardminish, East Tarbert Bay, Gigha.
NR 655523   LR: 62   (Map ref: 395)
The Druid's Stone is a tall standing stone, surviving to a height of over seven feet. It is near to two burial cairns, and is also known as the Hanging Stone, from a tradition that people found guilty at the nearby Court Hill met their deaths on it.

Dun Chibhich
Off unlisted road, 1 mile NW of Ardminish, S of Mill Loch, Gigha.
NR 645500   LR: 62   (Map ref: 396)
Standing on a rocky crag are the remains of an Iron Age fort. The fort was enclosed by a wall, sections of which remain to a height of about four feet. The entrance through the wall can be seen.

The fort is said to be named after 'Keefi', a great Pictish warrior, who is alleged to be buried near the fort; or from 'Keefie', a Fingalian character, who ran away with the wife of Diarmid. Diarmid pursued the couple to the fort, and here slew them both. Their burial place is also said to be near the fort.

Dunan an t-Seasgain
Off unlisted road, 1 mile N of Ardminish, Ardailly, Gigha.
NR 649507   LR: 62   (Map ref: 397)
A ruinous dun on a rocky crag, the walls of which survive to a height of about four feet. The entrance can be traced.

East Tarbert Bay Cairns
On unlisted road, 2 miles N of Ardminish, East Tarbert Bay, Gigha.
NR 656524   LR: 62   (Map ref: 398)
Two burial cairns are sited here, one larger than the other. The larger cairn is about 30 feet in diameter and rises to a height of about five feet, while the smaller – ten feet away – is some 25 feet round and about three feet high.

Historic and Heritage

Achamore Gardens
Off unlisted road, 1 mile SW of Ardminish, Achamore, Gigha.
NR 644477   LR: 62   (Map ref: 399)
The fine woodland gardens of rhododendrons and azaleas were created by Sir James Horlick, who purchased the estate in 1944. Many of the plants were brought in laundry baskets from his former home in Berkshire, and others were added over the following 29 years. Sub-tropical plants flourish in the virtually frost-free climate, and there is a walled garden for some of the finer specimens. There are good views over Islay and Jura, and two self-guided garden routes, one of 40 minutes, the other two hours.

The house was built in 1884 by Captain William Scarlett, Lord Abinger, after he had bought the island, but is not open to the public.

Open daily all year, dawn to dusk.
WC. Disabled access. Parking. £.
Tel: 01583 505254   Fax: 01583 505244

Holy Stone, Cairnvickuie
Off unlisted road, 1.5 miles N of Ardminish, Cairnvickuie, Gigha.
NR 654515   LR: 62   (Map ref: 400)
An early Christian stone, decorated with several crosses, is known as the Holy Stone. The broken cross stands nearby.

Kilchattan
Off unlisted road, 0.5 miles SW of Ardminish, Gigha.
NR 644482   LR: 62   (Map ref: 401)
The ruinous rectangular chapel, which was dedicated to St Cathan, dates from the 13th century. There are fine grave slabs, from as early as the 14th century, in the burial ground. One has been identified as that of Malcolm MacNeill of Gigha, who died in 1493.

There is a standing stone nearby [NR 642481], which survives to a height of over five feet, and is adorned with an ogham inscription, which may have read 'the son of Coiceile'. The inscription probably dates from the 7th century or later. The upper part of the stone may be part of a fence [NR 660540].

Ridh a' Chaibeil Cross

Off unlisted road, 1.5 miles N of Ardminish, Cairnwickuie, Gigha.
NR 655516 LR: 62 (Map ref: 402)
The broken 10th-century cross stands in an old burial ground.

Tobar a' Bheathaig

Off unlisted road, 2 miles N of Ardminish, S of East Tarbert Bay, Gigha.
NR 656519 LR: 62 (Map ref: 403)
The spring here is known as Tobar a' Bheathaig – 'well of the beech trees' or 'well of Beathag', a woman's name. The waters of the spring were said to have great beneficial powers, and used to wish for a fair wind: water being thrown in the direction from which the wind was to come.

Gigha Hotel, Gigha.

Map 11: Arran, Bute and Cumbrae

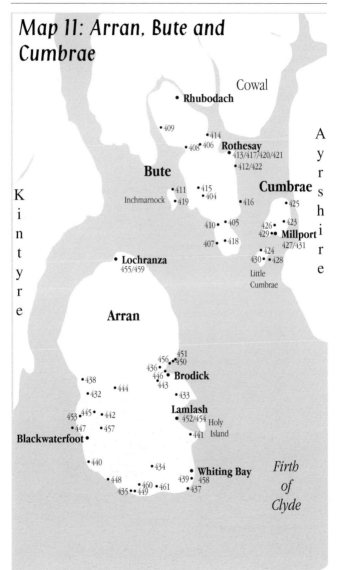

Cowal

• **Rhubodach**

•409

•414
•408 •406 **Rothesay**
•413/417/420/421
•412/422

Bute

A
y
r
s
h
i
r
e

•411 •415 **Cumbrae**
•404
Inchmarnock •419
•416 •425

K
i
n
t
y
r
e

410• •405 426• •423
429•• **Millport**
427/431

407• •418

•424
430• •428

• **Lochranza**
455/459

Little
Cumbrae

Arran

451
456• •450
436•
446• **Brodick**
443

•438
•432 •444 •433

Lamlash
453•445• •442 •452/454 Holy
•447 •457 •441 Island

Blackwaterfoot•

•440
•434

Firth
448• •439 •458 *of*
435•• •437 *Clyde*
449 460 461

•434 • **Whiting Bay**

Bute

('fire' or 'beacon fire' or 'victory Isle')

In Brief
Rothesay Castle. Kingarth. Mount Stuart. Victorian Rothesay (and its toilets).

Location (see map 11, p 156)
OS Landranger map 63
6.5 miles W of mainland at Largs, S of Cowal in Argyll, 8 miles NE of Arran

Tourist Information Centre
Rothesay (tel: 01700 502151; fax: 01700 505156)
Open Jan-Dec

How to Get There
By ferry from Wemyss Bay on mainland to Rothesay on Bute (1 hour; CalMac Tel: 01770 502707)
Also from Colintrave on Cowal to Rhubodach on N of Bute (15 mins; CalMac Tel: 01770 502707)

Notes
Sailing and cruises, and cycles can be hired. There are eight easy-to-follow walks of varying length and difficulty – maps from TIC. Angling and watersports available. Pony trekking. There is a hide at Loch Fad, from where many birds can be watched. There is an eighteen-hole golf course.

Rothesay Castle, Bute.

The Bute Highland Games are held in August and there is a Jazz Festival in April.

Hanging about in men's public conveniences should not always be encouraged, but the Victorian toilets in Rothesay are particularly impressive.

Basic Info

The island is about fifteen miles long and about three to five miles broad, and covers 48 square miles. Most of the island is very low and fertile, while the northern end is more hilly, rising to over 900 feet, as is the southern tip. There are fine beaches at Ettrick Bay, Scalpsie Bay, and at Kilchattan Bay, and the scenery at Kingarth is particularly fine.

Declared a Royal Burgh by Robert III in 1400, Rothesay is the main town on the island, dating mostly from Victorian times with its pier and Art Nouveau Winter Gardens of 1924 (now with a restaurant and cinema), and sweeps along Rothesay Bay and around Bogany Point. The Victorian toilets in Rothesay are a gem of a public convenience, although only for men.

There are villages at Port Bannatyne, Ascog, Kingarth and Kilchattan Bay.

Wildlife

Seals can be seen from Scalpsie Bay. There are a large number of birds – around 150 species have been recorded – including greylag, barnacle and Greenland geese and ducks in winter, and wheateaters, woodwarblers, redstart and blackcap in summer. Other birds include hawks, oystercatchers, curlews, redshank and eider ducks.

History

There are many prehistoric monuments, including standing stones or circles at Ettrick Bay, Largizean and Blackpark Plantation, as well as several chambered cairns, including those at Kilmichael, Northpark on Inchmarnock, Hilton and Bicker's Houses (there are also others: Carnbaan [NS 006693] and Glecknabae [NS 008682]). There are also several forts or duns: Little Dunagoil was occupied through the Bronze Age and by Vikings in the 12th and 13th centuries. The medieval chapel and early Christian monastery at Kingarth are set in a wonderful location, and there is also a chapel, St Mary's, in Rothesay, with the stone effigy of a warrior. The island was held by the Norsemen as part of the Hebrides, although seized by the Scots after the battle of Largs in 1263. The Stewarts held the island, and the fine castle at Rothesay, with its wet moat, before later moving to Mount Stuart. Other castles are at Kames, held by the Bannatyne family; Wester Kames [NS 062680], a property of the MacKinlays, Spences and Grahams; Meikle Kilmory, held by the Jamiesons; and Kelspoke [NS 106541]. Set in splendid grounds, Mount Stuart is the fine mansion of the Stewart Marquis of Bute, and is open to the public.

Today

Farming and fishing. Tourism.

Inchmarnock

Inchmarnock ('Isle of St Marnock') lies about one mile off the west coast of Bute at St Ninian's Bay. It is about two miles long and 0.5 miles wide and is relatively flat and fertile. The island was held by the Abbey at Saddell in Kintyre, and there are the remains of a small chapel, dedicated to St Marnock, the ruins of which were demolished 'by a vandal tenant' about 1850.

Places of Interest

Prehistoric

Bicker's Houses, Bute
Off A844, 3.5 miles SW of Rothesay, SW side of Barmore Hill, Bute.
NS 061604 LR: 63 (Map ref: 404)
Bicker's Houses is a long cairn, some 90 feet long and about 45 wide, which has been much robbed. The entrance to the partitioned burial chamber can be traced, and some upright slabs are still in place.

Blackpark Stone Circle
Off A844, 6 miles S of Rothesay, Blackpark Plantation, Bute.
NS 092556 LR: 63 (Map ref: 405)
A setting of three standing stones, the tallest of which rises to over nine feet. This may have been a

stone circle, and it is located in a clearing in a forestry plantation.

Dun Burgidale
Off A844, 2 miles NW of Rothesay, Dun Burgidale, Bute.
NS 063660 LR: 63 (Map ref: 406)
An oval dun or broch, with walls surviving to a height of about ten feet. The entrance can be

traced, and there has been a gallery within the wall.

Dunagoil
Off A844, 8 miles S of Rothesay, Dunagoil Bay, Bute.
NS 085531 LR: 63 (Map ref: 407)
Standing on a site defended by crags except on the landward side, the fort is encircled by the remains of a wall. Parts of the wall are vitrified. Finds from the fort, now in the Bute Museum, include glass and lignite bracelets, a brooch, ring-headed pins, pottery and axe-heads, dating from both the Bronze and Iron Age.

Nearby at Little Dunagoil [NS 087532] is another small fort, occupied from the Bronze Age until the 13th century. The remains of Viking longhouses were found here, and finds are also kept in the Bute Museum.

Ettrick Bay Stone Circle
Off A844, 4 miles NW of Rothesay, St Colmac, Bute.
NS 044668 LR: 63 (Map ref: 408)
The small stone circle now consists of four upright and four broken stones.

Kilmichael
Off A844, 9 miles NW of Rothesay, Kilmichael, Bute.
NR 994703 LR: 63 (Map ref: 409)
There are the remains of two chambered burial cairns at Kilmichael, one of which is known as 'St Michael's Grave' and has been excavated. Finds included pottery, animal remains and burnt human bone, and are in the Museum of Scotland. Nearby is another chambered cairn [NR 997705], and there are also the ruins of an old chapel, dedicated to St Michael or St Macaille [NR 992705], as well as a holy well, said to have been known as the 'Lovers' Well'.

The ruins of an oval fort [NR 994713] are sited on a gorge above the Aultmore Burn. A strong wall defends the weaker side, and survives to a height of six feet. The entrance, with a large upright, is at the north end. The dun can be overgrown and difficult to find.

Largizean Standing Stones
Off A844, 6 miles S of Rothesay, Largizean, Bute.
NS 084554 LR: 63 (Map ref: 410)
A setting of three large boulders in a line, about ten feet apart. The tallest is over seven feet high.

Northpark Cairn, Inchmarnock

Northpark, N tip of Inchmarnock.
NS 020613 LR: 63 (Map ref: 411)
A large burial cairn, which survives to a height of over six feet, with what may be the remains of kerb.

Historic and Heritage

Ascog House

On A844, 1.5 miles SE of Rothesay, Ascog, Bute.
NS 105633 LR: 63 (Map ref: 412)
Ascog House is an L-plan tower house, probably built in the 16th century. The lands may have been a property of the Glass family from the 15th century. They later passed to the Fairlies, but were acquired in 1587 by the Stewarts, who held the property until the middle of the 18th century.
Can be rented through the Landmark Trust.
Tel: 01628 825925

Bute Museum

Off A845, Stuart Street, Rothesay, Bute.
LR: 63 (Map ref: 413)
The Bute Museum has artefacts and displays from the island, and is housed in two galleries which cover the geology, archaeology, history and natural history of Bute.

The natural history room has birds, mammals and seashore items; while the history room has varied collections, such as models of Clyde steamers, old photographs of Rothesay, and farming and history items. There is a collection of early Christian crosses, and the prehistoric section has flints and pots from two Neolithic burial cairns. A comprehensive geological survey of the island can be seen, and there is also a children's 'touch table', toddlers' case, and small aquarium.
Open all year: Apr-Sep, Mon-Sat 10.30-16.30, Sun 14.30-16.30; Oct-Mar, Tue-Sat 14.30-16.30; closed Sun & Mon.
Guided tours by appt. Explanatory displays. Gift shop. WC. Disabled access and assistance. £.
Tel: 01700 502033

Kames Castle

Off A844, 2.5 miles NW of Rothesay, Kames, Bute.
NS 064676 LR: 63 (Map ref: 414)
Kames Castle is a massive 14th-century keep, formerly surrounded by a moat, to which later and lower buildings were added in the 18th century. Kames was a property of Bannatyne of Kames from

the beginning of the 14th century or earlier until 1780. The castle was extended in the 18th century, but later passed to the Stewarts.
Cottages in the courtyard of the castle can be rented.
Tel: 01700 504500

Kilmory Castle

On A844, 4 miles SW of Rothesay, Meikle Kilmory, Bute.
NS 051611 LR: 63 (Map ref: 415)
Not much remains of a tower house or castle, except one small turret. It was a property of the Jamiesons of Kilmorie, hereditary coroners of Bute, from the 15th century, but the property passed to the Stewarts in 1780.

Mount Stuart House

Off A844, 5 miles S of Rothesay, Mount Stuart, Bute.
NS 105595 LR: 63 (Map ref: 416)
A fine Victorian Gothic stately home with splendid interior decoration, Mount Stuart was designed by the Scottish architect Robert Rowand Anderson for the 3rd Marquis of Bute. The house is surrounded by 300 acres of fine landscaped grounds, gardens and woodlands. Octagonal glass pavilion with tropical plants.

A Special Day Return Ticket is available, which includes travel from Glasgow and admission to house and gardens – tel for details.
House & garden open Easter, then May-mid Oct, daily except closed Thu & Thu: house 11.00-16.30, gardens 10.00-17.00.
Visitor reception area. Guided tours. Gift shop. Tearoom. Picnic areas. Audio-visual presentation. Adventure play area. WC. Disabled facilities: access to house and most of gardens. Car and coach parking. Group concessions available. £££.
Tel: 01700 503877 Fax: 01700 505313
Email: contactus@mountstuart.com Web: www.mountstuart.com

Rothesay Castle

Off A845, Rothesay, Bute.
HS NS 086646 LR: 63 (Map ref: 417)
Surrounded by a wet moat and built on a mound or motte, Rothesay Castle consists of an enormous 12th-century shell keep, with four later round towers. In the late 15th century a large rectangular keep and gatehouse were added, which was completed

St Blane's Church, Kingarth, Bute.

by James V after 1541. The sea was formerly much closer to the castle.

The castle was attacked and taken by Norsemen in the 1230s, who cut a hole in the wall with their axes. It was captured in 1263 by King Hakon of Norway, before he was defeated at the battle of Largs, and Rothesay then returned to the king of Scots. The Stewarts were keepers of the castle. Rothesay was held by the English during the Wars of Independence, but was taken by Robert the Bruce, only to be captured again by the English under Edward Balliol in 1334, but was later recaptured by the Scots.

It was a favourite residence of Robert II and Robert III, who may have died here, rather than at Dundonald, in 1406. In 1401 Robert III made his son Duke of Rothesay, a title since taken by the eldest son of the kings of Scots and currently held by Prince Charles. The castle was besieged several times. Argyll's forces torched the castle in 1685, and it was very ruinous until the 19th century when it was partially rebuilt.

Finds from here, including weaponry, cannon balls, keys and candle-holders are in the Bute Museum. There is an exhibition on site.

Open daily all year: Apr-Sep 9.30-18.30; Oct-Mar Mon-Sat 9.30-16.30 except closed Thu PM and Fri, Sun 14.00-16.30; last ticket sold 30 mins before closing; closed 25/26 Dec & 1-3 Jan.

Explanatory panels. Car parking nearby. Group concessions. £.

Tel: 01700 502691

St Blane's Church, Kingarth

Off A844, 2 miles S of Kingarth, Bute.
HS NS 094535 LR: 63 (Map ref: 418)

In a peaceful and pleasant location is the site of a Christian monastery of the 6th century, founded by St Blane, who was born on Bute. The site is surrounded by an enclosure wall, and there are several ruinous buildings, including 'The Cauldron', the purpose of which is unclear. In the middle of the site is the fine ruinous 12th-century chapel. There is also an upper and lower burial yard with some fine gravestones, the upper yard being used for burying men, while the lower was for women.

A spring here, reputedly a holy well (and also believed by some to be a wishing well) is known as St Blane's Well.

Access at all times.
Parking.
Tel: 0131 668 8800   Fax: 0131 668 8888

St Marnock's Chapel, Inchmarnock

Off unlisted track, Midpark, Inchmarnock.
NS 024596 LR: 63 (Map ref: 419)

Not much remains of the small medieval rectangular chapel, dedicated to St Marnock. The associated burial ground was divided into two as a field adjoining has a 'women's burial place', a similar arrangement to that at St Blane's on Bute. The fragments of several crosses or carved stones have been found here, including one inscribed with runes, and are either in the Bute Museum or the Museum of Scotland. This may be the site of an early Christian monastery.

St Mary's Church, Rothesay

On A845, 0.5 miles S of Rothesay Castle, Bute.
HS NS 086637 LR: 63 (Map ref: 420)

The chapel, dedicated to St Mary and also known as Ladykirk, stands next to the modern parish church, and may date from as early as the 13th century. It is all that remains of a larger building, which was also dedicated to St Brioc, a 6th-century saint, and used as the Cathedral of the Isles. The chapel was roofless, but is being restored. It houses two well-preserved stone effigies: one of a warrior from the 14th century, probably a Stewart of Menteith. A sculptured stone, dating from around the 8th century, was found here and is now in the Bute Museum.

A spring, housed in a small building, is known as 'St Mary's Well'.

Access at all times.
Parking.
Tel: 0131 668 8800

Gardens, Animals and Miscellaneous

Ardencraig Garden

Off A844, S of Rothesay, Ardencraig, Bute.
LR: 63 (Map ref: 421)

Ardencraig Gardens feature a wide range of fine floral displays. The Cactus House has a huge variety of cacti, some large in size; and a Fuscia House with an impressive display of colour. There is a small aviary, stream and fish pond. Plants are available for sale.

Open May-Sep, Mon-Fri 9.00-16.30, Sat & Sun 13.00-16.30.
Gift shop. Tearoom. WC. Disabled access. Car and coach parking.
Tel: 01700 504225 ext 204 (council)/504644 (gardens) Fax: 01700 504225

Ascog Hall Fernery and Garden

On A886, 3 miles S of Rothesay, Ascog, Bute.
NS 106634 LR: 63 (Map ref: 422)

Built around 1870, the Victorian fernery, with fine rock work and water pools, has been restored and refurbished with a collection of sub-tropical ferns. The only surviving fern from the original collection, the 'Todea barbara', is said to be around 1000 years old. Ascog Hall was built in 1843, but had become ruinous before being restored only a few years ago.

Open Apr-Oct, Wed-Sun 10.00-17.00; last admission 16.30; closed Mon & Tue.
Guided tours. Partial disabled access. No dogs. Car parking; coaches by appt only. £.
Tel: 01700 504555
Web: www.york.ac.uk/depts/biol/web/units/ground/ascog/welcome.htm

Great and Little (or Lesser) Cumbrae

('isle of the Britons' or 'refuge')

In Brief
Doon the water. Cathedral of the Isles.

Location (see map 11, p 156)
OS Landranger map 63
2 miles SW of mainland at Largs
4 miles E of Bute at Kingarth

Tourist Information Centre
Millport (tel/fax: 01475 530753)
Open Easter-Jun wknds only; open daily Jun-Sep; closed Oct-Easter – contact Largs TIC
(mainland) if unavailable
Largs (mainland) (tel: 01475 673765; fax: 01475 676297)
Open Jan-Dec

How to Get There
Greater Cumbrae by ferry from Largs on mainland to Cumbrae Slip (Portyre) on Great Cumbrae
(15 mins; CalMac tel: 01475 674134). Buses connect to Millport

Notes
An easy way to get round is by bike, and there are also pony rides. There are several painted
rocks on the island, including the Crocodile Rock, Indian Rock and Lion Rock. The National
Watersports Centre (tel: 01475 530757) is located in Millport. There is an eighteen-hole golf
course. Funfair. Fishing. The Museum of the Cumbraes was located in The Garrison House,
but is currently homeless.

Basic Info
The islands of Cumbrae consist of Great Cumbrae Island and Little Cumbrae Island, and have
fine views to the mainland and across to Arran and Bute.

  Great Cumbrae Island is about four miles long and 2.5 miles at its widest. The island is quite
hilly and rises to just over 400 feet at Glaidstane, and the only town is Millport, which is
elegantly arranged around Millport Bay with its sandy beach. Millport is home to the Cathedral
of the Isles, a small church which can seat only 100 worshippers, believed to be the smallest
cathedral in Britain. Unlike many islands in the Hebrides, the population actually grew during
the 19th century, from 506 in 1801 to 1784 in 1891, and it is now around 1500. This was
mainly due to the island becoming a tourist attraction for visitors from Glasgow coming
'doon the water'. Little Cumbrae Island, 1.5 miles south of Great Cumbrae at Millport, is
about two miles long and one mile wide. The island is rocky and hilly, and also rises to over
400 feet.

History

Prehistoric monuments include several burial cairns, and there is an early Christian site at Mid Kirkton. The island was held by the Vikings, and King Hakon is said to have made camp here before going on to defeat at the battle of Largs. Great Cumbrae was a property of the Montgomerys, then the Stewarts, and there was a castle and mansion at Ballikillet [NS 172560], although little remains.

Little Cumbrae was held by the Hunters of Hunterston, then the Montgomery Earls of Eglinton, and was maintained as a hunting forest. There are the ruins of a small chapel dedicated to St Beye, and also of a castle, which was burned by Oliver Cromwell's troops in 1650.

Cathedral of the Isles, Millport, Cumbrae.

Today

Tourism.

Places of Interest

Prehistoric

Druids Stone, Craigengour
Off B899, 1 mile NE of Millport, Craigengour, Great Cumbrae.
NS 176564 LR: 63 (Map ref: 423)
A standing stone, six-feet high, which is said to be called the 'druids stone' or the 'Goulkan Stone', and to commemorate Vikings who were slain at the battle of Largs in 1263.

Sheanawally Cairns
Sheanawally Point, N tip of Little Cumbrae.
NS 155529 LR: 63 (Map ref: 424)
Three burial cairns. A suit of armour, helmet and two swords were reportedly found in one of the cairns in 1813. The two larger cairns are about 30 feet in diameter and survive to a height of about five feet, while the other is much smaller.

Tomont End Cairns
On A860, 3 miles NE of Millport, Tomont End, Great Cumbrae.
NS 183592 LR: 63 (Map ref: 425)
Two burial cairns, about 300 yards apart. The larger formerly had a diameter of about 60 feet and was twelve-feet high, but now much reduced. Urns and flint knives from here are in the Kelvingrove Museum and Bute Museum.

The cairn, lying to the south, is known as 'Lady's Grave' and survives to a height of about six feet with a diameter of some 40 feet. An urn found in the cist here is also in the Kelvingrove Museum.

Historic and Heritage

Ballikillet Castle
Off B899, 0.5 miles N of Millport, Ballikillet, Great Cumbrae.
NS 172560 LR: 63 (Map ref: 426)
Site of castle or mansion, some remains of which survive. It was a property of the Montgomerys, who owned much of the island until the early 18th century.

Cathedral of the Isles
Off A860, College Street, Millport, Great Cumbrae.
NS 166553 LR: 63 (Map ref: 427)
Britain's smallest cathedral, dating from 1851 and designed by William Butterfield. The cathedral has fine stained glass, and there is a collection of carved stones from Mid Kirkton.
Open daily all year.
Parking. Sales area. Picnic area. WC. Retreat House: accommodation available.
Tel: 01475 530353   Fax: 01475 530204
Email: TCCUMBRAE@ARGYLL.ANGLICAN.ORG
Web: WWW.SOL.CO.UK/S/SEDATI/MILLPORT/HTM

Little Cumbrae Castle
On an islet just E of Little Cumbrae.
NS 153514 LR: 63 (Map ref: 428)
Little Cumbrae Castle is a ruined 15th-century keep. It was a property of the Crown, and visited by Robert III, but held by the Hunters of Hunterston until 1515, when the Montgomerys acquired the property following a dispute between the Crown and the Hunters over the ownership of falcons. In the 1650s, the 6th Earl imprisoned Archibald Hamilton, a friend of Cromwell, in the castle before sending him to Stirling to be hanged. Cromwell had the castle sacked, and it was never reoccupied.

Mid Kirkton
Off A860, W of Millport, Mid Kirkton, Great Cumbrae.
NS 157551 LR: 63 (Map ref: 429)
A succession of churches were sited here, the earliest apparently dating from before 642. A later chapel here was dedicated to St Columba, but the last church on the site was abandoned in 1837. Several carved stones have been found here, as well as a cross-slab, and most are kept in the Cathedral of the Isles at Millport.

St Vey's Chapel, Little Cumbrae
Off track, E side of Little Cumbrae.
NS 148518 LR: 63 (Map ref: 430)
Little survives of St Vey's Chapel except foundations. The building was dedicated to St Beye, a 'Scottish virgin and saint', who is said to have died in 896. St Vey's Tomb [NS 147518], a ruinous rectangular structure, is believed to be her burial place.

Gardens, Animals and Miscellaneous

Museum and Marine Biological Station

On A860, 0.5 miles E of Millport, Keppel, Great Cumbrae.

NS 175545   LR: 63   (Map ref: 431)

This is a research centre of the Universities of Glasgow and London, founded in 1887 and extended in 1903. The recently refurbished museum and adjoining aquarium house a number of unique displays from the world of marine science.

Open all year: Oct-May, Mon-Fri 9.30-12.15 & 14.00-16.45; Jun-Sep also Sat.

One week courses available with accommodation and meals.

Tel: 01475 530581   Fax: 01475 530601

Email: d.murden@udcf.gla.ac.uk

Holy Island, Arran.

Arran

('peaked hill' or 'high')

In Brief
'Scotland in Miniature'. Brodick Castle. Machrie Moor Stone Circles. Goatfell.

Location (see map 11, p 156)
OS Landranger map 69
14 miles W of Ayrshire coast
4.5 miles E of Kintyre across Kilbrannan Sound
5 miles SW of S tip of Bute

Tourist Information Centre
Brodick (tel: 01770 302140/302401; fax: 01770 302395)
Open Jan-Dec

How to Get There
By vehicle ferry from Ardrossan on mainland to Brodick on Arran (55 mins; Cal Mac tel: 01294 463470 or 01770 302166)
By ferry from Claonaig on Kintyre to Lochranza on Arran (30 mins; CalMac tel: 01770 302166)

Notes
Boats, bicycles and cars can be hired from several places on the island, and there is paragliding at Kildonan (tel: 01770 820292). Horse riding, sailing, water-skiing, sailboarding and fishing. Outdoor Centre and Field Studies Centre. Seven golf courses.

Silk and Stained Glass Studio at Kinloch Hotel (tel: 01770 860444). Many arts and crafts shops and galleries round the island, as well as the Paterson Arran Kitchen Shop at Lamlash (tel: 01770 600606), Island Cheese Co (tel: 01770 302788) and Scottish Milk Products, which demonstrates cheese making, at Kilmory (tel: 01770 870240).

Basic Info
Sometimes called 'Scotland in Miniature' because of the variety of landscapes, Arran is one of the largest islands of the Hebrides, and is twenty miles long and some ten miles wide. The island has a range of scenery: wild, high and rugged to the north; rolling, green and fertile to the south. The north is quite mountainous, with ten peaks over 2000 feet, including Goatfell at 2868 feet, Caisteal Abhail at 2752 feet, and Ben Tarsuinn at 2706 feet. The island's profile is said to resemble a 'Sleeping Warrior', the effigy of a warrior laid out on a bier.

A relatively large proportion of the island is covered in coniferous forestry plantations, and there are a series of forest walks – information from Brodick TIC or Forest Enterprise (01770 302218).

The island has a population of 3500, although during the summer it is much higher. The largest village is at Brodick, but there are sizeable settlements at Lamlash, Whiting Bay, Blackwaterfoot, Lochranza and Sannox.

History

Arran has been occupied for thousands of years, and there are many prehistoric remains. The most impressive of these are the series of stone circles on Machrie Moor, which is one of the most important early sites in Scotland. There are other stones and circles, and also the remains of several chambered cairns, as well as several other impressive Iron Age fortifications.

The island was sacked by the Vikings in 797, and was long held by the Norsemen, being one of the islands claimed by Magnus Barelegs in 1098: Brodick means 'broad bay' (from the Norse *breithr-vik*). Somerled wrested the island from the Norsemen, but was assassinated at Renfrew in 1164. King Hakon of Norway marshalled his longships off the island before going on to defeat at Largs. Arran finally passed to the kingdom of Scots in 1266.

Robert the Bruce raised his standard on Arran in 1306, and along with Sir James Douglas, crossed back to Ayrshire – a standing stone on Kingscross Point is said to mark the place – after seizing Brodick Castle, and eventually drove the English from Scotland. A cave, known as King's Cave, is said to be where Bruce sheltered after his earlier defeat at Methven, and where he may have seen the famous spider, attempting to weave its web.

Arran was held by the Stewarts of Menteith, then briefly by the Boyds in 1467, but in 1503 was granted to the Hamiltons, eventually Earls then Dukes of Hamilton, who were important in the history of Scotland. Their base on Arran was at Brodick Castle, where there is a fine castle and mansion, now in the care of The National Trust for Scotland. There are other castles at Lochranza, which is particularly picturesque; Kildonan; and apparently two small towers defending Lamlash Bay, one at Whitehouse [NS 024308] in Lamlash itself, the other on the Holy Island.

Much of the island was cleared for sheep in the 19th century, but the island became very popular with holidaymakers from Glasgow going 'doon the water'. A distillery at Lochranza was recently opened.

Today

Tourism. Farming. Crafts. Cheese. Fishing. Whisky

Holy Island or Eilean Molaise

An island off the east coast of Arran, one mile east of Lamlash. It is two miles long and 0.5 miles wide, and is very hilly, rising to over 1000 feet. A private ferry runs an hourly service to the island (tel: 01770 600998). There was a monastery on the island, founded by St Molaise in the 6th century, and he is believed to be associated with a cave [NS 053303], known as the Smugglers' Cave, and one wall is inscribed with several crosses. A small tower was built on the north-west of the island to defend Lamlash Bay, a fragment of which stood until about 1879. It is said to have been built by Somerled. There is a now a Buddhist centre and retreat on the island.

Pladda

Islet ('flat island') 0.5 miles south of Arran at Kildonan. The island has associations with St Blaise of Pladda; and there is a lighthouse, which was first put here in 1790.

Places of Interest

Prehistoric

Auchgallon Cairn

Off A841, 4 miles N of Blackwaterfoot,
Auchgallon, Arran.

HS NR 893346 LR: 69 (Map ref: 432)

A Bronze Age burial cairn, 50 feet in diameter, surrounded by a circle or kerb of fifteen standing
stones. The stones vary in height but the tallest is
over seven feet.

Open all year.
Parking Nearby
Tel: 0131 668 8800   Fax: 0131 668 8888

Blairmore Glen Standing Stones

On A841, 2 miles S of Brodick, Blairmore Glen,
Arran.

NS 019334 LR: 69 (Map ref: 433)

By the road at the edge of the forestry plantation
are a group of four massive boulders, the biggest
of which stands to a height of nearly four feet. A
burial cist was found within the grouping.

Carn Ban

Off A841, 3.5 miles W of Whiting Bay, Carn Ban,
Arran.

HS NR 991262 LR: 69 (Map ref: 434)

In a clearing in a forestry plantation are the remains
of a Neolithic burial cairn, about 100 feet by 60 feet
with a forecourt. The cairn rises to fifteen feet in
height, and several upright stones can be seen forming the kerb and court. The chamber was divided
into four compartments, but is full of debris.

Access at all times.
Parking nearby
Tel: 0131 668 8800

Clachaig Cairn

Off A841, 5 miles SE of Blackwaterfoot, Clachaig,
Arran.

NR 949212 LR: 69 (Map ref: 435)

Not far west from Torrylin Cairn is another chambered cairn, which survives as a mound up to ten
feet high. A track cuts across the cairn at one end.

Deer Park Standing Stones

Off A841, 1 mile NW of Brodick, Deerpark,
Arran.

NS 006374 LR: 69 (Map ref: 436)

A group of three standing stones, located across
the road which leads from Brodick Castle. The tallest is over eleven feet high, while the other two
stones are about eight feet.

Dippen Head Fort

Off A841, 2 miles S of Whiting Bay, Dippin Head,
Arran.

NS 051224 LR: 69 (Map ref: 437)

The remains of a fort, defended on two sides by
gorges and on the third by a rampart, which survives to a height of eight feet. Traces of two entrances, one in the middle of the rampart, can be
seen.

Druid Stone, Auchencar

Off A841, 5 miles N of Blackwaterfoot,
Auchencar, Arran.

NR 891363 LR: 69 (Map ref: 438)

Standing on a stony knoll is a tall standing stone,
over fifteen feet high. A broken stone lies nearby.

Giants Graves, Whiting Bay

Off A841, 0.5 miles S of Whiting Bay, Giants
Graves, Arran.

NS 043247 LR: 69 (Map ref: 439)

The remains of two chambered cairns, known as
'Giants Graves'

The northernmost cairn is about four feet high
and 40 feet long and 36 feet wide. There are indications of the upright slabs forming the chamber.

The southernmost cairn is larger, being 70 feet
long and 40 feet at its widest. The cairn survives to
a height of five feet, and part of a forecourt is visible.

There is another cairn, Torr an Loisgte, nearby
[NS 040248].

Kilpatrick Prehistoric Settlement

Off A841, 1 mile S of Blackwaterfoot, Kilpatrick,
Arran.

HS NR 906262 LR: 69 (Map ref: 440)

The ruins of a round dry-stone homestead of un-
known date, with a more recent enclosure wall. 0.5
miles walk to site.

Access at all times.
Parking nearby.
Tel: 0131 668 8800   Fax: 0131 668 8888

Kingscross

Off A841, 2.5 miles SE of Lamlash, Kingscross Point, Arran.
NS 056283 LR: 69 (Map ref: 441)

The ruinous round dun survives to a height of just over five feet. The entrance can be traced.

A low mound [NS 056282], near to the dun, was the burial place of a Viking. The site has been excavated, and human bones were found here, along with rivets from a boat, decorated whalebone, a bronze coin and vitrified stone. These finds are in the Museum of Scotland.

A stone [NS 056282] is said to mark the place where Robert the Bruce set out for the Scottish mainland on his eventually successful attempt to drive the English out of Scotland.

Machrie Moor Stone Circles

Off A841, 3 miles N of Blackwaterfoot, Machrie Moor, Arran.
HS NR 910324 LR: 69 (Map ref: 442)

This is a very important and impressive complex of stone circles and cairns. There are the remains of five stone circles.

One circle [NR 912324] is made up of eleven stones, six granite boulders and five slabs, set alternately.

The stones of another circle [NR 911324] are the most memorable. Only three upright stones sur-

vive, but the tallest is over sixteen feet tall, while the lowest is still over twelve feet.

Of another circle [NR 910324] only one erect stone remains, although this stone is fourteen-feet high.

The fourth [910323] is a setting of four low boulders on the arc of an ellipse.

The fifth [NR 909323], and probably the most interesting is known as Suidhe Coire Fhionn ('Fingal's cauldron seat'). It consists of two rings of boulders. The inner is made up of eight stones, about three to four feet high. The outer consists of fifteen slightly smaller stones.

There has been at least one other circle [NR 912324].

Access at all times – involves 1.5 mile walk.
Tel: 0131 668 8800   Fax: 0131 668 8888

Mayish Standing Stone

Off A841, S of Brodick, Mayish, Arran.
NS 018355 LR: 69 (Map ref: 443)

A standing stone, which is over ten feet tall.

Monyquil Standing Stone

Off B880, 4.5 miles W of Brodick, Monyquil, Arran.
NR 941353 LR: 69 (Map ref: 444)

A large standing stone, over eight feet high, is located near a burial cairn.

Machrie Moor Standing Stones, Arran.

Brodick Castle, Arran.

Moss Farm Road Cairn

Off A841, 3 miles N of Blackwaterfoot, Tormore, Arran.

HS NR 901326 LR: 69 (Map ref: 445)

The remains of a Bronze Age cairn, about 75 feet in diameter, now surrounded by a kerb of several upright stones. The tallest of these is just over four feet high

Access at all times.

Parking nearby.

Tel: 0131 668 8800 Fax: 0131 668 8888

Stronach Standing Stone

On A841, 0.5 miles NW of Brodick, Stronach, Arran.

NS 010366 LR: 69 (Map ref: 446)

By the main road is a standing stone, over nine feet tall.

The Doon, Drumadoon

Off A841, 1 mile NW of Blackwaterfoot, Drumadoon, Arran.

NR 886292 LR: 69 (Map ref: 447)

Standing on a raised area on a headland near the sea, The Doon consists of an unusually large fort, which covers about twelve acres. A ruinous wall

encloses the area, and the entrance can be traced. A five-foot high standing stone survives within the wall.

Torr a' Chaisteal

Off A841, 3.5 miles S of Blackwaterfoot, Corriecravie, Arran.

HS NR 921232 LR: 69 (Map ref: 448)

The scant remains of a dun, round in shape, and defended by an outer rampart.

Access at all times.

Tel: 0131 668 8800 Fax: 0131 668 8888

Torrylinn Cairn

Off A841, 5 miles SE of Blackwaterfoot, Lagg, Arran.

HS NR 955211 LR: 69 (Map ref: 449)

A ruinous Neolithic chambered burial cairn, surviving to a height of six feet and about 65 feet in diameter. The cairn has been robbed and disturbed, and the chamber, with its compartments, is discernible.

Access at all times.

Parking nearby.

Tel: 0131 668 8800 Fax: 0131 668 8888

Historic and Heritage

Arran Heritage Museum

On A841, 1.5 miles N of Brodick, Rosaburn, Arran.

LR: 69   (Map ref: 450)

The museum features an original 18th-century croft farm with smiddy, cottage, dairy, coach house and stables. There is a large garden and special display area, which is changed annually, as well as exhibits on shipping, geology, archaeology, the Vikings and local history.

Open Easter-Oct, daily 10.30-1630.

Guided tours. Explanatory displays. Gift shop. Tearoom. Picnic area. Garden. WC. Disabled access. Car and coach parking. Group concessions. £.

Tel: 01770 302636   Fax: by arrangement
Email: tom.k.macleod@btinternet.com

Brodick Castle

Off A841, 1.5 miles N of Brodick, Cladach, Arran.

NTS NS 016378 LR: 69   (Map ref: 451)

Occupying a magnificent site overlooking Brodick Bay, Brodick Castle incorporates an ancient castle which was extended and remodelled in 1844 by the architect James Gillespie Graham.

Arran was held by the Norsemen until driven out by Somerled in the 12th century, although the property only passed to the Scottish Crown in 1266. The Stewarts of Menteith built the original castle, but it was held by the English during the Wars of Independence, until 1307 when recaptured by the Scots. Arran passed to the Hamiltons in 1503 and the castle saw much action down the centuries. The castle was remodelled for the marriage of Princess Marie of Baden to the 11th Duke of Hamilton. In 1958 Brodick was taken over by The National Trust for Scotland.

A 'Grey Lady' is said to haunt the older part of the castle, and a White Deer is apparently only seen when one of the chiefs of the Hamiltons is near death.

Castle open daily 1 Apr (or Good Friday if earlier)-Oct 11.00-16.30, last admission 16.00pm; Jul-Aug daily 11.00-17.00, last admission 16.30 restaurant 11.00-17.00; reception centre & shop 10.00-17.00; garden & country park open all year 9.30-sunset; Goatfell open all year.

Collections of furniture, porcelain, pictures and silver. Gift shop. Licensed restaurant. WC. Gardens and country park, ice house, summer house and adventure playground. Nature trail and access to Goatfell. Disabled WC and access. Car and coach parking. ££.

Tel: 01770 302202   Fax: 01770 302312

Kilbride

Off A841, NW of Lamlash, Kilbride, Arran.

NS 033323 LR: 69   (Map ref: 452)

The church of St Bride, dating from the 14th century, is now a shell, but several sculptured stones and grave slabs are built into the walls and lie in the burial ground. One is believed to be the grave of James Hamilton, 3rd Earl of Arran, who died in 1609. The chapel was used as the parish church for the east side of Arran.

Access at all reasonable times.
Parking.

King's Cave, Drumadoon

Off A841, 2 miles N of Blackwaterfoot, Torr Righ Mor, Arran.

NR 884309 LR: 69   (Map ref: 453)

The cliffs here have several caves, one of which is known as 'King's Cave' from the tradition that Robert the Bruce sheltered here after being crowned king in 1306 – one story is that it was here that he saw the famous spider. It was, however, apparently known as Fingal's Cave as late as the 18th century, and may have been used as a Christian retreat or hermitage.

The cave has numerous carvings, including crosses, the figure of a man, horses, deer and serpents, as well as more recent graffiti. A seat is carved into the rock. A grille has been fitted across the mouth of the cave.

Lamlash Parish Church

On A841, Shore Road, Lamlash, Arran.

NS 026309 LR: 69   (Map ref: 454)

The Victorian parish church has a 90-foot tower, and was built by the 12th Duke of Hamilton in 1886 to replace an earlier building. At the front of the church is an old cross and baptismal font, said to have been brought here from the chapel or monastery on Holy Island.

Open May-Sep, Mon-Fri – check opening times and days.
Sales area. WC. Parking Nearby.
Tel: 01770 600787

Lochranza Castle

Off A841, 10 miles N of Brodick, Lochranza, Arran.

HS NR 933507 LR: 69 (Map ref: 455)

In a beautiful location, Lochranza Castle is a ruined L-plan tower house, much of which dates from the 13th or 14th century, but which was remodelled in the late 16th century. Lochranza was used as a hunting lodge by the kings of Scots, and is said to have

been visited by Robert the Bruce. The castle may have been built by the Stewarts of Menteith, the MacDonald Lord of the Isles or the Campbells, who appear to have held the property in 1315. It passed to the Montgomerys, and James IV used it as a base to attack the Lords of the Isles in the 1490s.

There is said to have been a convent of nuns at Lochranza, dedicated to St Bridget.
Key available from Post Office/local shop.
Parking.
Tel: 0131 668 8800   Fax: 0131 668 8888

Arts, Crafts and Industry

Arran Aromatics

Off A841, 1 mile N of Brodick, Home Farm, Arran.

LR: 69 (Map ref: 456)

Set in a courtyard, Arran Aromatics is the home of Scotland's leading producer of natural soaps and body care products. The visitor centre features

Lochranza Castle, Arran.

Cleopatra's bath-time secrets and more with the 'History of Soap displays'. Production areas of the factory can be viewed from the gallery – where the newest Arran Candleworks products are being produced, along with many soaps and body care products. A full range of products are for sale in the shop.

Open all year: Easter- end Oct, daily 9.30-17.30; Nov-Easter please phone in advance.

Explanatory displays. Gift shop. Restaurant and tearoom. WC. Disabled access. Car parking.
Tel: 01770 302595   Fax: 01770 302599
Email: info@arran-aromatics.co.uk
Web: www.arran-aromatics.co.uk

Balmichael Visitor Centre

On B880, 7 miles SE of Brodick, Balmichael, Arran.

NR 925315   LR: 69   (Map ref: 457)

Converted from farm buildings and courtyard, the centre consists of a coffee shop, three craft shops, an antique shop and pottery. There is also an adventure playground and indoor play barn, as well as quad biking.

Open Easter-Oct, Mon-Sat 10.00-17.00, Sun 12.00-17.00; Nov-Easter, Wed-Sun 10.00-17.00.

Gift shop. Coffee shop. Picnic area. WC. Disabled access. Car and coach parking.
Tel: 01770 860430

Crafts of Arran

Off A841, Whiting Bay, Arran.

LR: 69   (Map ref: 458)

Quality crafts produced on Arran are featured here, including paintings, knitwear and jewellery as well as selected Scottish crafts.

Open Easter-Oct.
Tel: 01770 700251   Fax: 01770 700251

Isle of Arran Distillery

Off A841, 14 miles N of Brodick, Lochranza, Arran.

LR: 69   (Map ref: 459)

Set in a scenic location at Lochranza, Isle of Arran Distillery is the newest single malt whisky distillery in Scotland, having only been in production since 1995. The visitor centre features interactive displays and a short film illustrating whisky production on Arran over the last 150 years; and a tour concludes with a free dram. An audio-visual room is located

in the mock 18th-century crofter's inn.

Open daily all year 10.00-17.00; closed Christmas and New Year; for group booking contact the distillery; restaurant open 11.00-22.00; closed Wed evening; winter opening times vary.

Visitor centre. Guided tours. Audio-visual programme and explanatory displays. Gift shop. Restaurant. Picnic area. Garden. WC. Disabled access. Induction loop for audio-visual programme. Car and coach parking. ££. Coach parties welcome but should tel in advance. Private functions and conference facilities.
Tel: 01770 830264   Fax: 01770 830364
Email: arran.distillers@btinternet.com
Web: www.arranwhisky.com

Kilmory Workshop

Off A841, N of Kilmory, Cloined, Arran.

LR: 69   (Map ref: 460)

The workshop features woodwork and pottery, all items hand-made on the premises. The woodwork is made from local timber, sawn and seasoned in Kilmory, and includes turned work, furniture and toys. There is also hand-thrown stoneware domestic pottery. Fine views to Kintyre and Ayrshire.

Open summer, Tue-Fri 10.00-17.30; winter, Mon & Wed-Fri 10.00-17.30; tel to check other times.
Tel: 01770 870310   Fax: 01770 870310

Gardens, Animals and Miscellaneous

South Bank Farm Park

On A841, 14 miles S of Brodick, East Bennan, Arran.

NR 993217   LR: 69   (Map ref: 461)

A 60 acre working farm with various rare and minority breeds of farm animals: poultry, Highland cattle, red deer, and Clydesdale horse. Other features are a farm trail and superb views, as well as sheepdog demonstration on Tuesday and Thursday at 14.30.

Open Easter-Sep, daily 10.00-17.00.

Picnic area. WC. Disabled access. Car and limited coach parking. Group concessions. £.
Tel: 01770 820221

Other inshore islands

Handa

Island ('sand') two miles north-west of mainland at Scourie, across Sound of Handa. The island has steep cliffs and rises to 406 feet. Thousands of seabirds nest in the cliffs and the island is a nature reserve.

Calbha Mor and Calbha Beag

Islets off coast in Eddrachillis Bay.

Oldany Island

Island, 1.5 miles long, just off coast, three miles east of Point of Stoer, which has fine pasture. There is an old burial ground here.

Isle Ristol

Island, one mile in diameter and rising to 234 feet, just off coast, three miles north-west of Achiltibuie. An islet **Eilean Mullagrach** is to the west.

Summer Isles (Tanera Mor and Tanera Beg)

Group of islands 1.5 miles west of coast at Achiltibuie. Tanera Mor ('big harbour island') is about two miles long and rises to 406 feet in height, while Tanera Beg ('small harbour island') is to the west. The islands are bare and rocky, but Tanera Mor supported a population if 119 in 1881, although it had been abandoned by the 1930s. There are a few crofters on the island.

Other nearby islets include **Glas-leac Mor**, **Eilean Fada Mor**, **Eilean Dubh**, and two miles to the south-east **Horse Island**, as well as **Priest Island** and **Bottle Island**.

Isle Martin

Triangular-shaped island just off coast, three miles north-west of Ullapool, which is owned by the RSPB.

Gruinard

Island ('green bay'), 1.5 miles long and 0.5 miles wide, in Gruinard Bay. It was infected with anthrax in 1942 during the World War II as an experiment to test its effectiveness for biological warfare. It was not pronounced safe until 1987.

Isle of Ewe

Island, two miles long, in Loch Ewe, which had a 'pleasant cultivated surface'.

Longa Island

Island, one mile long, at the mouth of Loch Gairloch.

Island Macaskin, Eilean Righ, and Eilean Mhic Chrion

Partly wooded islands in Loch Craignish off Argyll. Eilean Righ is some two miles long but is very thin, and there are the remains of two duns. Off Craignish Point are several islets including

Garbh Reisa, Reisa ant-Sruith and **Reisa Mhic Phaidean**.

Island of Danna

Island, about 1.5 miles long, joined to the mainland by a causeway, at the mouth of Loch Sween. It is said to have once had a castle.

Island Davaar

Small island at the mouth of Campbeltown Loch. It rises to 379 feet and has a lighthouse.

Sanda Island

Island, about one mile long, off the south-eastern tip of the Mull of Kintyre, two miles south of the coast. It has steep cliffs to the west, rises to 404 feet, and also has a lighthouse on the south coast. There are also the remains of an old chapel. To the north is **Sheep Island**.

Index of Islands

A

Am Fraoch Eilean (Jura), 139, 140

Arran, 167-174

Ascrib Islands (Skye), 76

B

Bac Mor(Dutchman's Cap), Treshnish (Mull), 110

Baleshare and Illeray (North Uist), 46, 47

Barra, 64-65, 67-68

Belnahua (Slate Island), 128

Benbecula, 53-56

Bernera Island (Lismore), 123

Berneray (Barra), 66, 67

Berneray (Sound of Harris), 45, 47, 49, 51

Boreray (Sound of Harris), 45

Boreray (St Kilda), 40

Bottle Island (Summer Isles, Wester Ross), 175

Brosdale Island (Jura), 139

Bute, 157-162

C

Cairnburg, Treshnish (Mull), 110

Calbha Mor and Calbha Beag (Eddrachillis Bay), 175

Calvay (Loch Eynort, South Uist), 60

Calvay (South Uist), 60, 62

Calve Island (Mull), 106, 110

Calve Island (Mull), 107

Canna, 92-96

Cara (Gigha), 153

Coll, 97-99

Colonsay, 134-137

Crowlin Islands (Skye), 75

Cumbrae, 163-166

E

Earraid (Mull), 110

Easdale (Slate Islands), 128

Eigg, 92-96

Eileach an Naoimh, Garvellachs (Slate Islands), 129

Eilean Chaluim Chille (Lewis), 26

Eilean Dubh (Summer Isles, Wester Ross), 175

Eilean Dubh Beag (Slate Islands), 128

Eilean Dubh Mor (Slate Islands), 128

Eilean Fada (Summer Isles, Wester Ross), 175

Eilean Fladday (Raasay), 78

Eilean Iasgaich (South Uist), 60

Eilean Iubhard (Lewis), 26

Eilean Kearstay (Loch Roag, Lewis), 26

Eilean Mhic Chrion (Loch Craignish, Argyll), 175

Eilean Molaise (Arran), 168

Eilean Mor (Knapdale), 141

Eilean Mor (South Uist), 60

Eilean Mullacrach (Achiltibuie), 175

Eilean Righ (Loch Craignish, Argyll), 175

Eilean Tigh (Raasay), 78

Eilean Trodday (Skye), 76

Ensay (Sound of Harris), 29

Eorsa (Mull), 109

Eriska (Lismore), 123

Eriskay , 60, 63

F

Fiaray (Barra), 65

Fiola Meadhonach (Slate Islands), 128

Fladda, Treshnish (Mull), 110

Fladda-Chuain (Skye), 76

Flannan Isles (Lewis), 27

Floday (Loch Roag, Lewis), 26

Flodda (Benbecula), 54

Flodday (Vatersay), 66

Flodday More and Flodday Beg (North Uist), 46

Fuday and Orosay (Barra), 65

Fuiay and Flodday (Barra), 65

G

Garbh Reisa (Craignish Point, Argyll), 176

Garvellachs (Slate Islands), 129, 130-131

Gasay (South Uist), 60

Gasker (Harris), 29

Gigha, 152-155

Gigulum (Gigha), 153

Glas-Leac Mor (Summer Isles, Wester Ross), 175

Gometra (Mull), 109, 112

Great Bernera (Lewis), 25, 32, 34

Great Cumbrae, 163-166

Grimsay (North Uist), 45-6, 48, 51

Gruinard (Wester Ross), 175

Gunna (Coll), 98

H

Handa (Scourie), 175,

Harlosh Island (Skye), 76

Harris, 22-23, 28-29, 31-39

Heisker or Monach Islands (North Uist), 46

Hellisay and Gighay (Barra), 65

Hirta see St Kilda, 40-41

Holy Island or Eilean Molaise (Arran), 168

Horse Island (Summer Isles, Wester Ross), 175

I

Inch Kenneth (Mull), 109-110, 113, 115

Inchmarnock (Bute), 158, 162

Insh Island (Slate Islands), 128

Iona, 119-121

Isay (Skye), 76

Island Davaar (Campbeltown Loch, Kintyre), 176

Island Macaskin (Loch Craignish, Argyll), 175,

Island of Danna (Loch Sween, Argyll), 176
Islay, 142-151
Isle Martin (Ullapool, Wester Ross), 175
Isle of Ewe (Loch Ewe, Wester Ross), 175
Isle Ristol (Achiltibuie), 175

J
Jura, 138-141

K
Keava (Loch Roag, Lewis), 26
Keiravagh Islands (Benbecula), 54
Kerrera, 125-126
Killegray (Sound of Harris), 30
Kirkibost Island (North Uist), 45

L
Lewis , 22-25, 31-39
Lingay (Sound of Harris), 45
Lingay (Vatersay), 66
Lismore, 122-124
Little Bernera (Lewis), 26
Little Colonsay (Mull), 109
Little Cumbrae, 163-166
Longa Island (Loch Gairloch, Wester Ross), 175
Longay (Skye), 75
Luing (Slate Islands), 128, 130
Luirsay (South Uist), 60
Lunga (Slate Islands), 128
Lunga, Treshnish (Mull), 110

M
Mingulay (Barra), 66
Monach Islands see Heisker, 46
Muck, 92-96
Muldoanich (Vatersay), 66
Mull, 106-107, 111-118

N
Nave Island (Islay), 144
North Uist, 43-45, 47-52

O
Oldany Island (Point of Stoer), 175
Oransay (North Uist), 45

Orasay Island (Loch Roag, Lewis), 26
Ornish (South Uist), 60
Oronsay (Colonsay), 134-137
Oronsay (Skye), 76
Orosay (South Uist), 60
Orsay and Eilean Mhic Coinnich (Islay), 144

P
Pabay (Skye), 76
Pabbay (Sound of Harris), 30
Pabbay (Vatersay), 66, 68
Pabbay (South Uist), 60
Pabay Mor (Lewis), 26
Pladda (Arran), 168
Pladda and Eilean Dubh (Lismore), 123
Priest Island (Summer Isles, Wester Ross), 175

R
Raasay, 77-91
Reisa Ant-Sruith (Craignish Point, Argyll), 176
Reisa Mhic Phaidean (Craignish Point, Argyll), 176
Rona (Lewis), 26, 37
Rona (Raasay), 77-78
Ronay (North Uist), 46
Rubha Fiola (Slate Islands), 128
Rum, 92-96

S
Sanday (Small Isles), 92-96
Sanday Island (Mull of Kintyre), 176
Sandray (Vatersay), 66, 67
Scalpay (Harris), 29
Scalpay (Skye), 75
Scarba (Slate Islands), 129
Scarp (Harris), 29
Scotasay (Harris), 29
Seaforth Island (Lewis), 26
Seil (Slate Islands), 128, 130, 131
Sheep Island (Mull of Kintyre), 176
Shiant Isles (Lewis), 26
Shillay (Sound of Harris), 30
Shillay Mor (South Uist), 60

Shuna (Slate Islands), 128
Shuna Island (Lismore), 123, 124
Skye, 72-75, 79-91
Slate Islands, 127-131
Small Isles (Jura), 139
Small Isles, 92-96
Soay (Skye), 76
Soay (St Kilda), 40
Soay Mor and Soay Beg (Harris), 29
South Uist, 58-59, 61-63
St Kilda or Hirta, 40-41
Stack Islands (Eriskay), 60
Staffa (Mull), 108-9
Stockinish Island (Harris), 29
Stuley (South Uist), 60
Summer Isles (Wester Ross), 175

T
Tanera Mor and Tanera Beag (Summer Isles, Wester Ross), 175
Taransay (Harris), 29, 31, 33, 37
Tarner Island (Skye), 76
Texa (Islay), 144
Tiree, 100-103
Torsa (Slate Islands), 128, 130
Treshnish Islands (Mull), 110, 113-114

U
Ulva (Mull), 109, 112, 114, 117

V
Vacsay (Loch Roag, Lewis), 26
Vallay (North Uist), 45, 48
Vatersay, 65-66
Vuia Mor (Loch Roag, Lewis), 26

W
Wiay (Benbecula), 54
Wiay (Skye), 76

Index of Places of Interest

A

Achadun Castle (Lismore), 124
Achamore Gardens (Gigha), 154
Achnancarranan Standing Stones (Islay), 145
Aird an Runair Settlement (North Uist), 47
Aird a' Mhorlan Burial Ground (North Uist), 50
Airidh na h-Aon Oidhche Cairn (Benbecula), 55
Airidhan an t-Sruthain Gairbh Cairn (North Uist), 47
Alt nan Ba (Islay), 145
An Cala Garden (Seil), 131
An Cara, Loch an Athain (South Uist), 61
An Carra, Beinn a' Charra (North Uist), 47
An Dunan, Lowlandman's Bay (Jura), 140
An Lanntair (Lewis), 37
An Sean Chaisteal (Mull), 111
An Sgurr Fort (Eigg), 95
An Tuireann Arts Centre (Skye), 88
Annait, Skye (Skye), 82
Ardbeg Distillery (Islay), 149
Ardencraig Garden (Bute), 162
Ardfad Castle (Seil), 130
Ardlamey Cairn (Gigha), 154
Ardnacross Cairns and Standing Stones (Mull), 111
Arnol Blackhouse Museum (Lewis), 34
Aros Castle (Mull), 113
Aros Castle (Jura), 140
Aros Experience (Skye), 82
Arran Aromatics (Arran), 173-174
Arran Heritage Museum (Arran), 172
Ascog Hall Fernery and Garden (Bute), 162
Ascog House (Bute), 160
Auchgallon Cairn (Arran), 169
Aurora Crafts (Skye), 88

B

Bagh na h-Uamha Stone (Rum), 95
Balinoe Standing Stone (Tiree), 102
Baliscate Standing Stones (Mull), 111
Ballikillet Castle (Great Cumbrae), 165
Ballinaby Standing Stones (Islay), 145
Ballycastle Dun (Luing), 130
Balmichael Visitor Centre (Arran), 174
Barp Reineval (South Uist), 61

Barpa Langass (North Uist), 47
Barpa nam Feannag (North Uist), 47
Barr Leathan Standing Stone (Mull), 111
Barra Heritage and Cultural Centre (Barra), 67
Beinn Tighe Souterrain (Canna), 95
Beinn a' Chlaidh Stone (Berneray), 47
Ben Hogh Rocking Stone (Coll), 99
Bernera Centre (Great Bernera), 34
Bicker's Houses, Bute (Bute), 159
Blackpark Stone Circle (Bute), 159
Blairmore Glen Standing Stones (Arran), 169
Borgh Pottery (Lewis), 37
Borline Church and Cross (Skye), 82
Borve Castle (Benbecula), 55
Borve Standing Stones (Barra), 67
Borve Standing Stones (Skye), 79
Borvemore Studios and Cafe (Harris), 38
Bowmore Distillery (Islay), 149
Breachacha Castle (Coll), 99
Brochel Castle (Raasay), 82
Brodick Castle (Arran), 172
Bunnahabhain Distillery (Islay), 149-150
Burg (Mull), 111
Bute Museum (Bute), 160

C

Cairnburg Castle (Treshnish Islands), 113-114
Caisteal Bheagram (South Uist), 62
Caisteal Calvay (South Uist), 62
Caisteal Camus (Skye), 82
Caisteal Maol (Skye), 82
Caisteal Uisdein (Skye), 82-83
Caisteal nan Con (Torsa), 130
Callanish Standing Stones (Lewis), 31
Camus an Staca Standing Stone (Jura), 140
Canna Cross (Canna), 95
Caol Ila Distillery (Islay), 150
Caolas Standing Stone (Tiree), 102
Caravat Barp (North Uist), 47
Carinish Stone Circle (North Uist), 47
Carn Ban (Arran), 169
Carn Liath, Balgown (Skye), 79
Carn Liath, Kensaleyre (Skye), 79
Carn Liath, Struanmore (Skye), 79
Carn a' Mharc (Lewis), 31
Carnan a' Ghrodhair Souterrain (Lewis), 31

Carnan nan Long Cairn (Illeray), 47
Carnduncan (Islay), 145
Carrachan Standing Stones (Mull), 111
Carraigh Bhan (Islay), 145
Castle Coeffin (Lismore), 124
Castle Keep (Skye), 88
Castle Loch Heylipol (Tiree), 102
Castle Shuna (Lismore), 124
Castle Sinclair (Barra), 68
Cathedral of St Moluag, Lismore (Lismore), 124
Cathedral of the Isles (Great Cumbrae), 165
Ceann Hulavig Stone Circle (Lewis), 31
Cill Chaitriona (Colonsay), 136
Cill Chroisd (Skye), 83
Cill an Ailein, Glen Aros (Mull), 114
Cill an t-Suidhe (Lismore), 124
Cillchriosd Standing Stone (Mull), 111
Cille Bharra (Barra), 68
Cille Mhic Eoghainn (Ulva), 114
Clac Mhic Leoid (Harris), 31
Clach Ard (Skye), 79
Clach Mhic-'Illean (Islay), 145
Clach Mhor a' Che (North Uist), 47
Clach an Teampull (Taransay), 31
Clach an Trushal (Lewis), 31
Clach an Tursa (Lewis), 31
Clach an t-Sagairt (North Uist), 50-51
Clach na Gruagach Standing Stone (Colonsay), 136
Clach na h-Annait (Skye), 79
Clachaig Cairn (Arran), 169
Clachan Cross (Lismore), 124
Cladh Maolrithe (Berneray), 51
Cladh Orain (Tiree), 102
Cladh a' Bhearnaig (Kerrera), 126
Claig Castle (Jura), 140
Clan Donald Centre (Skye), 83
Clettraval Chambered Cairn (North Uist), 47-48
Cloch-thuill Stone (Oronsay), 136
Cnoc Ceann a' Gharaidh Stone Circle (Lewis), 32
Cnoc Fillibhir Bheag Stone Circle (Lewis), 32
Cnoc Nan Guaillean Standing Stone (Islay), 145
Cnoc a' Bhadain (Coll), 99
Cnoc nan Gobhar, Kilmarie (Skye), 79
Co Leis Thu? Genealogy and Exhibition Centre (Harris), 35
Colbost Croft Museum (Skye), 83

The Hebrides

Colonsay House Gardens (Colonsay), 136-137
Columba Centre (Mull), 114
Coroghon Castle (Canna), 95
Coultoon Stone Circle (Islay), 145
Crafts of Arran (Arran), 174
Croft Crafts (Harris), 38
Croft Studio (Skye), 88

D

Dandelion Designs and Images Gallery (Skye), 88-89
Deer Park Standing Stones (Arran), 169
Dervaig Standing Stones (Mull), 111-112
Dippen Head Fort (Arran), 169
Doune Broch Centre (Lewis), 32
Druid Stone, Auchencar (Arran), 169
Druids Stone, Craigengour (Great Cumbrae), 165
Druid's Stone, East Tarbert Bay (Gigha), 154
Druim an Airidh Fhada Cairn (Coll), 99
Druim na h-Uamha Souterrain (North Uist), 48
Duart Castle (Mull), 114-115
Dun Aisgain (Mull), 112
Dun Ara (Mull), 112
Dun Ardtreck (Skye), 79
Dun Ban, Grimsay (Grimsay), 48
Dun Ban, Loch Caravat (North Uist), 48
Dun Ban, Ulva (Ulva), 112
Dun Baravat (Great Bernera), 32
Dun Beag (Skye), 79
Dun Bharpa Chambered Cairn (Barra), 67
Dun Bhoraraic (Islay), 145
Dun Boreraig (Skye), 79
Dun Borodale (Raasay), 79-80
Dun Borrafiach (Skye), 80
Dun Borranish (Lewis), 32-33
Dun Borve (Harris), 33
Dun Bragar (Lewis), 33
Dun Briste (Berneray), 67
Dun Buidhe (Benbecula), 55
Dun Burgidale (Bute), 159
Dun Carloway (Lewis), 33
Dun Channa (Canna), 95
Dun Chibhich (Gigha), 154
Dun Choinichean (Mull), 112
Dun Cholla (Colonsay), 136
Dun Chonnuill (Garvellach Islands), 130
Dun Chruban (Lismore), 123
Dun Cruinn (Skye), 80
Dun Cuier (Barra), 67
Dun Eibhinn (Colonsay), 136

Dun Eiphinn, Gometra (Gometra), 112
Dun Fiadhairt (Skye), 80
Dun Gearymore (Skye), 80
Dun Grugaig (Skye), 80
Dun Hallin (Skye), 81
Dun Mor a' Chaolais (Tiree), 102
Dun Mor, Vaul (Tiree), 102
Dun Mor, West Gerinish (South Uist), 61
Dun Mucaig (Seil), 130
Dun Nighean Righ Lochlainn, Breinish (North Uist), 48
Dun Nosebridge (Islay), 145
Dun Ringill (Skye), 81
Dun Scurrival (Barra), 67
Dun Sgathaich (Skye), 83-84
Dun Suladale (Skye), 81
Dun Torcuill (North Uist), 48
Dun Torcusay (Benbecula), 55
Dun Trudernish (Islay), 146
Dun Uiselan (South Uist), 61
Dun Vulan (South Uist), 61
Dunan Achaidh (Coll), 99
Dun an Fheurain (Mull), 112
Dun an Sticar (North Uist), 48
Dun na Cleite (Tiree), 102
Dun na Muirgheidh (Mull), 112
Dun nan Gall (Mull), 112
Dunagoil (Bute), 159
Dunan an t-Seasgain (Gigha), 154
Dunan nan Nighean (Colonsay), 136
Duntulm Castle (Skye), 84
Dunvegan Castle (Skye), 84-85
Dunyvaig Castle (Islay), 146-147

E

Easdale Folk Museum (Easdale), 130
East Tarbert Bay Cairns (Gigha), 154
Edinbane Pottery (Skye), 89
Eileach an Naoimh (Garvellach Islands), 130-131
Eilean Amalaig Castle (Mull), 115
Eilean Chaluim Chille (Skye), 85
Eilean Mor, South Knapdale (Eilean Mor), 141
Eligar Souterrain (South Uist), 61
Ettrick Bay Stone Circle (Bute), 159
Eyre Standing Stones (Skye), 81

F

Fairy Bridge (Skye), 85
Fear an Eich (Lewis), 38
Fingal's Limpet Hammers Standing Stones (Colonsay), 136
Finlaggan (Islay), 147
Fir Bhreige Standing Stones (North Uist), 48
Fivepennies Well (Eigg), 95

Foshigarry Prehistoric Settlement (North Uist), 48

G

Gaelic Whiskies – Whisky Exhibition (Skye), 89
Gearrannan Blackhouse Village (Lewis), 35
Giant Angus MacAskill Museum (Skye), 85
Giants Graves, Whiting Bay (Arran), 169
Gisla Woodcraft (Lewis), 38
Glac Hukarvat (South Uist), 61
Gleann Droighneach Standing Stone (Islay), 146
Glendale Toy Museum (Skye), 85
Glendale Watermill (Skye), 85
Glengorm Standing Stones (Mull), 112
Gorm Castle (Islay), 147
Gramisdale Stone Circle (Benbecula), 55
Gruline Standing Stones (Mull), 112
Gunnery of MacLeod (Berneray), 51
Gylen Castle (Kerrera), 126

H

Harbour View Gallery (Lewis), 38
Hebridean Jewellery (South Uist), 63
Holy Stone, Cairnvickuie (Gigha), 154
Hough Stone Circles (Tiree), 102
Howmore Church and Chapels (South Uist), 62

I

Inchkenneth Cairn (Inchkenneth), 113
Inchkenneth Chapel (Inchkenneth), 115
Iona Abbey (Iona), 120
Iona Heritage Centre (Iona), 120-121
Iona Pottery and Gallery (Iona), 121
Island Crafts (North Uist/Grimsay), 51
Islay Woollen Mill (Islay), 150
Isle of Arran Distillery (Arran), 174
Isle of Jura Distillery (Jura), 141
Isle of Mull Angora Rabbit Farm (Mull), 117
Isle of Mull Museum (Mull), 115
Isle of Mull Weavers (Mull), 117
Isle of Skye Brewing Company (Leann an Eilein) Ltd (Skye), 89

J

Joan MacLennan Tweeds (Harris), 38
Jura House Walled Garden (Jura), 141

K

Kames Castle (Bute), 160
Keills Cross Shaft (Islay), 147

Kenneth MacLeod Harris Tweed Mill (Lewis), 38
Kiessimul Castle (Barra), 68
Kilarrow (Bowmore) Parish Church (Islay), 147
Kilashik (Skye), 86
Kilbride (Arran), 172
Kilbride Chapel (Islay), 147-148
Kilchattan (Luing), 131
Kilchattan (Gigha), 154-155
Kilchiaran Chapel (Islay), 148
Kilchoman Cross (Islay), 148
Kildalton Cross and Chapel (Islay), 148
Kildonan Museum, Cafe and Crafts (South Uist), 62
Kildonnan, Eigg (Eigg), 96
Kilearnadil Burial Ground (Jura), 141
Killarow Graveyard (Islay), 148
Killunaig (Coll), 99
Kilmhoire Chapel (Jura), 141
Kilmichael (Bute), 159
Kilmore Old Parish Church (Skye), 86
Kilmory Castle (Bute), 160
Kilmory Workshop (Arran), 174
Kilmory, Rum (Rum), 96
Kilmuir Church (Skye), 86
Kilnaughton (Islay), 148
Kilnave Chapel and Cross (Islay), 149
Kilninian Cairn (Mull), 113
Kilninian Chapel (Mull), 115
Kilpatrick Prehistoric Settlement (Arran), 169
Kilphedder Cross (North Uist), 51
Kilpheder Aisled (Wheel) House (South Uist), 61
Kilvickeon Church (Mull), 115
Kingscross (Arran), 170
King's Cave, Drumadoon (Arran), 172-173
Kneep Prehistoric Settlement (Lewis), 33
Knock Ullinish Souterrain (Skye), 81
Knockrome Standing Stones (Jura), 140
Kylerhea Otter Haven (Skye), 91

L
Lagavulin Distillery (Islay), 150-151
Lamlash Parish Church (Arran), 172
Laphroaig Distillery (Islay), 151
Largizean Standing Stones (Bute), 159
Leac nan Cailleachan Dubha (Vallay), 48
Leccamore Dun (Luing), 130
Lewis Loom Centre (Lewis), 38
Lews Castle and Lady Lever Park (Lewis), 39
Little Cumbrae Castle (Little Cumbrae), 165

Little Gallery (Skye), 89
Liveras Cairn (Skye), 81
Loch Hunder Dun (North Uist), 48-49
Loch Seaforth Stone Circle (Lewis), 33
Loch Siant Well (Skye), 86
Loch an Duin Dun, Taransay (Taransay), 33
Loch an Sgoltaire Castle (Colonsay), 137
Loch a' Bharp Cairn (South Uist), 61
Loch a' Gheadais Dun (North Uist), 49
Loch nam Ban Mora (Eigg), 95
Lochbuie Stone Circle (Mull), 113
Lochranza Castle (Arran), 173
Luchruban (Lewis), 35
Luib Croft Museum (Skye), 86
Luskentyre Harris Tweed Co (Harris), 39

M
Maari Standing Stone (North Uist), 49
MacGillivray Centre (Harris), 39
MacGillivrays (Benbecula), 56
MacLeod's Castle (Lewis), 35
Machrie Moor Stone Circles (Arran), 170
Margaret Curtis (Lewis), 33
Mayish Standing Stone (Arran), 170
Mhiann Arts (Iona), 121
Mid Kirkton (Great Cumbrae), 165
Milbuie Cairn (Colonsay), 136
Milton (South Uist), 62
Mingary Standing Stone (Mull), 113
Monyquil Standing Stone (Arran), 170
Morven Gallery (Lewis), 39
Moss Farm Road Cairn (Arran), 171
Mount Stuart House (Bute), 160
Moy Castle (Mull), 115-116
Mull & West Highland Narrow Gauge Railway (Mull), 118
Mull Theatre (Mull), 117
Museum and Marine Biological Station (Great Cumbrae), 166
Museum nan Eilean, Lionacleit (Benbecula), 55
Museum nan Eilean, Stornoway (Lewis), 35
Museum of Islay Life (Islay), 149

N
Na Clachan Bhreige, Kilmarie (Skye), 81
Na Fir Bhreige Standing Stones (North Uist), 49
Nerabus Chapel and Burial Ground (Islay), 149
Ness Heritage Centre (Lewis), 35
North Locheynort Cairn (South Uist), 61

Northpark Cairn, Inchmarnock (Inchmarnock), 160
Nuns' Cave, Carsaig (Mull), 116
Nunton (Benbecula), 56

O
Oiseval Gallery (Lewis), 39
Old Byre Heritage Centre (Mull), 116
Old Parish Church, Sorobaidh (Tiree), 103
Ormacleit Castle (South Uist), 62-63
Oronsay Priory (Oronsay), 137
Our Lady of the Isles (South Uist), 63

P
Pabbay (Pabbay), 68
Pennycross (Mull), 116
Pennygown Chapel (Mull), 116
Pilgrims Way to Iona (Mull), 116-117
Pobull Fhinn Stone Circle (North Uist), 49
Pollachar Standing Stone (South Uist), 61
Port Charlotte Cairn (Islay), 146
Port Donain Cairns (Mull), 113
Port Ellen Pottery (Islay), 151
Port Ellen Standing Stone (Islay), 146
Pottie Standing Stone (Mull), 113
Prince Charles's Cave (Skye), 91

R
Raasay House (Raasay), 86-87
Ravenspoint (Lewis), 39
Ridh a' Chaibeil Cross (Gigha), 155
Rothesay Castle (Bute), 160-161
Rubha na Crannaig (Eigg), 95
Rubh' an Dunain Cairn and Dun (Skye), 81

S
St Blane's Church, Kingarth (Bute), 161
St Catherine's Well (Eigg), 96
St Clement's Church, Rodel (Harris), 36
St Columba's Church (Uí), Aignish (Lewis), 36-37
St Marnock's Chapel, Inchmarnock (Inchmarnock), 162
St Mary's Chapel, Dunvegan (Skye), 87
St Mary's Church, Rothesay (Bute), 162
St Michael's Chapel, Grimsay (Grimsay), 51
St Moluag's Chapel, Raasay (Raasay), 87
St Moluag's Church, Eoropie (Lewis), 37
St Ronan's Church, Rona (Rona), 37

St Vey's Chapel, Little Cumbrae (Little Cumbrae), 165
Sandray (Sandray), 67
Sgalabraig Souterrain (Berneray), 49
Shawbost Crofting Museum (Lewis), 36
Sheanawally Cairns (Little Cumbrae), 165
Skeabost Island (Skye), 87
Skerryvore Museum (Tiree), 103
Skye Batiks (Skye), 89-90
Skye Jewellery (Skye), 90
Skye Museum of Island Life (Skye), 87
Skye Serpentarium Reptile World (Skye), 91
Skye Woollen Mill (Skye), 90
Skyeskyns (Skye), 90
Slaterich Cists (Kerrera), 126
Soay Studio (Harris), 39
Sornach a' Phobuill Stone Circle (North Uist), 50
South Bank Farm Park (Arran), 174
Sron an Duin Dun (Berneray), 67
Staffin Museum (Skye), 87
Steinacleit Prehistoric Site (Lewis), 34
Stiaraval Cairn (Benbecula), 55
Stone of Punishment, Canna (Canna), 95
Storab's Grave, Raasay (Raasay), 81
Stornoway Castle (Lewis), 37
Stronach Standing Stone (Arran), 171
Studio Gallery (South Uist), 63

T

Taigh Chearsabhagh Museum and Art Centre (North Uist), 51-52
Taigh an t-Sithiche, St Kilda (St Kilda), 41
Talisker Distillery (Skye), 90
Tarbert Standing Stones (Jura), 140
Teampull Chaluim Chille (Benbecula), 56
Teampull Tharain (Taransay), 37
Teampull na Trionaid (North Uist), 51
The Barn (Colonsay), 137
The Doon, Drumadoon (Arran), 171
The Gallery, Colonsay and Oronsay Heritage Trust (Colonsay), 137
Tigh Cloiche Cairn (North Uist), 50
Tigh Talamhant Souterrain, North Uist (North Uist), 50
Tigh Talamhanta, Barra (Barra), 67
Tirefour Broch (Lismore), 123
Tobar a' Bheathaig (Gigha), 155
Tobar na Cille (St Kilda), 41
Tobar na Suil (Luing), 131
Tobar nam Buaidh (St Kilda), 41
Tobar nan Gaeth Deas (Colonsay), 137

Tobermory Distillery (Mull), 118
Tomont End Cairns (Great Cumbrae), 165
Tormisdale Croft Crafts (Islay), 151
Torosay Castle (Mull), 117
Torr a' Chaisteal (Arran), 171
Torrylinn Cairn (Arran), 171
Totronald Standing Stones (Coll), 99
Traigh Ghrianal Cairn (Tiree), 102
Trotternish Art Gallery (Skye), 90
Trumpan Church (Skye), 87-88
Tungadale Souterrain (Skye), 81
Tursachan Standing Stones, Barraglom (Great Bernera), 34

U

Uamh Fhraing, Eigg (Eigg), 96
Uamh Ghrantriach Souterrain (South Uist), 62
Uamh Iosal Souterrain (South Uist), 62
Uamh nan Ramh Souterrain (Raasay), 81
Uig Heritage Centre (Lewis), 37
Uig Pottery (Skye), 90
Uiskentuie Standing Stone (Islay), 146
Uist Animal Visitor Centre (North Uist), 52
Uist Craft Workshop (South Uist), 63
Uist Outdoor Centre (North Uist), 52
Ulva Heritage Centre (Ulva), 117
Uneval Chambered Cairn (North Uist), 50

V

Vatten Chambered Cairns (Skye), 81-82
Weaver's Castle (Eriskay), 63

W

West Highland Heavy Horse Tours (Skye), 91
World of Wood (Skye), 91